Canada: The Stat of the Federation 1989

Edited by
Ronald L. Watts and
Douglas M. Brown

Institute of
Intergovernmental
Relations

Queen's University
Kingston, Ontario
Canada

Canadian Cataloguing in Publication Data

The National Library of Canada has catalogued this serial as follows:

Canada, the state of the federation

Annual.
1985-
Vols. for 1985-   edited by Peter M. Leslie ;
vols. for   edited by Ronald L. Watts and Douglas M. Brown.
ISSN 0827-0708.
ISBN 0-88911-556-7 (1989)

1. Federal-provincial relations — Canada — Periodicals.*
2. Federal government — Canada — Periodicals.
I. Queen's University (Kingston, Ont.). Institute of Intergovernmental
Relations.   II. Leslie, Peter M.   III. Watts, Ronald L.
IV. Brown, Douglas Mitchell, 1954-   .

JL27.F42   321.02'3'0971   C86-030713-1

The Institute of Intergovernmental Relations

The Institute is the only organization in Canada whose mandate is solely to promote research and communication on the challenges facing the federal system.

Current research interests include fiscal federalism, constitutional reform, the reform of federal political institutions and the machinery of federal-provincial relations, Canadian federalism and the global economy, and comparative federalism.

The Institute pursues these objectives through research conducted by its own staff and other scholars through its publications program, seminars and conferences.

The Institute links academics and practitioners of federalism in federal and provincial governments and the private sector.

CONTENTS

PREFACE

This is the fourth edition of the annual series of the Institute of Intergovernmental Relations, *Canada: The State of the Federation*. With this edition the Institute returns to the original scheduling envisaged for the series with publication in the late summer of each calendar year. This edition also returns, after last year's special focus on the Meech Lake Accord and the Free Trade Agreement, to the original format of a more varied collection of articles focusing on a selection of individual provinces and on a set of discrete issues in intergovermental relations and Canadian federalism.

The fourth edition also continues with a Chronology of Events, in this edition covering the period January 1988 to June 1989.

The editors wish to acknowledge the cooperation and promptness of all of the authors in this volume for meeting our deadlines and in complying at short notice with suggested revisions. Each article has had the benefit of independent reading by other scholars in the field outside the Institute. We are most grateful for the contribution of these referees, again at very short notice.

The preparation of this volume has been the result of the usual excellent team effort at the Institute. We would like to thank Valerie Jarus and Patti Candido for preparing the text, Daniel Bonin for preparing the "sommaires", Marilyn Banting and Margaret Day for proofreading and Mary Kennedy for assistance in distribution.

Ronald L. Watts
Douglas M. Brown
September, 1989

CONTRIBUTORS

Robin Boadway is a Professor of Economics at Queen's University and the author of many books and articles on fiscal federalism, including *Intergovernmental Transfers in Canada.*

Douglas M. Brown is Associate Director of the Institute of Intergovernmental Relations.

Yvon Fontaine, Dean of the Law School at L'Université de Moncton, is a past president of the Fédération des francophones hors Québec.

Roger Gibbins, Professor of Political Science at the University of Calgary, is the editor of *Meech Lake and Canada: Perspectives From the West.*

Dwight Herperger is a Research Assistant at the Institute of Intergovernmental Relations.

Derek P.J. Hum is Professor of Economics at St. John's College, University of Manitoba. He is the author of *Federalism and the Poor: A Review of the Canada Assistance Plan*

Alastair R. Lucas, a long time associate of the Canadian Institute of Resources Law, is Associate Professor in the Faculty of Law, University of Calgary and has written widely in the area of environmental and natural resource law.

Darrel R. Reid is the Information Officer/Bibliographer of the Institute of Intergovernmental Relations.

Donald W. Stevenson, recently retired from a distinguished career in the Ontario Public Service and Deputy Minister of the Ministry of Intergovernmental Affairs, is Associate to the Principal at Glendon College, York University.

Paul G. Thomas is Associate Professor of Political Studies at the University of Manitoba and co-author of *Canadian Public Administration: Problematical Perspectives.*

Ronald L. Watts, former Principal of Queen's University, 1974-84 and a member of the 1977-79 Task Force on Canadian Unity, is the Director of the Institute of Intergovernmental Relations.

I

Introduction

ONE

An Overview

Ronald L. Watts

Comme par le passé, cette nouvelle édition de "Canada: The State of the Federation" traite de questions d'importance touchant le fédéralisme canadien. En première partie l'intérêt se porte sur l'Ontario et le Manitoba, à la lumière des divers changements survenus depuis quelque temps dans ces deux provinces. Sont ensuite abordés des problèmes d'actualité affectant singulièrement les relations fédérales-provinciales, à savoir: la réduction du déficit fédéral et la réforme fiscale, les politiques relatives aux minorités linguistiques, la stratégie nationale en matière de garderie, la législation environnementale canadienne, la réforme du Sénat et la participation provinciale aux négociations du GATT. L'élection fédérale de novembre 1988 fait l'objet, par ailleurs, d'une analyse détaillée. Au demeurant le scrutin fédéral a peut-être réglé la question du libre-échange mais il aura eu pour effet, en revanche, de fragiliser l'Accord du lac Meech. A telle enseigne qu'on pourrait presque parler maintenant du "désaccord" de Meech...

La présente introduction dégage d'abord la signification intrinsèque de l'Accord et rappelle ses principaux traits caractéristiques. Puis, on y montre pourquoi l'entente constitutionnelle—en dépit du concert d'approbations qui marqua initialement son adoption—a commencé à être critiquée de toutes parts et, en particulier, au Canada anglais. Le débat entre pro et anti-Meech s'articule, grosso modo, autour des quatre points suivants: 1) fédéralisme centralisateur vs fédéralisme coopératif 2) prise en charge nationale ou provinciale de la dualité linguistique canadienne 3) primauté ou non de la Charte des droits et libertés sur la "société distincte" 4) légitimité ou non des mécanismes "exécutifs" de la réforme constitutionnelle.

La Loi constitutionnelle de 1982 contenait déjà en germe les motifs de dispute cristallisés subséquemment par le Lac Meech. Un échec éventuel de l'Accord provoquerait à coup sûr une crise importante au sein du système fédéral canadien. Mais la longévité manifeste de la fédération canadienne constitue peut-être le garant d'une prochaine solution politique au problème constitutionnel vécu pour l'heure au Canada.

INTRODUCTION

The previous volume in this series, *Canada: The State of the Federation, 1987-88*, departed from the format of earlier volumes to concentrate upon the two major issues preoccupying Canadian political debate at that time: the Canada-U.S. Trade Agreement and the Meech Lake Accord. Both of these initiatives had fundamental implications for the development of the Canadian federal system. Moreover, in both cases the dispute between supporters and opponents turned on similar clashes between the advocates of "collaborative federalism" and of "nation-centred federalism" and both aroused public debate about the appropriate processes for arriving at fundamental constitutional and economic changes.

The federal general election of 21 November 1988 settled, at least in principle, the issue of the free trade agreement which was quickly adopted after the Progressive Conservative victory. But the election and its aftermath contributed to unsettling the issues surrounding the Meech Lake Accord as the critics of the trade agreement now turned their attention to the Accord. In the aftermath of the election a number of new issues and some old ones also came to the fore. The pressure on the federal government to reduce its deficit and to press its agenda of tax reform has given new prominence to issues of fiscal federalism leading to increased federal-provincial contention. Language legislation in Parliament, Saskatchewan, and Alberta and particularly Bill 178 in Quebec has rekindled controversy over minority language rights and policies. The effort to develop a federal-provincial program on child care has failed, at least for the time being, to produce national consensus. The pressure for a new more comprehensive federal role in environmental legislation has posed questions about the appropriate relative roles of the federal and provincial governments in this area. Alberta's initiative in selecting its Senate nominees by election has introduced a new dynamic into the movement for Senate reform. The Uruguay Round of GATT negotiations has raised again the issue of the role of provincial governments in the negotiating and implementing of international trade agreements.

This volume, therefore, returns to the earlier format of this series. In addition to an introductory overview of the state of the Canadian federation and an analysis of the significance for Canadian federalism of the federal general election of 1988, there is a section of two chapters that focuses on developments in two particular provinces and a section of six chapters that focuses on a number of topical issues affecting the current development of Canadian federalism.

THE 1988 FEDERAL GENERAL ELECTION

While the Canada-U.S.Trade Agreement was the dominant campaign issue in the federal general election, other issues of significance to Canadian federalism were raised. In chapter two, Darrel Reid tracks and assesses the significance of six policy areas affecting federal-provincial relations to which attention was given during the campaign: language and the Constitution Act, 1982; the Meech Lake Accord; environmental regulation; regional development; tax reform; Canada-U.S. free trade. A number of these issues are also addressed in more depth in later chapters in this volume.

The issue which dominated the election was, of course, the Canada-U.S. Trade Agreement upon which the campaign focused almost totally. When the election was called in September, Brian Mulroney's Progressive Conservatives had a substantial lead in the polls and the trade agreement appeared secure. But during the campaign both opposition parties hammered away at the agreement and John Turner's performance in the mid-campaign leaders' debate on television produced a massive shift of public opinion against the government and the agreement. The vigour of the Conservative counter-attack in the final weeks produced, however, an unprecedented second shift in public opinion during the campaign. As a result the Conservatives were re-elected with a significant majority. That virtually decided the issue and in the following month Parliament ratified the Canada-U.S. Trade Agreement.

The election results provided some interesting insights into regional attitudes towards the trade agreement. Traditionally, it had been the peripheries that had espoused free trade with the United States, whereas central Canada had opposed it. During 1987 and 1988 the premiers of the various provinces generally followed this pattern with only the premiers of Ontario and Prince Edward Island, and for a time, Manitoba opposing the agreement. The one major exception to the historical tradition was the strong support of Mr. Bourassa for the agreement. In the actual election results, support for and against the trade agreement to a considerable extent cut across regional lines. By contrast with the positions taken by the premiers, it was only Quebec, Alberta, Ontario, and Manitoba that gave the Conservatives either a clear majority or a plurality of the seats. Indeed, 110 of the 180 seats that they captured were in Quebec (63) and Ontario (47). Thus, ironically, it appeared that in broad terms central Canada had again ultimately determined Canadian trade policy over the peripheries, except that in this election the electorates in central Canada and in the peripheries both reversed their traditional positions on free trade with the United States. This pattern may be explained in part by the dependency of most of the noncentral provinces upon federal regional development and social welfare programs (Alberta being a notable exception in this regard) and the portrayal by the opposition parties of the trade agreement as threatening these programs. It may also be explained in part by the active support and advocacy of the business interests in central Canada who, by contrast with their position in earlier periods when free trade with the United States was proposed, were now confident that they could compete effectively in a continental market. Equally important was the strong advocacy of the Quebec government in support of the burgeoning entrepreneurial interests in that province.

The election and its aftermath also further illustrated the linkages between the Canada-U.S. Free Trade Agreement and the Meech Lake Accord. Once the election had decided the trade agreement issue, opposition began almost immediately to harden against the Accord. With the approval of the trade agreement certain, critics of that agreement turned their attention to the Meech Lake Accord. They argued that the Accord, on top of the trade agreement, would further erode the federal government's power to establish national programs, and that the combination of free trade and the "distinct society" clause in the Accord would lead de facto to Quebec's economic and political independence from the rest of Canada. Their opposition to the Accord was further hardened by the prominent role Quebec had played in support of a trade agreement which in the view of its critics undermined Canada's sovereignty as a nation.

In the election the Conservatives had swept Quebec, increasing their representation from that province. This emphasized to Canadians in the other provinces the almost decisive voice of Quebec in the federal government reducing sympathies for Quebec's "plight" in the other provinces. The election result also accentuated the predominantly English-speaking representation of the two opposition party caucuses in Ottawa and consequently strengthened the influence within the national Liberal and NDP parties of those critical of the Accord. Although the leaders of both parties had previously supported the Accord in the hope of improving the representation of their parties from Quebec, the election result left them having to cope with the rising criticism of the Accord within their own ranks, especially from some of the new members elected from western Canada. Moreover, the positions of both Mr. Turner and Mr. Broadbent were further weakened after both announced that they would vacate their positions as party leaders.

Thus, the general impact of the federal general election was to settle the issue of the Canada-U.S. Trade Agreement but to unsettle the issue of the Meech Lake Accord. The trade agreement has become law, finally settling the major policy issue of 1988 although by no means ending the continuing debate over its merits and consequences. But the effect of the election and its aftermath has been to leave the fate of the Meech Lake Accord as the major issue dominating Canadian federalism during 1989 and 1990.

FOCUS ON THE PROVINCES

Interesting developments of relevance to the evolution of Canadian federalism occurred during 1988 and the first half of 1989 in virtually every province.

In a number of them, most notably Saskatchewan, Alberta, and Quebec, minority language legislation during 1988 contributed to a heightening of tensions, a subject dealt with more fully in chapter six of this volume by Yvon Fontaine. In New Brunswick, too, minority language rights have been an important issue, while Premier McKenna's reservations about the Meech Lake Accord have attracted much national attention since New Brunswick remains one of the two provinces that has yet to ratify the Accord.

In five of the provinces and in the Yukon, general elections were held during 1988 and the first half of 1989. In Manitoba (26 April 1988) and Newfoundland (20 April 1989), the provincial elections changed the party in power. In the former, the election of a minority Progressive Conservative government with new opposition party leaders opposed to the Meech Lake Accord in its present form, created a political dynamic making the adoption of the Accord by the legislature doubtful. In Newfoundland, the provincial election brought into power a Liberal government whose leader, Clyde Wells, is committed to rescinding that province's endorsement of the Accord. In the three other provincial elections, Nova Scotia (6 September 1988), Alberta (20 March 1989), and Prince Edward Island (29 May 1989), the incumbent governments were returned, but in the two latter cases the elections were fought in considerable measure on federal-provincial issues: a mandate for electing senate nominees being the ostensible reason for the Alberta election and a protest against the impact of federal defence expenditure reductions within P.E.I. being the central issue in the provincial election campaign there. In the Yukon election (20 February 1989) an NDP majority was returned. Territorial concerns about the barriers to provincehood imposed by the proposed Meech Lake Accord alterations to the constitutional amendment process clearly remained alive.

For this year's volume, in the section "Focus on the Provinces", Ontario and Manitoba have been selected for particular analysis. Ontario, during the Robarts and Davis years, had tended to identify federal interests as coinciding with those of Ontario. But Tom Courchene, in his provocative Robarts Lecture in 1988, drew attention to the need to reassess Ontario's position within the federation.[1] He suggested that under the Peterson government, in power since 1985, the Ontario government has appeared to isolate itself from both the federal government and the other provinces by its opposition to the Canada-U.S. Trade Agreement, by its emphasis upon a social policy agenda rather than economic policy, and by distinguishing Ontario interests from national interests. Courchene's reassessment occasioned considerable soul-searching within Ontario governmental circles. In chapter three of this volume, Don Stevenson examines critically the Courchene analysis pointing to a greater continuity in the Ontario role than Courchene had allowed.

Manitoba will play a key role in whether the Meech Lake Accord is in the end adopted or rejected and given the minority government situation that followed the provincial election of 1988 this is one province where the outcome will depend on more than the views of the premier. This points to the importance of understanding the economic and political dynamics of developments within Manitoba. In chapter four, Paul Thomas analyses such factors as the economic situation, attitudes to federalism, and patterns of party politics for their impact on the Meech Lake process and on federal-provincial relations. The latter have been seriously affected by the impact of the federal government's deficit-reduction efforts upon federal transfers and regional development programs. Both geographically and in terms of its position in federal-provincial relations Manitoba is significant as a province very much "in the middle."

FOCUS ON ISSUES

Although overclouded during the federal general election by the preoccupation of that campaign with the Canada-U.S. Trade Agreement, the election campaign itself identified and events following the campaign have accentuated attention to a number of issues, some new and others revived. These will have an increasingly powerful impact on federal-provincial relations.

Particularly important are the combined effect of federal deficit-reduction and tax reform efforts. Robin Boadway, in chapter five, examines the likely impact of these issues and suggests that federal-provincial fiscal relations in Canada have arrived at an important crossroads. The impact of the effort to reduce the federal deficit upon the size and form of fiscal transfers to the provinces and the federal determination to pursue tax reform, particularly a federal general sales tax, have in the short-term already accentuated controversies and tensions. But both these developments also have important long term consequences: they will affect the federal government's ability to fulfil its obligations for equalization that were constitutionalized in section 36 of the Charter; they will leave the federal government in a less dominant position in terms of the relative occupancy of tax fields by the federal and provincial governments; and there are signs of a serious erosion of intergovernmental tax harmonization.

In the realm of official language policy, despite the advances achieved by Ottawa's Official Language Act of 1988, developments in Saskatchewan and Alberta, and particularly Bill 178 in Quebec have been seen by the linguistic minorities in these provinces as retrograde and even repressive measures.

Consequently, during 1988 the salience of the minority languages issue was heightened and tensions were aroused. Particularly significant was the passage in December of Bill 178 in the Quebec National Assembly, involving resort to the "notwithstanding" clause in the Charter. This followed the Supreme Court ruling of 15 December 1988, that certain sections of Quebec's Bill 101 prohibiting commercial signs except in French violated the Quebec and the Canadian Charters of Rights and Freedoms.[2] Bill 178 was seen by the Quebec government as a necessary response to the concerns of francophone Québécois about the preservation of their language and culture surrounded as they were by an anglophone North America and with heightened vulnerability due to their own sharply declining birthrate.

The Quebec government viewed the legislation as a compromise less oppressive than the original Bill 101 imposed by the Parti Québécois. But the impact of this legislation and particularly the use of the "notwithstanding" clause to safeguard it, had a traumatic impact on anglophones in Quebec and English Canadians outside Quebec. It was viewed as repressive because of the use of the "notwithstanding" clause to deny rights identified by the Supreme Court as embodied in the Charter. Moreover, to liberal English Canadians who had supported bilingualism as a concession to national unity, Bill 178 was seen as a repudiation of the Trudeau policy of national bilingualism as the means to bicommunal accommodation. The degree to which Bill 178 symbolized the continuing two solitudes within Canada on linguistic issues was illustrated by the subsequent Gallup poll of 20 July 1989. This reported that while 77 per cent of Canadian francophones thought that English rights were well protected in Quebec only 24 per cent of Canadian anglophones thought so and that while 81 per cent of anglophone citizens believed French language rights outside Quebec were well protected, only 28 per cent of Canadian French-speakers thought likewise.[3] In chapter six, Yvon Fontaine examines this linguistic impasse and argues for the importance of the recognition of official language minorities both outside and inside Quebec as functional minority communities.

During the latter half of the 1980s, child care came to the fore as the major candidate for a new national federal-provincial program. Following the report of the Task Force on Child Care (Cooke Report) in 1986 and the report of the House of Commons Special Committee on Child Care in 1987, the development of a National Child Care Strategy resulted in the introduction in Parliament of Bill C-144, *The Canada Child Care Act 1988*. But despite the apprehension of Canadians about any limitation of social programs, the pressures for deficit-reduction and the polarization between the supporters of commercial and non-profit child care led to the post-election deferral of action in this area by the federal government. In chapter seven, Derek Hum analyses the "rise and stall" of the federal national child care strategy and the issues which the

Mulroney government will have to confront in this area before it faces the electorate again.

The federal election also indicated a greatly increased public concern about the environment. Indeed, the subsequent public attention in the summer of 1989 given to the PCB disposal issue in Quebec illustrates the increasing importance of environmental issues. In chapter eight, Alastair Lucas examines legal developments such as recent court decisions, the development of new comprehensive federal environmental legislation in 1988 and major new or amending environmental legislation in many provinces. He points to the flurry of analyses, consultation and negotiation in this field in which Canadian governments have recently been engaged. But particularly important, he emphasizes the longer-term implications for the redefinition of federal and provincial roles in this area arising from the trend to broadening federal jurisdiction and the impact of this upon provincial jurisdiction in such areas as natural resources.

Senate reform has been a perennial issue in Canadian constitutional politics, and a variety of models for Senate reform and improved "intrastate federalism" were advocated in the decade leading up to the Macdonald Commission report in 1985. The issue has currently taken a particular dynamic, however, from a number of factors. One has been the resurgence of western Canadian alienation in the period after the 1984 federal election. The West perceived that, despite the election of a Conservative national government, its own influence on national policy remained weak by comparison with that of Quebec and Ontario. This has led to the advocacy under Albertan leadership of the "Triple E" (elected, equal provincial representation, and effective) Senate as a means of strengthening western influence in national politics. A second factor has been the Meech Lake Accord which identified Senate reform as an item on the constitutional agenda and which, as an interim measure, gave provinces the right to nominate candidates for federal appointments to the Senate. But the Accord, by making the process for constitutional amendment more rigid, also raised fears among many westerners that further progress to Senate reform might be blocked rather than facilitated. A third factor has been the initiative of the Alberta government to exploit these developments by passing the *Senatorial Selection Act, 1989*. This provides for the holding of elections to select Alberta's nominees for the Senate. Alberta clearly hopes that this will lever progress towards an elected Senate. In chapter nine, Roger Gibbins discusses these developments and their likely impact on the dynamics of Senate reform as Canada moves into the 1990s. Of particular interest is whether this focus on one "e" will help keep the issue of Senate reform in play, or whether it will put the focus upon "election" at the expense of provincial "equality" within the Senate. The degree of voter interest which the electorate displays in the first senatorial election campaign will also give some indication of the strength of popular pressure for an elected Senate.

With the heated election debate over the Canada-U.S. Trade Agreement behind us, the focus of trade policy has shifted to the Uruguay Round of multilateral negotiations under the auspices of the General Agreement on Tariffs and Trade (GATT). These negotiations raise questions about the degree to which the particular character of Canadian federalism limits the ability of Canada to respond to global economic and trade challenges. In chapter ten, Douglas Brown examines the implications of the Uruguay Round negotiations for the jurisdictional responsibilities of the federal and provincial governments and for the processes of federal-provincial consultation on trade policy. The Canada-U.S. Trade Agreement, as finally adopted, to a large extent finessed the question of provincial implementation in areas of provincial jurisdiction. In the Uruguay Round of GATT negotiations, however, as the international negotiating agenda moves into issues of developing rules for trade in services and investment, this is likely to pose particular challenges for the distribution of constitutional jurisdiction between the federal and provincial governments.

MEECH LAKE: ACCORD OR DISCORD?

Such issues as federal deficit reduction and tax reform, minority language rights and policies, the need for a national child care strategy, jurisdiction over environmental legislation, Senate reform, and provincial involvement in the GATT negotiations have heightened federal-provincial tensions. But the unsettled prospects for the adoption of the Meech Lake Accord has been the fundamental factor contributing to a growing sense of malaise and even potential crisis within the Canadian federation at the current time. By mid-1989 this situation was increasingly drawing comment from leading Canadian columnists.[4] Indeed, Pierre Pettigrew has been quoted as saying: "I am more uneasy about the future of the federation today than I was nine years ago, on the eve of the Quebec referendum."[5]

The intent of the Meech Lake Accord was to rectify the lack of Quebec's assent to the constitutional amendment of 1982. While the 1982 revisions to the constitution were legally binding on Quebec, the 1982 constitutional amendment had in effect been imposed on that province because its legislature had refused to endorse it. The Meech Lake Accord, negotiated in 1987 was intended to define the terms on which the provincial government of Quebec could formally add its assent to the revised constitution of 1982. Thus, its aim was to bring Canada closer to the ideal of a constitutional regime based on the consent of the governed, including the consent of Quebec.

The Accord was the product of a First Ministers' meeting at Meech Lake on 30 April 1987 at which Prime Minister Mulroney and the ten provincial premiers including Robert Bourassa, premier of Quebec, agreed unanimously on the features of a constitutional amendment that would have Quebec's support. On 3 June 1987, at a further meeting of the First Ministers in Ottawa, unanimous agreement was reached upon the legal form of the constitutional amendment that would implement the Accord. Since then the proposed constitutional amendment has received approval by Parliament and by eight of the provincial legislatures. The Accord still requires the assent of the legislatures of New Brunswick and Manitoba if it is to come into effect. In both provinces new premiers who did not participate in the Meech Lake meeting have come into office and these premiers have been pressing for revisions to the Accord. More recently, in Newfoundland, whose legislature had assented earlier to the Accord, a provincial election has returned to power a new Premier, Clyde Wells. He has threatened to rescind Newfoundland's assent to the Accord if it is not amended. Consequently, there are now serious questions about whether the Accord will receive the required unanimous assent of the provincial legislatures to come into effect.

The seven major elements of the Accord involve: (1) explicitly recognizing in the constitution linguistic duality as a characteristic of Canada, and Quebec as constituting "a distinct society within Canada;" (2) providing certain guarantees to Quebec about jurisdiction over immigration which would constitutionalize existing administrative agreements; (3) clarifying the federal spending power in areas of exclusive provincial jurisdiction; (4) extending the currently somewhat limited number of constitutional provisions which would require unanimous agreement of the provinces for formal ratification; (5) constitutionalizing the Supreme Court and providing that in future appointments would be made by the central government from among provincial nominees; (6) providing that appointments to the Senate would also in future be made by the central government from among provincial nominees; (7) providing for annual First Ministers' conferences on the economy and on the constitution.

While the Accord was initially hailed as the product of a unanimous agreement among all 11 first ministers and had the support of all three national party leaders in the Federal Parliament at the time, since then it has become the subject of bitter attack and criticism by a variety of groups within Canada. The debate has turned around four sets of issues, each revolving around different conceptions of Canadian federalism.

The first has been the clash between "nation-centred federalism" and "collaborative federalism."[6] Advocates of the former, typified by the Trudeau Liberals, see as essential for the future of Canada: strong national government leadership, the development of national standards in social policies, a national approach to protecting the rights of national and provincial linguistic minorities, and a national government relatively unconstrained by the requirement of intergovernmental agreement. They fear that the Meech Lake Accord would dangerously weaken the central government. The "distinct society" provision for Quebec would in their view undermine the sense of Canadian nationhood. The immigration and spending power provisions are seen as constraining federal jurisdiction and the more rigid constitutional amendment procedure would make adaptation to global and domestic challenges more difficult. They are concerned that the provisions relating to Supreme Court and Senate appointments and for First Ministers' Conferences would complicate national decision making. Furthermore, they taunt, in an obviously rhetorical yet emotive exaggeration, that the Canada-U.S. Trade Agreement has given Washington half the Canadian federal government's powers and that now the Meech Lake Accord would give the other half to the provinces.

On the other side, supporters of "collaborative federalism" argue that the provinces are vital communities and that only by accommodating these realities, rather than by suppressing them, can true Canadian unity be achieved. Mechanisms to build upon consensus and collaboration strengthen Canadian unity rather than weaken it, they argue. Furthermore, they point out that, although the collaborative role of the provinces would be enhanced under the Accord, specific provisions in the text of the proposed constitutional amendment would ensure that federal jurisdiction remains undiminished.[7]

A second source of debate upon the Accord has been the continued tension between those advocating competing models of how to accommodate linguistic duality within Canada. Critics of the Accord, such as Pierre Trudeau and his followers, see the responsibilities assigned to the Quebec government to promote that province's character as a "distinct society" as undermining their own advocacy of linguistic dualism as a pan-Canadian national policy. In their view the responsibility for the protection of the rights of official language minorities across the country, including those of Quebecers, should lie with the federal government. Supporters of the Accord, on the other hand, view the distinctiveness of Quebec with its French-speaking majority as a sociological fact and see the need, both symbolically and in order to undercut future Quebec separatism, to recognize that reality in the constitution. In varying degrees this has been the position of all the major provincial political parties within Quebec including the "federalist" non-separatist parties.

A third source of contention has been the emerging clash between pluralism rooted in territorially based interests and pluralism within Canada which is based on non-territorial interests. Among the most bitter opponents of the Accord have been those who have criticized the Accord's preoccupation with the concerns of territorially based interests which find their focus in such issues as language and intergovernmental relations.[8] The representatives of non-territorial interests argue that with the addition of the Charter of Rights and Freedoms in 1982, the Canadian Constitution is as much about relations between the individual and the state as about federalism and relations between governments. The Meech Lake Accord, they complain, attempts to tilt the balance back to the pre-Charter era by its focus on territorially based interests and intergovernmental relations. Thus, women's groups, multicultural groups, organizations representing aboriginal peoples, and liberal intellectuals have expressed concerns that the Accord's identification of Quebec as a "distinct society" might in that province undermine the primacy of the Charter. Among these critics have been a number of federally funded advocacy groups. They have argued that the criteria of rights and social justice are more important than accommodating the concerns of Quebec or of provincial groups. The defenders of the Accord have responded that fears that the Accord would undermine the Charter have been exaggerated. Furthermore, they emphasize that the concerns of territorially based minorities remain a legitimate political reality within Canada which cannot be simply ignored.

The fourth source of contention has been over the processes appropriate for constitutional reform. Critics of the Accord have pointed out that there was little prior public discussion, that the Accord was negotiated in two closed meetings of a group of 11 male First Ministers with only a few officials involved and that when the Accord was placed before Parliament and the Legislatures, the public debate was a sham because the Accord had to be either accepted or rejected with no opportunity for amendment.[9] These critics have attacked the processes of "executive federalism" as undemocratic, even to the point of challenging the legitimacy of responsible parliamentary government which gives rise to these processes. Their demand has been for a more participatory process of constitutional reform. The supporters of the Accord, on the other hand, point out that the process followed has met in every particular the requirements for constitutional amendments incorporated in the revised Constitution of 1982. Furthermore, that with the requirement of ratification by Parliament and the provincial legislatures the process has provided in this instance for more extensive public examination than the process by which the 1982 constitutional amendment establishing the Charter was ratified. They suggest, as well, that effective resolutions are unlikely to emerge from generalized processes of participatory democracy. There is a genuine dilemma here. The "elite accommodation" model represented by the Meech Lake process has offended the advocates of participatory democracy. But there have been few practical proposals for maximizing public and group participation in the negotiation of constitutional reform which would not at the same time minimize the chances of reaching Canada-wide compromise and agreement.

The debate over the Meech Lake Accord has brought out in full the contradictions embodied in the constitutional amendments of 1982. That resolution had attempted to combine the elements most sought after by both the Trudeau national government and the majority of premiers. The struggles between the charterists and the federalists, between advocates of "nation-centred" and of "collaborative" federalism, between insistence upon uniform national rights and the recognition of diversity, and between the supremacy of the charter and the judiciary versus legislative supremacy as retained through the "notwithstanding" clause, represent clashes between different elements embodied in the 1982 compromise. Each now claims that their element must prevail.

Since the federal election in November 1988, support for the Accord appears to have deteriorated significantly within English Canada. Where in previous periods the erosion of faith in the English-French partnership in Canada has usually come from Quebec nationalism, uncharacteristically it now is most marked among the anglophone majority. A number of factors have contributed to this. First, with the settlement of the free trade issue, the focus of its nationalist opponents within English Canada has been transferred to the Accord. Throughout the debate on the trade agreement its opponents were concerned that it would both weaken the east-west economic ties between the regions within Canada by expanding the north-south trading links and that it would restrict the ability of future federal governments to implement national economic and social programs. With that battle lost, the attention has turned to the Meech Lake Accord which it is feared would, by recognizing Quebec's distinctiveness, further weaken its ties with the rest of Canada and would at the same time increase the role of the provincial governments generally at the expense of the federal government.

A second factor has been the impact of the election upon the composition of the opposition caucuses in Ottawa. The leaders of both the national opposition parties had endorsed the Accord in Parliament, but the sweeping Conservative success in Quebec in the 1988 federal election has meant that the representation of both opposition parties in the House of Commons is dominated by anglophone Canadians from outside Quebec and contains a larger proportion of members critical of the Accord.

A particularly influential factor was Quebec's decision in December, by the passage of Bill 178, to reaffirm the prohibition of using languages other than French on outdoor commercial signs, overriding a Supreme Court ruling and the Charter of Rights and Freedoms in the process. The use of the "notwithstanding" clause in the Charter and the repudiation by Bourassa of his earlier campaign promises had a dramatic effect. This action shocked the national anglophone majority, including many who had previously been supportive of Quebec's aspirations, by its repudiation of bilingualism, its emphasis upon the minority status of anglophones in Quebec, and by the primacy given to the distinctiveness of Quebec's majority over the safeguards for minority rights embodied in the Charter. Indeed, it may, by itself, in the long-run have sounded the death-knell of the Accord.

A more subtle but insidious factor has been the realization among Canadians outside Quebec, not just those who were opposed to the Canada-U.S. Trade Agreement, that it was Quebecers who in the 1988 federal election had effectively decided that Canada would implement the free-trade agreement. This was seen as yet another case of Quebec setting the national agenda as it had previously done for so many years in its support for the Trudeau Liberal government. Sympathy for the need to make concessions to a Quebec which was able to exercise so much influence and power on the national scene, became even harder to muster. In the words of Grant Devine, premier of Saskatchewan: "No matter how hard you try to explain that Quebec did not make it into the Constitution in 1981, they don't understand and they are tired of hearing about it....Anything you do now to try to make Quebec a part of the country and the Constitution appears to them as if everybody's dropping on their knees to do something special for Quebec."[10]

The general effect, as a Gallup poll in June 1989 indicated, has been a sharp deterioration in support for the Meech Lake Accord since the beginning of 1989.[11] This has not been the result of greater knowledge of the Accord, for fully 60 per cent of the Gallup respondents indicated that they were not familiar with the Accord. It represents, instead, a growing weariness with the issue among English Canadians. By contrast with the concern and anxiety expressed in English Canada during the crises of 1979-81 and the desire at that time to help the federalist cause within Quebec, it seems that now many English Canadians no longer seem to care. Indeed, a Gallup poll in July 1989 suggested that more than one in four English Canadians (27 per cent) favoured Quebec separating from the rest of Canada and becoming an independent country, the highest level since Gallup first posed the question more than 20 years ago.[12] Thus, it would appear that the tolerance and concern that typified the views of English Canada about Quebec's aspirations in the period 1979-82 have been replaced by indifference and impatience. In the process those fighting for the federalist cause within Quebec, opposing separatism, have felt increasingly abandoned and discouraged.

The result has been a reversion to the old stereotyped polarization between an English Canada insistent upon a "nation-centred" federation and emphasizing the primacy of national programs and rights and a Quebec determined to use whatever tools it has at hand to ensure its distinctiveness. Meech Lake has come to represent this polarization. For Quebec it is seen as the irreducible minimum for further accommodation. Indeed, English Canadian critics of the Accord seem to have consistently underestimated the degree to which the Accord has been criticized within Quebec for gaining that province too little.[13] For large parts of English Canada, on the other hand, the Accord represents too large and unacceptable a concession towards a part of the country that seems to manifest so little commitment to the objectives of the rest of the country.

Although Gordon Robertson has argued cogently that the time limit for ratification of constitutional amendments does not apply to those requiring the unanimous consent of the provinces,[14] the governments involved in the process have been assuming that the deadline of 23 June 1990 must be met. As that date approaches the emotional polarization has become increasingly difficult to bridge. As Jeffrey Simpson has put it:

> Each time a leading politician puts the argument in terms of Meech Lake or disaster, Quebecers are reminded that Meech Lake will be the one and only litmus test of English-Canadian accommodation, and English-Canadians recall that Meech Lake is the latest in a series of what many of them consider endless and profoundly fatiguing demands for accommodation coming from the same place.[15]

One thing is certain. There will be no return to the status quo which existed before the Meech Lake Accord was proposed. The debate over the Accord has itself deeply affected the psyches of English Canada and Quebec. Consequently, the failure to ratify the Accord will leave serious scars, even if it does not unravel Confederation, as it well might. The political climate for reconciliation will be poisoned for a considerable period to come. Furthermore, the clear indication of the unworkability of the constitutional amendment process adopted in 1982 is likely to mean that other proposals for constitutional amendment, such as senate reform, will stand little chance of success for a long period to come. Almost inevitably, Canada would revert to the situation prior to 1982 when the evolution and development of its federal system had to be achieved incrementally through a variety of extraconstitutional amendments and accommodations rather than through formal constitutional amendments. It is one of the ironies of the Meech Lake saga that the careful process of prior intergovernmental negotiation which preceded the Accord and which was adopted in order to avoid the explosive effects of a failure to reach resolution, has itself, by attracting the stigma of "elite decision making," helped to produce the very disaster that it was intended to avoid.

Of course, Canadians may again, as in 1981, through a realization of the serious implications of the current polarization, find a political resolution before it is too late. But indifference and fatigue will need to be replaced by a conscious and extraordinary effort. Over the years, sometimes at the last minute, Canadians have worked out solutions to their political problems. Indeed, 1867 was one such example, as was 1982. Compared to the experience of other nations, including other federations such as the United States and Switzerland which have experienced the upheavals of civil war during their history, Canada's 122 years of stable government has been a remarkable achievement. Canada is one of the longest surviving federations in the world. But no constitution settles all issues once and for all. Constitutional systems by their very nature are constantly evolving and federal unity requires continuous work in every generation. Perhaps the realization of what is really at stake, of what kind of country Canada or Quebec would be without each other, may in the end help Canadians, and particularly their political leaders, yet again to summon the political will to heal the rifts.

Notes

1.   T. Courchene, "What Does Ontario Want?," The Robarts Lecture (Toronto: York University, 26 April 1988).

2.   *Allan Singer* v. *Attorney-General of Quebec* and *Attorney-General of Quebec* v. *La Chaussure Brown, Inc.*, 15 December 1988.

3.   Lorne Boginoff and Peter MacIntosh, *Support for Separatism Reaches All-Time High* (Toronto: Gallup Canada, Inc., 20 July 1989).

4.   See, for instance, Jeffrey Simpson, "Accord and Discord" and "Meech Lake visions" in *Globe and Mail*, 1 August 1989; William Thorsell, "Missing the boat" *Globe and Mail*, 6 May 1989, and "Important voices silent as resentment toward Quebec grows" *Globe and Mail*, 19 August 1989; Carol Goar, "Drifting Apart" three part series in the *Toronto Star*, 22, 23, 24 July 1989.

5.   Pierre Pettigrew, vice-president of Samson Bellair International Inc. and a leading Quebec federalist, quoted by Carol Goar, "Is Canada starting to fall apart?" *Toronto Star*, 22 July 1989, p. D1.

6.   On this, see especially Richard Simeon, "Meech Lake and Shifting Conceptions of Canadian Federalism" *Canadian Public Policy*, XIV Supplement (1988), pp. S13-S19.

7.   *Constitution Amendment Bill, 1987,* ss. 1, 3 and 7 inserting ss.2(4), 95B(2), and 106A(2) in the *Constitution Act, 1867*.

8.   See, for instance, Alan C. Cairns, "Citizens (Outsiders) and Governments (Insiders) in Constitution-Making: The Case of Meech Lake" *Canadian Public Policy* XIV Supplement (1988), pp. S121-S145.

9.   See Simeon, "Meech Lake and Shifting Conceptions," pp. S21-S23 and Cairns, "Citizens (Outsiders) and Governments (Insiders)," pp. S125-S127.

10. Quoted by Carol Goar, "Is Canada starting to fall apart?" *Toronto Star*, 22 July 1989, p. D1.

11. *Globe and Mail*, 22 June 1989. See also the comments of Jeffrey Simpson, "Meech Lake visions" *Globe and Mail*, 23 June 1989, p. A6.

12. Lorne Bozinoff and Peter MacIntosh, *Support for Separatism Reaches All-Time High* (Toronto: Gallup Canada, Inc., 20 July 1989). The percentage of those favouring Quebec's separation was in fact higher in B.C. (36 per cent) than in Quebec (34 per cent). Furthermore, in Quebec at 34 per cent it was substantially higher than in 1979 (18 per cent) or 1978 (12 per cent).

13. See Denis Robert, "La signification de l'Accord du lac Meech au Canada anglais et au Québec francophone: un tour d'horizon du débat public," in Peter M. Leslie and Ronald L. Watts (eds.), *Canada: The State of the Federation, 1987-88* (Kingston: Institute of Intergovernmental Relations, Queen's University, 1988), pp. 117-156.

14. Gordon Robertson, "Meech Lake—the myth of the time limit" Supplement to Institute for Research on Public Policy *Newsletter*, vol. 11, no. 3, May/June 1989.

15. Jeffrey Simpson, "Accord and Discord" *Globe and Mail*, 22 June 1989, p. A6.

TWO

The Election of 1988 and Canadian Federalism

Darrel R. Reid

Le chapitre ci-dessous présente un tour d'horizon de la dernière campagne électorale fédérale qui s'est soldée par une seconde victoire majoritaire des conservateurs de Brian Mulroney avec, en toile de fond, l'enjeu-clé du libre-échange. Plus spécifiquement, l'auteur aborde quelques thèmes majeurs de la campagne apparentés directement au fédéralisme canadien.

Concernant d'abord la question linguistique, la plupart des acteurs fédéraux auront été embarrassés par l'intention manifestée par le gouvernement Bourassa de recourir à la fameuse clause nonobstant pour légitimer le caractère distinct du Québec, à l'encontre de la Charte canadienne des droits et libertés. Parallèlement, chez les ultras du Canada anglais, on vouait aux gémonies le bilinguisme institutionnel.

L'Accord du lac Meech, avalisé antérieurement par les trois partis fédéraux, aura été évoqué surtout pour rappeler l'importance—cruciale pour la fédération—d'un retour du Québec au sein du giron constitutionnel canadien. Au plan environnemental, malgré certaines critiques circonstancielles de l'opposition, les trois partis ont fait chorus à propos du règlement des grands problèmes environnementaux auxquels fait face le Canada. En matière de développement régional, le gouvernement conservateur s'est fait l'apôtre de la décentralisation—plutôt bien agréée par les provinces—avec, à la clé, un certain nombre de projets nouveaux devenus toutefois vulnérables depuis le dernier budget Wilson.

La réforme fiscale fut, contre toute attente, à peu près escamotée durant la campagne électorale au profit du libre-échange. Ce dernier thème aura, de loin, dominé le débat électoral et opéré d'importants clivages idéologiques entre partisans et détracteurs de l'entente, la polémique portant notamment sur les risques—ou non—d'un étiolement de l'identité canadienne par suite d'une intensification de nos échanges économiques avec les Etats-Unis.

Pour terminer, l'auteur propose une brève analyse des résultats du scrutin fédéral pour chaque région de même qu'une explication de l'appui variable obtenu par les principaux partis en cette occasion. Qui plus est, D. Reid se livre à une supputation des priorités du gouvernement Mulroney aux fins de son second mandat. En conclusion, l'auteur explique le nouveau succès conservateur moins comme une adhésion populaire au crédo gouvernemental que comme la nécessité, ressentie par plusieurs, d'opter pour du "connu", face à une situation politique mouvante.

INTRODUCTION

It was an impressive victory after one of the most divisive elections in Canada's history. After a bitterly-contested 51-day campaign Brian Mulroney's Progressive Conservative Party did what no federal government had been able to do for 35 years and no Conservative government had done this century: it won a second consecutive parliamentary majority. In this election free trade became *the* central issue of the election and the campaign a national obsession with the future of the country and how best to safeguard it.

Among those observers with more than a passing interest in the results of this election were Canada's ten provinces and two territories, each of which had its own policy agenda, and each tracked events related to its interests with great care. Some, like Ontario and Quebec, were active participants across the policy spectrum in a campaign both believed to be crucial to their interests; others entered the fray reluctantly and only when challenged to do so. And, although the free trade debate dominated the election campaign, the provinces were no less interested in other issues of importance to Canadian federalism. It is the purpose of this paper, accordingly, to survey those issues which have been of ongoing interest to the Canadian federation and to suggest how those results might affect the Canadian federation during the government's next term of office.[1]

The first section of this paper, entitled Campaign Issues/Non-Issues, tracks six policy areas that have been of ongoing interest to federal-provincial relations in Canada and assesses the significance—if any—of the following issues in the federal election: language and the Constitution Act, 1982; the Meech Lake Accord; environmental regulation; regional development; tax reform; and free trade. The second section briefly examines the results of the election before offering some tentative suggestions as to what the government's new agenda might mean for federal-provincial relations in the future.

CAMPAIGN ISSUES/NON-ISSUES

LANGUAGE AND THE CONSTITUTION ACT, 1982

Although language became an issue in the West, most of the political action on this subject during the election of 1988 occurred in Quebec and was related to the inextricably intertwined issues of language and constitutional language rights. These issues were given an added urgency by an impending Supreme Court of Canada decision on the constitutional validity of the commercial speech provisions of Quebec's Charter of the French Language (Bill 101). Closely related to the case before the Court was the question of whether the

Quebec government ought to invoke Section 33 of the *Constitution Act, 1982*—known as the "notwithstanding clause"—to defend the status of French in the province should the decision go against the government. Both issues had come to dominate political discourse in Quebec over the previous year; both therefore, attracted attention from federal and provincial politicians who recognized that victory in the election would most likely be decided in Quebec.

Prior to the election call and during the campaign itself the Quebec government had made it clear not only that the "distinct society" provision of the Meech Lake Accord was to have priority over the Canadian Charter of Rights and Freedoms, but also that the notwithstanding clause remained the single most important guarantor of Quebec's newly-won distinct society status. Language, it was asserted, was the single most important symbol of Quebec's cultural distinctness and therefore was to be diligently defended. According to Quebec Premier Bourassa,

> La clause de la société distincte a pour but d'augmenter la force de l'article 1 de la Charte, qui permet à des gouvernements démocratiques de limiter certains droits, dans certaines circonstances... Si la Charte a priorité sur la clause de la société distincte, nous nous retrouverons dans une situation empirée au Québec. C'est pourquoi actuellement, selon la Charte canadienne des droits, nous pouvons utiliser le fait que le Québec est une société culturellement distincte, à tout le moins, nous pouvons l'invoquer devant les tribunaux....[2]

Exactly opposite Bourassa's provincial Liberals on this issue were their federal Liberal counterparts, whose desire to see the notwithstanding clause dropped from the Constitution Act, 1982 had been clear from as far back as September 1987, with the *Report* of the Special Joint Committee on the 1987 Constitutional Accord. In an addendum to the Committee's report, Liberal members stated their belief that "section 33 of the Constitution Act, 1982 should be repealed. We consider the paramountcy of the Charter essential, and do not feel that this power of derogation can any longer be justified."[3] In Quebec, Liberal leader John Turner reaffirmed this position on 8 October, suggesting to interviewers not only that Bill 101 and the upcoming Supreme Court judgement should be of national concern, but that the federal government was fully justified in using its funds to promote bilingualism in Quebec.[4]

This assertion, among others, attracted a harsh attack from the federal Secretary of State, Lucien Bouchard. According to Bouchard, the Liberal leader's commitment to abolish the notwithstanding clause made him more dangerous to Quebec than former Prime Minister Pierre Trudeau had been: "Is it possible," he asked, "that there is, in the Liberal party, a neo-Trudeauist who wants to be even tougher on Quebec than Trudeau was when he shoved down our throats (the Constitution of 1982), which we Quebecers did not want?"[5] Speaking, as he put it, as a citizen of Quebec, Bouchard affirmed the notwithstanding clause as being essential to the survival of Quebec. "In Quebec, this clause is perceived as a safety net to protect Quebec against federal initiatives that could be damaging. Abolishing it would have far-reaching consequences and I am concerned (that someone would propose it)." He went on to assert that "I know of no one in the Conservative party who would want to do such a thing..."[6] Mr. Bouchard's stand, while undoubtedly making for good press in Quebec, appears to have directly contradicted the position of his party and of the party's leader, Prime Minister Brian Mulroney.[7]

The Conservatives were not the only party seen to be in confusion over the notwithstanding clause during the election campaign. Like the other two parties, the New Democrats, while not calling for the outright revocation of Section 33, were clearly uncomfortable with its existence. NDP members of the Joint Committee had recommended that "serious attention" be given to its repeal in a second round of constitutional negotiations.[8] Such concerns notwithstanding, NDP leader Ed Broadbent's position on the issue throughout the campaign was that since the clause existed in law, it was none of his business if the Government of Quebec chose to invoke it in defense of its language or culture.[9] When officials and candidates from the Quebec wing of the party suggested that the notwithstanding clause should be available *only* to Quebec and *only* to safeguard French language rights, however, Broadbent, who at first dismissed their comments as a difference of nuance, later was forced to distance himself from those comments, asserting that the position of these Quebec candidates was "Not the position of the party as a whole."[10]

The West: Bilingualism and Bill C-72

To many in Western Canada, language was an issue as well, but for entirely different reasons. Here, voters were concerned not with the preservation of the French language, but with implications of Bill C-72, the federal government's overhaul during the last session of Parliament of the 20-year-old *Official Languages Act*. Just days before the election, Alberta premier Don Getty had launched a complaint about the federal government's bilingualism policy being "shoved down the throats" of westerners. According to Getty, the federal government's insistence upon bilingualism was limiting the jobs for unilingual westerners in the federal civil service.[11] While at any other time such complaints might have been dismissed as typical western spleen, this time Getty's remarks provoked a measured response from Getty's federal Conservative counterparts and a more hostile one from Quebecers.[12] External Affairs Minister Joe Clark, locked in a struggle with Reform Party leader Preston Manning in his Alberta riding of Yellowhead, allowed that: "There is obviously a language issue waiting to be stirred up among some Albertans. In my mind, it's an old issue, a very divisive issue ... the kind of issue that doesn't help the country."[13] Despite the press coverage Getty's comments received in central Canada, however, they were received with rather more sympathy by westerners than the Conservatives would have liked to have seen.[14]

While during the election campaign Getty was somewhat restrained in his language complaints by his strong support of the Free Trade Agreement, other western parties were only too happy to take up the cause—one for which many commentators acknowledged there was a ready audience in the West. Most notable among these was the Reform Party of Canada, led by Preston Manning, that drew readily upon the hostility generated by the perceived inequalities of official bilingualism. In Regina, for example, Mr. Manning asked his audience why it is that one who supports francophone rights in Quebec is described as a "Quebec nationalist," while one in the West who promotes English is often dismissed as a "racist, Western redneck." In a reference to the Quebec signs case he observed that "Nobody gets arrested in Western Canada for putting a sign up in French .... It's the double standard."[15] Mr. Manning pledged the Reform Party to bring "some rational thinking into the way the French language issue is dealt with in Ottawa." The priorities of the federal government "are distorted when $60 million is injected into the province (of Saskatchewan) to further the expansion of the French language," when those funds might have been more usefully spent on drought relief.[16]

Farther to the East, rumblings of discontent with Ottawa's bilingualism policy were heard as well. Candidates from the Confederation of Regions Party (CoR), hoping to capitalize upon anti-bilingualism sentiment in Northern Ontario, targeted the ridings of Sudbury and Nickel Belt, where the victory margins of Liberal Douglas Frith and New Democrat John Rodriguez had been less than 3,000 votes in 1984. While CoR candidates managed to top the 3000-vote mark, however, both Mr. Rodriguez and Sudbury Liberal candidate Diane Marleau posted strong victories in their ridings, actually increasing their margins of victory.[17] Here, as in the West, the major concern was the perceived lack of access to jobs for unilingual anglophones. CoR candidates also linked the government-sponsored encouragement of French to the Meech Lake Accord and, more particularly, its distinct society clause, which they perceived as giving Quebec a power held by no other province.[18]

MEECH LAKE ACCORD

Outside the tangled language-culture-constitution politics of Quebec, the Meech Lake Constitutional Accord did not become an election issue. This was primarily because the Accord itself had already passed Parliament with all-party support, and the party leaders—each hoping for a strong showing in Quebec—

had little desire to see the issue re-debated on a political stage anywhere near so volatile as this election had become. The government's campaign on the issue was restrained, to say the least; with the agreement of the legislatures of New Brunswick and Manitoba still necessary to complete the Accord, the matter remained a delicate one that uncontrolled regional bickering could do much to undermine. For their part, Turner and Broadbent faced rising opposition from within their own parties to their support of the Accord. Together, all three parties managed to keep discord over Meech Lake to manageable proportions throughout much of the country during the election campaign.

According to their official platforms, all three parties agreed that the Accord should be ratified as quickly as possible. In fact, their platforms looked remarkably similar. Each party promised:

- to ratify the Meech Lake Accord and bring it into effect;
- to support the concept of Quebec as a "distinct society" within Canada;
- to pursue negotiations with the governments of New Brunswick and Manitoba in order to obtain their assent to the Accord; and,
- to begin a second round of constitutional negotiations (post-ratification) aimed at addressing the concerns of womens' groups, aboriginal peoples and linguistic minorities.

Only in Quebec did this seeming unanimity break down. Here, Mulroney pursued his party's strategy of portraying both the Accord and the Free Trade Agreement (FTA) as being two substantial means for Quebec to realize its constitutional and economic destiny. He was largely successful in keeping Turner and the Liberals on the defensive by pointing both to Turner's discomfort with certain aspects of the Accord and his attempts to modify it in the Commons.[19] Further, he was able to point to the bitter—albeit temporarily muffled—discord within the Liberal party on the issue and ask Quebec voters who they trusted to carry the Accord through to completion.

On this point, the Conservatives scored heavily in Quebec. They had, moreover, an important ally in this fight. No sooner had the election begun than Bourassa launched an attack against "dissident Liberals" in the federal caucus who had voted against the Accord and were still working within the party to undermine support for it. These Liberals wanted to "weaken Quebec" by making the Accord's distinct society clause subordinate to the Canadian Charter of Rights and Freedoms. This, according to Bourassa, was clearly unacceptable.

> I want to clear up this constant assertion by those Liberals who oppose Meech Lake.... What is most important for us in the Meech Lake accord is to give Quebec more power to protect its cultural future. The recognition in the Constitution of a distinct society would give more strength to the charter and would allow us to protect our future more effectively."[20]

For their part, those federal Liberals who had voted for the Accord complained that Bourassa was not showing enough gratitude for the federal Liberal Party's official support of the Accord.

Despite the turmoil in Quebec, however, the other parties to the constitutional agreement—the provinces—did not enter the debate. None of these, facing political opposition from within their own territory, wished to see the debate on their carefully-crafted agreement re-opened. And at election call, the prospects for the successful completion of the Accord looked reasonably good. Eight of the ten provincial legislatures had already ratified the Accord and the minority government of Manitoba Premier Gary Filmon, who at that time personally supported the Accord, had plans to introduce a motion of support for the agreement into the Manitoba legislature. Despite the outspoken opposition of Manitoba Liberal leader Sharon Carstairs, it seemed likely that NDP leader Gary Doer, who had supported the agreement earlier, would do so once again. Only New Brunswick Premier Frank McKenna remained to be convinced of the need for his support of the agreement. Although events that followed the election would complicate matters greatly, the attitude of the provinces during the campaign was one of quiet—albeit guarded—optimism.[21]

ENVIRONMENT

Campaigning on their environmental record, the Conservative strategy was to emphasize the need for a collective commitment required of Canadians to effect an improvement in the environment. By most indications, this approach seemed to be the one most likely to succeed with the Canadian electorate on two fronts: it would address what earlier polls had repeatedly shown to be high public concern over the environment[22] and would strike a cooperative note with the provinces, with whom the federal government shares jurisdiction in environmental matters.

The centrepiece of the Tories' election platform was their *Canadian Environmental Protection Act* (CEPA), passed by Parliament the previous June. When it was introduced, it was portrayed by the Conservative government as a tough-minded answer to Canada's environmental concerns. As described by then-Environment Minister Tom McMillan it was to be "the most progressive in the western hemisphere [which would be] backed up by a compliance and enforcement schedule that will demonstrate to Canadians this government means business when it's going to take on polluters."[23] Critics charged that the Act weakened federal powers by reducing the federal role in environmental protection largely to one of consultation with the provinces. At the time, Liberal environment critic Charles Caccia pronounced the Act a victim of the "Meech Lake virus."[24]

On the popular level there was, from the beginning, little voter interest in the environment issue. Although there had been a pre-election bulge in popular concern about environmental matters in the wake of the St.-Basile-le-Grand accident—which, for example, led the NDP to stress environmental issues above free trade in early campaign ads—polls throughout the campaign consistently ranked the environment well down the list of voter concerns.[25] From the federal-provincial perspective as well, environmental issues generated little debate among Canada's federal players for the reasons that follow.

First, the opposition parties were unable to take the initiative on environmental matters from the Conservatives. Prior to the election, the government had seized the environmental "high ground" with its much-ballyhooed CEPA; a renewed commitment to get tough with environmental offenders; and a pledge to increase the visibility of environmental matters within the cabinet. Although both opposition parties hammered away at what was termed the "deathbed repentance" of the Conservatives on environmental matters, neither managed to offer alternatives significantly different in substance from those of the Conservatives. In fact, the platforms of all three parties were remarkably similar, with each party pledging:

- to give environmental matters a higher profile within government;
- increased funds for a cleanup of the Great Lakes region;
- to sign an acid rain accord with the United States;
- to eliminate PCBs from the country in the near future; and
- to toughen penalties against polluters.

Neither the Liberals nor New Democrats were able to produce a credible alternative to the CEPA that would redress the "sellout of federal authority" they had denounced earlier in such strong terms. Their reluctance to promise tougher federal government action vis-à-vis the provinces seems to indicate a de facto acceptance by the parties of the provinces' more active role in environmental regulation. This state of affairs could only work in the Conservatives' favour.

Finally, external events seemed to give more urgency to the ongoing federal-provincial process for handling environmental matters. The Conservatives could rightly claim that the wheels were turning. During the election campaign, for example, the provinces continued to meet with the federal government to press it to use its federal powers over taxation to create a "superfund" from which funds could be drawn for the cleanup of hazardous wastes. As well, the provinces urged Ottawa to use its powers over interprovincial and international transportation to ban the marine and air transportation of PCBs and other hazardous wastes sent to foreign countries for destruction. As any of these provincial initiatives would almost certainly be stalled by a change in government, there was little provincial challenge to the status quo ante in environmental matters during the election campaign.

REGIONAL DEVELOPMENT

Given the high profile that regional development has between elections, its economic impact upon all regions, and recent spending commitments by the Conservatives, it seemed likely that regional development would be one of the major issues of the campaign. Traditionally, this policy area has served as a sort of lightning rod to which such issues as regional discontent and the allocation of regional benefits have been drawn. Yet, with all its potential, regional development did not become an election issue for a number of reasons ranging from general agreement on the philosophy of regional development to its being upstaged by the free trade debate.

In reality, the Conservative campaign on regional development had begun long before the 1 October election call. Between May and September 1988 the government announced a series of major regional development initiatives to be spread across the country. And although the Conservatives insisted that the timing of these announcements was coincidental to that of the election call, their announcement certainly did no harm to the Conservatives who were campaigning on their commitment to regional development across the country. The list of pre-election spending commitments was both long and expensive, including, among other things:

- the Hibernia mega-project off Newfoundland, for which Ottawa was to supply $1 billion in grants and $1.66 billion in loan guarantees;
- the concluding of a $970 million, five-year major regional development pact with Quebec aimed at encouraging regional participation in the regional economic development process;
- the announcement of joint federal-provincial funding for a $1.3 billion heavy oil upgrader in Lloydminster, in which Ottawa would hold a 31.6 per cent equity;
- participation with the government of Alberta in a $4 billion Alberta oil sands project, in which Ottawa and Alberta were to provide $850 million in cash and up to $1.2 billion in loan guarantees;
- the signing of an energy accord with the government of the Northwest Territories giving them a say in the future development of energy resources in the region; and
- a commitment to help finance a $485 million natural gas pipeline to Vancouver Island, of which the federal stake was to be a $100 million grant plus a $50 million interest-free loan.

For the Conservatives, the announcement of such major commitments before the election had two main advantages: first, having formally committed themselves, they could portray these initiatives as already-concluded agreements rather that campaign promises; and second, these projects provided the Conservatives with an effective counter-argument to those complaining of Conservative inattention to a given region. Having made most of their initiatives before the election call, the Conservatives were able to proceed with a business-as-usual approach, announcing several small projects through their new regional development agencies—the Atlantic Canada Opportunities Agency (ACOA) and the Western Diversification Office (WDO)—while keeping actual election commitments to a minimum.

Of almost as much value to the Conservatives as the big announcements was the widespread perception, even among the opposition parties, that their reorganization of regional development along more decentralized lines was, if not an unqualified success, at least a step in the right direction. Since the Conservatives came to power in 1984 Canada's regional development agencies had undergone both a major reorganization and a shift in philosophy. In 1987 the Conservative government announced that the Department of Regional Industrial Expansion (DRIE), which had been responsible for regional development, would be folded into the new Department of Industry, Science and Technology. ACOA and WDO were to take over most of DRIE's regional development concerns. With the establishment of these two agencies, the Conservatives announced their intention to decentralize regional development decision making. No longer would decisions affecting the economic well-being of the Atlantic or Western regions be made in far-off Ottawa, but rather would be made locally by an agency responsive to local needs and concerns, and with the money and authority to carry them out. This approach was further enforced by the recent Ottawa-Quebec development accord that pledged the two governments to encourage the making of development decisions according to regional objectives. Thus it would appear that there was enough interest in all of these fledgling regional initiatives that opposition was muted by those advocating a wait-and-see approach.

Finally, despite some differences in their platforms, both opposition parties saw some utility in the Conservatives' new approach to regional development, and incorporated aspects of it into their own election promises. The Liberal Party, while promising a "new approach" to regional development through a return to "traditional principles," saw enough merit in the new approach to promise the retention of many of the Conservatives' innovations. The Liberals promised a new Ministry of Regional Development, but this department was to act as an umbrella organization for those agencies already in place. Their platform amounted, in effect, to an improvement upon—not a fundamental reorganization of—the present government's regional development policies. Even more than the Liberals, the New Democrats proposed policies that supported the Conservatives' decentralized approach to regional development. Ed Broadbent made his support for the decentralized approach of the Conservatives plain during the campaign by promising, among other things, to double the annual budget of ACOA[26] and to substantially boost the budget of WDO.[27]

On the policy level—if not necessarily at the level of voter response—this working consensus among the political parties and various regional interests that the new approach deserved a chance represented a vindication of sorts for the Conservative approach to regional development.[28] Post-election events, however, have thrown into question how thoroughly and how quickly the Conservatives will be able to carry out their agenda for change. Shortly after the election the new government announced, in light of a worsening budgetary deficit situation, that all its regional programs would be reevaluated because of the harsh new realities. While this will likely result in less money to the regions and the delay of some projects, barring a major change in philosophy, the Conservatives' two-track approach of mega-projects and decentralized regional development agencies will continue throughout the next term. By the end of that period, more data may be available on how successful their new approach has been, and will push regional development issues onto the electoral stage.

TAX REFORM

As with many of the issues in this election, tax reform has long been the subject of intensive federal-provincial negotiations. Indeed, at the time of the election call federal and provincial officials were putting the final touches on a general framework for the implementation of Finance Minister Michael Wilson's proposed multi-stage tax.[29] Despite the universal unpopularity of tax changes, the opposition was unable—and the provinces were unwilling—to make tax reform an election issue for two main reasons: first, there was enough provincial interest in the rough outline of the proposed national sales tax to suspend their criticisms; and second, the Conservatives managed, with one or two exceptions, to keep the issue out of the election spotlight.

Since Wilson announced his intention to produce a national sales tax in 1987, all the provinces had indicated an interest in pursuing the option further. To this end, they had been holding technical discussions regularly with federal officials for more than a year to hammer out the details of what such a tax might look like. From the beginning, the provinces had a number of jurisdictional concerns, including how the different tax rates in the provinces would be handled, and the implications of turning over the collection of provincial taxes to the federal government.

There were clearly some advantages to the proposal. First, there were obvious cost advantages to having both levels of tax collected at the national level; this would avoid the costly duplication of having to maintain tax collection agencies at both levels of government. Further, Ontario and Quebec have long maintained that the federal Manufacturers' Sales Tax, which taxes goods at the manufacturing level, has had a disproportionate effect upon their manufacturing-based economies. Under the tax reform proposals, this tax would be spread throughout the economy, lowering the tax burden on industries and leading to enhanced competitiveness, increased profits, and job creation. Finally—and no mean consideration in itself—there was a political attraction to having the federal government perform the ever-thankless function of collecting taxes. (For the provinces, though, this latter consideration had to be weighed against the fact that the public would hold them also responsible for higher prices at the cash register.) An additional incentive to talk had been given the provinces by the federal government's commitment to proceed unilaterally, if need be, with its new tax regime.

In the early stages discussions had gone well. By the time of the election call a preliminary administrative framework had been worked out and federal-provincial meetings continued throughout the election to clean up the remaining details. With these nearly out of the way, federal and provincial negotiators had finally reached the big issues: "what goods and services were to be included in the tax base; what the federal and provincial rates would be; whether the tax would be visible to the consumer or hidden; the size of the federal sales tax credit; and most important, whether the provinces would cooperate."[30] During the election these decisions—the truly political decisions—had yet to be made, and the provinces were not willing to broadcast their positions on them prematurely.

If the provinces were unwilling to make tax reform an election issue, the Liberals and New Democrats, despite wanting very much to do just that, were unable to do so. From the beginning, both opposition parties had accused the Conservatives of effecting a "tax grab." They almost succeeded in raising the profile of the issue when Don Blenkarn, chairman of the Commons Finance Committee, suggested that Ottawa's proposed national sales tax could net the government as much as $10 billion more that previously announced. Both opposition leaders were quick to pounce on Blenkarn's pronouncements, accusing the Conservatives of having a hidden tax agenda for Canadians. The Prime Minister was quick to distance his party from Blenkarn's comments, however. Restating the government's promise that any new tax would be "revenue-neutral"—that is, that the sum total of taxes collected would remain unchanged— Mulroney stated that Blenkarn's suggestions were "out of line," and did not represent the government's calculations: "Finance Minister Michael

Wilson speaks for the government and he has already expressed the government's position" on the impact of tax reform.[31] His quick action succeeded in defusing what might have become a major election issue for the opposition parties.

More than anything else, however, the positions of the opposition parties on tax reform were undermined by the high level of support they had previously shown for the concept of tax reform in general. Earlier in the year, the all-party Commons Finance Committee had unanimously recommended that Ottawa produce proposals on a new sales tax at the earliest possible date and had urged the government to give high priority to negotiations with the provinces. While the general outline of the proposed tax had been made public, so few of the actual details had been announced either by Ottawa or the provinces that opposition attacks never gathered the needed momentum to make tax reform a full-fledged election issue.

FREE TRADE

During the 1988 federal election, free trade, or more particularly the Canada-U.S. Free Trade Agreement (FTA) signed between the two countries on 2 January 1988, became *the* election issue, sweeping all other issues before it. In retrospect, it is hard to imagine how anyone could have expected otherwise. The principal reason for the election call was Turner's request that the Liberal majority in the Senate block the government's free trade legislation until after an election on the issue. A Gallup poll conducted the week of the election call indicated that 57 per cent of respondants believed that free trade would be the principle election issue; environmental issues and the Meech Lake Accord, by comparison, were cited by 1 and 2 per cent respectively.[32]

In federal-provincial terms, free trade was already a well-worn issue and had been the subject of protracted federal-provincial consultation earlier in 1987-88.[33] During this election, however, the federal-provincial debate, which had already generated no small amount of interprovincial tension, was subsumed by a broader ideological one. Although this did little to reduce those tensions, it shifted the centre of the debate away from the federal-provincial dimension. Discussions now shifted from jurisdiction, tariff schedules, and level playing fields to ones of national identity and purpose. On this level, two very different visions of the Canadian federation emerged and were debated upon the electoral stage.

From the beginning, the Conservatives' strategy for selling free trade was to include it as part of its larger "Managing Change" campaign, which emphasized their party's qualifications to carry Canada into the twenty-first century. It was to be but a part of the new agenda for Canada's future. Where its merits were to be stressed was in the regions that had expressed support for free trade and which viewed enhanced Canada-U.S. trade as their way to prosperity. The West was particularly receptive to the themes used by Mulroney, who was prepared to exploit regional grievances to gain support for the agreement. In fact, it became part of Conservative strategy to invite the other regions to share in the prosperity that Ontario had enjoyed through such free trade-like arrangements with the United States as the Auto Pact. In Winnipeg, for example, Mulroney asked his audience: "Why is there no manufacturing base here? Because, for one thing, western producers have been exploited by unjust tariff rates to the East."[34] Free trade, according to this vision, was to offer the western provinces the historic possibility of freeing themselves from this traditional state of affairs favouring Ontario.

Western politicians were willing to take up this time-honoured theme in defense of free trade. Saskatchewan Premier Grant Devine, for example, had carried his defense of the agreement into Broadbent's home-riding of Oshawa, Ontario, where he explained that all that the West was seeking was the same benefits that had accrued to Ontario as a result of their favoured trading status with the United States. Don Getty, for his part, fumed about the parade of "eastern jokers" headed Alberta-wards with their anti-free trade sermons; commenting on a series of visits by Broadbent, Canadian Auto Workers president Bob White, and author Pierre Berton, Getty exclaimed: "To have them come out here and say 'if you guys got this it'd be terrible,' it's really a joke and I'm getting tired of it."[35]

For the federal government, the most outspoken Ontario-basher was Lucien Bouchard who called the rest of the country to oppose Ontario's anti-free trade campaign, accusing the "Ontario establishment" of opposing the FTA in order to retain its wealth and privilege at the expense of the rest of the country.

> Look at this debate (on free trade) with the eyes of a Quebecer from the yes side. In 1980, Ontarians came to Quebec to tell us 'you are ghettoizing yourselves. Don't do that. Open up to the world instead; do like us.' Well, they convinced us. Quebec chose not to separate, and to become an active partner in Confederation, and to open up to the world. Now they want us to stop? That happens every time Quebec is on the verge of a significant breakthrough. Quebec has decided to do things right, and to play the game by the book. We have become a vibrant, aggressive partner in Confederation. And now Ontario tells us: 'Hold it. You, in Quebec, just stay at home, and just be an economic ghetto *vis-à-vis* the United States. We'll do the trading with them and you'll get the equalization payments.' It gives me the impression that Quebec is the one playing straight inside Confederation, and that Ontario has become the separatist force, the one which wants to go it alone. That makes me angry.[36]

Such attacks, their effects upon Quebecers aside, certainly had an effect upon Ontarians, and Bouchard's attacks provoked a bitter response from Premier Peterson:

> This is a man that tried to ruin the country over a separatist vote and now he's trying to do it over free trade... Presumably when one aspires to be a national politician and be in the cabinet, as he is, one has to have some kind of comprehension of the rest of the country and some kind of a national vision. I would hope that he isn't going into the cabinet just to further some of his old ambitions about Quebec separatism.[37]

The sparring between Bouchard and Peterson underlined a widening rift between Ontario and Quebec over the free trade issue. Bourassa, for example, while officially eschewing involvement in the federal campaign, in reality vigorously defended the agreement in any forum available to him. This brought him into conflict, at various times, with John Turner, members of the federal Liberal caucus, and Premier Peterson.

As portrayed by both Bourassa and the Conservatives, the free trade issue represented nothing less than a battle for the future of Quebec. In language reminiscent of the 1980 referendum campaign, Mulroney told a Quebec audience that:

> Quebecers are fed up with the old tactics of those who are contemptuous of our intelligence and insult our dignity. They say no to these prophets of doom, these professional pessimists, and yes to the builders of a new Quebec prosperity. ... (Quebec's Liberal Premier) Robert Bourassa supports free trade! (Parti Québécois leader) Jacques Parizeau supports free trade! And Brian Mulroney supports free trade![38]

As the Conservatives had planned it, the issue of free trade was to be only one part of the larger vision for Canada presented to the Canadian electorate. Mulroney portrayed the FTA as playing a vital role in what he termed the "national reconciliation" that free trade would bring about. Just as the Meech Lake Accord would bring Quebec back "into the constitutional fold," thereby making it a full partner in Confederation, so the FTA would do the same for the entire country in an economic sense, distributing the economic benefits of liberalized trade across the nation, not just to the few. No one region would be penalized by the gains of others. Alberta would profit, but not at the expense of Ontario. Ontario would benefit, but not at the expense of Alberta. This was his vision: a less centralist Canada that would allow maximum freedom of action to provinces wanting to realize their economic potential, free from undue influence by an overbearing federal government. The nation could only be strong as its individual members are strong.[39]

Opposition to this view came in two forms, each passionately opposed to the FTA but each with differing emphases. One view held that the FTA would have a decentralizing effect upon the country and foster its breakup; the other, that the FTA's effect would be to weaken governments uniformly at both the federal and provincial levels, thereby endangering the give-and-take of Canadian federalism.[40] The first view, as proposed by the Liberals and anti-free trade groups such as the Council of Canadians, was that Canada's interests could be adequately defended only by a strong federal government. The FTA, so their argument ran, loosened these bonds by restricting the federal government's ability to act in energy, regional development and, especially, social programs. In the leaders' debate of 25 September Turner stated

> Above all, we will never, never sign a deal which surrenders our control and ability to manage our economy, or our social and regional equality programs, or our destiny as a people. Mr. Mulroney's trade deal does just that.[41]

The second group, of which Saskatchewan NDP leader Roy Romanow was one of the more articulate spokesmen, argued that the agreement would weaken the powers of both the federal and provincial governments to the point where policies desired by the United States would eventually predominate. This, according to Romanow, would destroy Canada's unique form of federalism, with its careful balance of national and regional interests. The perceived threat to Canada was twofold. First, the FTA would give the United States more influence over what policies governments would pursue and would lock the country into a bilateral system where American interests would eventually come to dominate Canadian ones in the formulation of both provincial and national policies. Second, the agreement would create instability in the carefully developed federal-provincial-regional relationship by the treaty's insistence that the federal government ensure provincial compliance to the agreement— even in areas of provincial jurisdiction. This would undermine the give-and-take of the Canadian federation.

> No more discussion of federal-provincial negotiations. No more of that genius of compromise for a better Canada. They can override .... the federal system of compromise [that] is the source of strength that keeps [Canada] together and that provides the bonds that unite the country. But out of that need to compromise and cooperate we have built as a consequence a far different world and certainly a nation different from the U.S. where, as I see it, the pre-eminent ethic has been emphasis on individual rights (and) to a predominant commitment to the market-place and the development of private enterprise.[42]

Thus, during this election the free trade issue proceeded along both regional and ideological lines. And while it is true that ideological factors exerted the greater influence upon the election of the two, it can also be said that even these were influenced by factors of ongoing concern about the impact on the Canadian federation.

THE RESULTS

REGIONAL DIFFERENTIATION

The Conservative victory has meant different things in different regions of the country. Whether these regional variations point to broader electoral trends remains to be seen, but they testify to a wide diversity of voting patterns in the Canadian federation.

The West/North

With the sole exception of Alberta, where support for the party remained strong, the electoral fortunes of the Conservatives declined throughout the West in the 1988 election; in the four western provinces overall seats held by the Tories dropped from 58 of 77 in 1984, or 75 per cent to 48 of 96 in 1988, or 50 per cent (see Table 2.1). Popular support declined in all four western provinces, by as little as 4 per cent in Alberta to as much as 18.5 per cent in Yukon and the Northwest Territories (see Table 2.2). Underlying these results are a number of factors which could indicate increasing problems for the government in the West in years to come.

After a period of relative inactivity, a number of protest parties have emerged and may become a significant new factor in the West, since 1957 a bastion of Conservative support. These parties attempted to mobilize voter discontent with the main parties, appealing to the traditional roots of western alienation: the perception of the West's lack of clout in the national parliament; Ottawa's language polices; and perceived discrimination against the West in the awarding of government contracts.

As is shown in Table 2.2, the most successful of these protest parties was the Reform Party of Canada, which made reasonably strong showings in Alberta, B.C., and Manitoba. In Alberta, the party ran third in overall votes, gathering 15 per cent of the popular vote in that province. This was good enough to place them ahead of the Liberal Party and they came within 20,000 votes of being runner up to the Conservatives.[43] Although the Reform Party won no seats during the election proper, it sent its first member to the federal house after a by-election victory in the Alberta riding of Beaver River held after the death of Conservative member John Dahmer. Despite these numbers in Alberta, the Reform Party's largest impact may have been felt in B.C., where, arguably, the

Table 2.1
Party Support by MPs Elected by Province, 1984 and 1988

Party	B.C.		Yukon/ NWT		Alta.		Sask.		Man.		Ont.		Que.		N.B.		N.S.		P.E.I.		Nfld.		National	
	84	88	84	88	84	88	84	88	84	88	84	88	84	88	84	88	84	88	84	88	84	88	84	88
PC	19	12	3	0	21	25	9	4	9	7	67	47	58	63	9	5	9	6	3	0	4	2	211	170
Liberal	1	1	0	2	0	0	0	0	1	5	14	42	17	12	1	5	2	5	1	4	3	5	40	82
NDP	8	19	0	1	0	1	5	10	4	2	13	10	0	0	0	0	0	0	0	0	0	0	30	43
Other	0	0	0	0	0	0*	0	0	0	0	1	0	0	0	0	0	0	0	0	0	0	0	1	0
Total	28	32	3	3	21	26	14	14	14	14	95	99	75	75	10	10	11	11	4	4	7	7	282	295

* The PC member for the constituency of Beaver River died before taking his seat in the Commons; in a byelection a Reform Party candidate was elected.
Source: *Globe and Mail*, "How Canada Voted, 1984, 1988", 23 November 1988, A14, A15; (Canada: Report of the Chief Electoral Officer, 1984).

Table 2.2
Party Support by Per cent of Popular Vote by Province, 1984 and 1988
Totals may not equal 100 due to rounding

Party	B.C.		Yukon/ NWT		Alta.		Sask.		Man.		Ont.		Que.		N.B.		N.S.		P.E.I.		Nfld.		National	
	84	88	84	88	84	88	84	88	84	88	84	88	84	88	84	88	84	88	84	88	84	88	84	88
PC	47	35	49	30	69	52	42	36	43	37	47	38	50	53	54	40	51	41	52	41	58	40	50	43
Liberal	16	20	24	30	13	14	18	18	22	37	30	39	35	30	32	45	34	46	41	50	36	41	28	32
NDP	35	37	22	37	14	17	38	44	27	21	21	20	14	14	14	9	14	11	7	8	6	12	19	20
Other	2	8	5	3	4	17	2	1	8	5	1	3	6	3	0	5	0	1	1	1	0	0	3	5

Source: *Globe and Mail*, "How Canada Voted, 1984, 1988", 23 November 1988, A14, A15; (Canada: Report of the Chief Electoral Officer, 1984).

party's 5 per cent of the popular vote may have cost the Conservative Party four seats.[44]

Another factor evident in the West was the changing political orientation of Manitoba. Commentators have noted that Canada's electoral map consists of two overlapping two-party systems: from the Ottawa River eastwards the Liberals and Conservatives dominate; from Manitoba westwards the Conservatives and NDP dominate; and in Ontario, where the two systems overlap, all three parties contest elections.[45] Where once Manitoba had more in common with its sister provinces to the West, significant Liberal gains both in the federal and the provincial election earlier in the year, suggest that the overlap once confined to Ontario has moved westwards to include Manitoba. Results from the federal election and the provincial election of April in Manitoba are almost identical to the popular vote figures in Ontario for the federal election.[46]

One final point of interest is that in the West, where regional issues have traditionally played a large part in its politics, it was the trans-regional free trade issue that dominated the election. Although at the outset of the campaign western voters were almost evenly split on the merits of the agreement,[47] by early November support had fallen sharply.[48] It is possible that, of the 17 seats lost by the Conservatives in British Columbia, Saskatchewan, Manitoba, and the North (Table 2.1), many can be most directly attributed to voter concerns about free trade. This result was all the more noteworthy given the enthusiastic support of the FTA by the region's four premiers. An Environics poll taken late in the campaign indicated that in B.C., Saskatchewan, and Manitoba a solid majority of those polled opposed the FTA in its current form despite the endorsement of the provincial premiers.[49] Such a cleavage of public opinion in these provinces indicates that, despite the best efforts of the premiers to rally public support for the agreement within their provinces, they were not the prime spokesmen for their constituencies. Although it is too soon to tell whether this sharp variance is part of a developing trend or not, it is clear that, for this issue at least, factors other than regional interests played a greater part in the voters' minds. Indeed polls throughout the campaign indicated that such factors as age, sex, and socio-economic status were better indicators of voter intention on this issue than geographical location. At the very least, the trans-regional cleavage of opinion bears witness to the dominance of the free trade issue and the passions that the free trade issue brought to the surface in the 1988 election. This appears to have been true in other regions of Canada as well, including Ontario.

Ontario

As in the West, support for the federal Tories fell, but not as far as some commentators had predicted, given the Ontario government's vociferous opposition to the FTA. There was a deep division of opinion in Ontario over the free trade agreement. The relative strength of the Tory showing in Ontario indicates the depth of support for the agreement both by the business community and among voters in higher income brackets. Popular opposition to the agreement, nevertheless, was higher in this province than in any other.[50]

Here, as in the West, two protest parties—the Christian Heritage Party (CHP) and the Confederation of Regions Party (CoR) played a role, although their effect was not nearly so pronounced. While in actual numbers, the returns of these parties were not all that significant (together, the two polled 82,500 votes), their impact upon the results may have been much greater. Together, they may have played a significant role in taking as many as five seats away from the Conservatives.[51]

Quebec

In Quebec, the Conservatives found rock-solid support for their twin initiatives of free trade and the Meech Lake Accord. As is shown in Tables 2.1 and 2.2, Quebec was the only region of the country in which the Conservatives increased both their percentage of the popular vote and the number of seats won over their 1984 results.

A major factor in these improved results for the Conservatives was the active role taken by Bourassa in supporting the Conservative campaign for free trade against all opponents declared or otherwise. Throughout most of the election Bourassa steadfastly denied any partisanship. When polls one week before the election indicated that the Conservatives and Liberals were virtually deadlocked, however, Bourassa took to the floor of Quebec's National Assembly to warn Quebecers of possible job losses due to punitive U.S. trade actions should the FTA not be implemented.[52] Because both the Liberals and NDP had vowed to scrap the agreement, Bourassa's remarks were widely interpreted to be an endorsement of the Progressive Conservatives.

Language, too, became a factor in the province's electoral results. Although the Quebec electorate as a whole gave Mulroney's Conservatives heavy support, some interesting results emerged from the Montreal area, home to many of Quebec's anglophones. The federal Liberals won their best results here in an otherwise bleak electoral landscape, gathering ten seats of the 18 they won in the entire province. Much of this support came from the anglophone community and may be as a result both of the perceived abandonment of Quebec anglophones by the Conservative government through the granting of the distinct society provision to the Quebec government and the frankly nationalistic tone of federal politicians campaigning in Quebec.

As in the Atlantic provinces, the New Democratic Party failed to win any seats in the province. This result was particularly disappointing to NDP strategists in light of the energy and money spent to win a breakthrough in Quebec. The party, it seems, was the victim of the electoral dynamics in Quebec. On the one hand, their failure to gain the support of francophones may have been because of their opposition to free trade and because the nationalistic tone of the Quebec campaign polarized voters, making it primarily a two-party race. On the other hand, the party may have been unable to attract anglophone support because of it's acceptance of Quebec's right to override minority language rights in the province.

Atlantic Provinces

Voters in the Atlantic provinces showed a major rejection of the Conservative Party in this election, with results indicating a 12 per cent drop in public opinion and a loss of 13 seats. While it is difficult to attribute this result to any single factor, it is clear that voter concerns over the impact of free trade upon their region were a major factor in this shift. These election results demonstrate conflicting concerns between what has been traditional Atlantic support for freer trade with the United States and the possible negative effects of the particular agreement the Conservatives were proposing. Chief among regional concerns was a general uneasiness about the effect of the FTA on social programs. Residents of the four provinces are more dependent on these than other Canadians. The Conservative losses in the region are all the more significant given the strong support of the agreement by three of the regions' four premiers.

THE NEW AGENDA

The election results of 21 November gave Brian Mulroney's Conservatives a broad mandate to pursue their agenda for change. Although the voters were clearly uncomfortable with the Conservatives' position on free trade, it appears that most, after having been bombarded for six weeks by conflicting claim and counterclaim, returned to the opinion, recorded in polls early in the election, that the Conservatives were the party best able to deal with a wide variety of policy issues and was the party best able to manage the country during rapidly changing times. In a Globe-Environics poll taken between 2 and 10 October respondents rated the Conservatives as the party best able, among other things, to handle Canada-U.S. relations; manage foreign policy and international relations; manage the economy; encourage regional economic development; handle federal-provincial relations; create jobs; and manage French-English relations.[53] Forty-two per cent of respondents indicated their support for the Conservatives. Within a pollster's margin of error this result was duplicated exactly on election day six weeks later. Given the prominence of free trade, economic and national sovereignty-related issues in this election, it seems likely that this confidence in the Conservatives, despite a significant hiatus in mid-campaign, had reasserted itself by election day.

In light of the clear majority the new government has received, it is likely that it will move ahead in a number of policy areas with renewed confidence; following are several areas that will have some impact upon federal-provincial relations in the next term.

Free Trade

Because the principal election issue was free trade, the Conservatives have moved quickly to ratify and implement the agreement with the United States. Although detractors have pointed out that more voters voted for parties against the deal than for it, among those who fought the election on the issue there was little doubt that the Conservatives had now won the right to proceed. In post-election comments John Turner stated: "You know that we let the people decide. The people have decided, so that, having stated our case, we'll let matters proceed."[54] Turner's interpretation of the election outcome was shared by Ed Broadbent who, in referring to the Prime Minister's future course of action stated: "He has the right, he has a mandate that's clear... The Canadian people have taken a decision and Mulroney certainly has the right to continue with passage of free trade."[55] Peterson, who had been the FTA's most vocal provincial opponent allowed that the fight was now over: "There's no sense refighting the battle. I think that one has to admit that in a sense we lost."[56] With the FTA in place, the provinces will continue to monitor closely the impact the agreement will have upon their own policy agendas. Of these, social programs and regional development may receive special attention in federal-provincial discussions. Another area of interest to the provinces will be the definition of what constitutes unfair subsidies under the FTA; this has been one of the main concerns of those regions heavily dependent upon regional development aid. The deadline for the completion of these negotiations is seven years, however, and it is reasonable to expect that this issue may recur in the next election.

Meech Lake Accord

The election results have made the prospects for the ratification of the Meech
Lake Constitutional Accord much less bright than they were before the election.
Among those taking their seats in the new Parliament are many who are either
opposed to or have strong reservations about the Accord. Included in this
number are francophone Liberal Acadians such as Douglas Young (Gloucester),
a former minister in Frank McKenna's cabinet; a strong delegation of Manitoba
Liberals who, along with Sharon Carstairs, have voiced concerns about the
Accord; and anglophone Liberals from Quebec, several of whom have openly
questioned the wisdom of John Turner's support for the Accord in light of the
Liberal Party's poor showing in Quebec.

Significant changes have occurred in the outlook of western NDP members
as well. Gary Doer has taken the position that the need for amendments to the
Accord has increased because of the Conservative victory and the impending
passage of the FTA. His fear is that the Accord could further weaken Ottawa's
powers, especially in the establishment of new social programs. "Mr.
Mulroney," he stated "has been given a blank cheque on social services by the
people of Canada with the approval of the free trade agreement and we'll [the
Manitoba New Democrats] be very careful on a second blank cheque on the
spending power provision of Meech lake."[57] Although in principle Doer's
concerns are at variance with those of his Saskatchewan counterpart Roy
Romanow, who regards the FTA as strengthening Ottawa's hand, both agree
that the Accord is a decentralizing document and that it requires careful
reexamination in light of the passage of the FTA.

Events subsequent to the election campaign have further complicated the
Accord's path to successful completion. In the wake of Bourassa's invocation
in December of the notwithstanding clause to protect the French language in
Quebec, a number of his fellow premiers have expressed their concern about
the "distinct society" status granted to Quebec by the Accord. Premiers Gary
Filmon of Manitoba, William Vander Zalm of British Columbia and newly-
elected Clyde Wells of Newfoundland have all questioned whether the Accord
is too flawed to be allowed to pass in its present state.

Outside these provincial concerns, opposition to the Accord is on the up-
swing as well. The election has boosted the number of those opposed to the
Accord within both opposition parties, with the result that the continued
unanimous support of the three major national political parties is not nearly so
solid as it was before the election. Whatever the future of the Meech Lake
Accord, it is clear that the new Conservative government's path towards its
ratification has become more—not less—tortuous as a result of this election.

Tax Reform

How the government will proceed with its tax reform plans, and whether the provincial governments will cooperate remains unclear. Shortly before delivering his budget in April 1989, Wilson indicated that since provincial agreement on a joint tax was not forthcoming, the federal government would proceed unilaterally with its own tax, since called the "Goods and Services Tax" (GST). Although prior to the election Alberta was the only province to state its opposition to the plan, there are now rising indications of wider provincial hostility to the plan for a federal GST. In May 1989, for example, Bourassa proposed that Ontario join his province to fight the new tax. His comments were received favourably not just by Peterson, but by Vander Zalm, Wells and Getty. Chief among their concerns is that Ottawa's imposition of the new tax will make it more difficult for the provinces to raise revenues.[58] Clearly, this matter is a long way from being resolved and will continue on federal-provincial agendas for some time to come.

Environment

During the next four years, environmental issues are likely to become more important to federal-provincial relations in Canada. This is not just because of heightened public awareness of environmental issues, but because the federal government's commitment to increasing the profile of environmental matters within cabinet and the concept of "sustainable development" will generate more controversy with the provinces when federal and provincial interests collide. Such a divergence of interests has already been apparent, for example, in the postponement of the Rafferty-Alameda dam project in southern Saskatchewan.[59] Given the increased role of both levels of government in environmental regulation, this trend may be expected to increase.

CONCLUSION

Whether it was because the campaign was dominated so completely by the emotional free trade issue, or because federal-provincial relations, due in part, to the technical nature of many of the issues, seldom grip the emotions of voters, there is little evidence to suggest that federal-provincial issues per se influenced the outcome of the election to any significant degree. Even so, it cannot be said that the election has had no influence upon federal-provincial relations. For election rhetoric has added to the intensity of discussions most notably in the areas of language and the constitution, the related area of Meech Lake, the role of Quebec in Confederation, and regional development. These intensified discussions can hardly be expected to bring forth smoother federal-provincial, interprovincial and interregional relations than heretofore.

The new Conservative government has interpreted its electoral victory as constituting a broad mandate to govern and can be expected to move on a broad range of initiatives during its next term in office. Across such policy areas as Meech Lake and environmental regulation the government has been pursuing a broadly decentralist agenda consistent with Mulroney's philosophy of "collaborative" federalism. This can be expected to continue throughout the next term. Complicating matters, however, was the government announcement shortly after the election that budgetary concerns caused by rising interest rates have forced it to reevaluate all spending commitments. In areas of joint federal-provincial funding—most notably regional development and social policy—any significant funding cuts to the provinces will certainly raise tensions as the policy focus shifts from program to program. From the standpoint of the Canadian federation, the election of 1988 may have served, nevertheless, as a foretaste of the variety of issues which will predominate in the days to come.

Notes

1. It is not the intent of this article to suggest that strictly federal-provincial issues played a major role in either the campaign or its eventual outcome. They did not. Nevertheless, from the point of view of those engaged in the practice of federal-provincial relations there was the potential for any one of a number of issues to rapidly gain prominence during the election. It is on a collection of these policy areas that this article will focus.
2. *Le Devoir*, 21 October 1988, 1.
3. Canada, Special Joint Committee of the Senate and the House of Commons on the 1987 Constitutional Accord, *Report* (Ottawa: Queen's Printer, 1987) p. 150.
4. *Toronto Star*, 12 October 1988, A-18.
5. Ibid.
6. Ibid.
7. As with the Liberals, Conservative members of the Joint Committee had registered their concerns about Section 33, suggesting that it might need to be reconsidered in light of the risk it presented to Charter rights. (Joint Committee, *Report*, p.142). Earlier, Mulroney's press secretary had observed that "The Prime Minister has always said that there were two flaws in the 1982 Constitution, that it was patriated without Quebec, and that the notwithstanding clause was conceded to the provinces." *Globe and Mail*, 17 October 1988, A6.
8. Joint Committee, *Report*, p.157.

9.   On a campaign swing through Quebec, for example, Broadbent, when asked if the Quebec government should invoke the notwithstanding clause, asserted "It's not up to me. Quebec has the right to use the clause if it wants to." *Montreal Gazette*, 15 October 1988, C1.

10. *Montreal Gazette*, 9 November 1988, B4.

11. *Edmonton Journal*, 27 September 1988, A1.

12. In one of the more colorful responses Quebec Liberal MP Jean-Claude Malepart called Getty a "stumbling dinosaur wallowing in an intellectual swamp" *Edmonton Journal*, 29 September 1988, A1.

13. *Financial Post*, 21 October 1988, p.14.

14. See, for example, "Getty is just telling the truth about bilingualism," *Winnipeg Free Press*, 3 October 1988.

15. *Regina Leader-Post*, 9 September 1988: "Reform Party takes aim at language double standard."

16. Ibid.

17. The margins of victory of the two candidates were as follows: Rodriguez, 8,296; Marleau, 5,971, Source: *Globe and Mail*, Nov. 23, 1988, A14-15: "How Canada voted 1988".

18. *Globe and Mail*, 16 November 1988, A-9.

19. Mr. Turner had moved amendments to several sections of the agreement. Among the changes he sought were the recognition that aboriginal peoples constitute a distinctive and fundamental characteristic of Canada and the recognition of the multicultural nature of Canada. His motion was defeated. Canada. *House of Commons Debates*, 2 October 1987, p. 9585.

20. Among those named were Sheila Finestone (Mount Royal), David Berger (Laurier) and Don Johnston (St. Henri-Westmount), all of whom had voted against the Meech Lake Accord in the House, *Montreal Gazette*, 4 October 1988, A9.

21. Events subsequent to the election changed the dynamics of the debate both in Manitoba and elsewhere. In response to a Supreme Court striking down the commercial speech provisions of Quebec Bill 101 Quebec Premier Bourassa announced the intention of his government to invoke the notwithstanding clause in defense of the French language in Quebec. Two days later Premier Filmon announced that his government would drop their Meech Lake bill from its legislative agenda in protest of the Quebec government's action. Since then, Newfoundland has elected a government determined to see changes to the Accord.

22. One principle reason for this concern was the July 1988 toxic chemical fire at St.-Basile-le-Grand, Quebec that forced the evacuation of more than 3000 residents.

23. *Ottawa Citizen*, 6 May 1988: "Environment act clears Commons."

24. Liberal critic Charles Caccia attached this term to what he perceived as the growing provincial clout on environmental matters, *Financial Times*, 12 September 1988, p.6.

25. One example is the Gallup poll reported in the *Toronto Star*, 3 October 1988 "Tories top poll at 43 per cent, trade seen as key issue", where free trade is listed as the main election issue by 59 per cent of respondents, environment by 2 per cent.

26. *Halifax Chronicle-Herald*, 10 November 1988, p.1.

27. *Globe and Mail*, 31 October 1988, B1: "Western fund wins credibility."

28. It should be noted that if such a regional consensus existed, it does not appear to have affected voter response. The Atlantic provinces, which are major recipients of regional aid, rejected the Conservatives in this election.

29. This tax was first proposed in Wilson's *White Paper* of 18 June 1987. The proposals called for a two-stage tax reform: the first stage involved the restructuring of personal and corporate income taxes; the second stage, to follow later, was to involve the introduction of a multi-stage, or value-added tax which would replace both the federal Manufacturers' Sales Tax and provincial sales taxes.

30. *Financial Post*, 22 October 1988, p.4.

31. *Globe and Mail*, 8 October 1988, A1.

32. *Toronto Star*, 3 October 1988: "Tories top poll at 43 per cent, trade seen as key issue."

33. For a good description of the federal-provincial consultations leading up to the trade agreement, see Douglas M. Brown, "The federal-provincial consultation process," In P.M. Leslie and R.L. Watts (eds.), *Canada: The State of the Federation 1987-88* (Kingston: Institute of Intergovernmental Relations, 1988).

34. *La Presse*, 5 November 1988, A14 (translation).

35. *Calgary Herald*, 6 October 1988: "Getty fumes at eastern jokers."

36. *Globe and Mail*, 4 November 1988, A1.

37. *Globe and Mail*, 5 November 1988, A1.

38. *Globe and Mail*, 24 October 1988, A10.

39. *Le Devoir*, 5 October 1988, p.2: "Mulroney associe le libre-échange à la réconciliation nationale."

40. The dynamics of these two views are more fully described in Peter Leslie, "The Peripheral Predicament: Federalism and Continentalism," in Leslie and Watts (eds.), *Canada: The State of the Federation 1987-88*.

41. *Winnipeg Free Press*, 3 November 1988, p.7.

42. *Toronto Star*, 16 October 1988, A6: "Federalism at risk in trade deal, NDP's Romanow says."

43. Vote tallies for Alberta were as follows: P.C. 601,648; NDP 201,879; Reform Party 178, 224; Liberal Party 158,492.
44. Reform Party candidates in the B.C. ridings of Victoria, Saanich-Gulf Islands, Okanagan-Similkameen and Kootenay West polled more votes than the margin between the NDP winner and the Conservative loser, *Globe and Mail*, 25 October 1988, A6: "Jostled from the right."
45. This analysis was made by Prof. William Irvine, Queen's University, at a post-election seminar entitled "The Election Results: Polls, Parties and Campaigns" at Queen's University, 23 November 1988.
46. On 21 November 1988 the popular vote breakdown in Manitoba was as follows: P.C. 37 per cent; Liberal Party 37 per cent; NDP 21 per cent. In the 26 April 1988 provincial election the popular vote was P.C. 38 per cent; Liberal Party 35 per cent; NDP 23.5 per cent. Both these breakdowns compare favourably with the Ontario results for the federal election: P.C. 38 per cent; Liberal Party 39 per cent; NDP 20 per cent.
47. A Globe-Environics poll in October showed regional support for the agreement almost evenly divided at 42 per cent for and 41 per cent against the agreement, with 18 per cent undecided, *Globe and Mail*, 14 October 1988, A1.
48. A Globe-Environics poll one month later indicated that opposition to the agreement had risen to 48 per cent, with 40 per cent in support and 12 per cent undecided, *Globe and Mail*, 11 November 1988, A1. This change is all the more significant when it is noted that support for the agreement in Alberta remained at 56 per cent.
49. *Globe and Mail*, 11 November 1988, A1. In British Columbia 59 per cent were against, 31 per cent for; Saskatchewan, 58 per cent against, 39 per cent for; Manitoba, 48 per cent against, 38 per cent for. Alberta respondents, on the other hand were 56 per cent for the agreement, 32 against.
50. Sixty per cent of Ontarians polled in November indicated their opposition to the FTA. Globe-Environics poll, *Globe and Mail*, 11 November 1988, A1.
51. Those ridings where these parties may have deprived the Conservatives of victory include: Lambton-Middlesex, Haldiman-Norfolk, Leeds-Grenville, Northumberland, and Hamilton Mountain.
52. *Montreal Gazette*, 17 November 1988, A11.
53. *Globe and Mail*, 15 October 1988, A7. It is acknowledged that the use of such subjective terms as "best able" by the polling firm raises significant questions of definition, thereby limiting the usefulness of this poll. Nevertheless, the results do point to an identifiable body of opinion which was also reflected in early election polls on voter preference.
54. *Globe and Mail*, 23 November 1988, A1.

55. Ibid.
56. *Globe and Mail*, 24 November 1988, A4.
57. *Winnipeg Free Press*, 24 November 1988, p.2.
58. *Toronto Star*, 15 May 1989, A23.
59. For more examples of increasing federal-provincial interaction in this area see Alistair Lucas, "The New Environmental Law" in this volume.

II

Focus on the Provinces

THREE

Ontario and Confederation: A Reassessment

Donald W. Stevenson

Réagissant à d'autres réflexions sur le même thème, le présent article procède à un réexamen attentif du rôle exercé jusqu'à maintenant par l'Ontario au sein de la fédération canadienne.

Depuis longtemps enfant chéri du gouvernement central sur le plan économique, l'Ontario se sera employé jusque dans les années '70 à cultiver son image de province élitaire et désintéressée. Grand-seigneur politique, l'ex-premier ministre John Robarts amena l'Ontario, durant son règne, à se poser en "sage" de la fédération; ainsi, le gouvernement ontarien usa d'une approche pragmatique en regard de certains problèmes inhérents au fédéralisme canadien: en font foi principalement l'initiative de la conférence interprovinciale sur la "Confédération de demain" en 1967, le soutien au principe de péréquation et l'appui à l'"opting-out" défendu par le Québec.

Mais aussitôt confronté à la crise énergétique qui menaçait du coup ses privilèges fiscaux et économiques, l'Ontario aura troqué, fin '70, son rôle traditionnel d'arbitre national au bénéfice d'un profil partisan qui conduisit cette province à s'aligner inconditionnellement sur les politiques centralisatrices du gouvernement Trudeau. S'en suivit dès lors un isolement face à ses partenaires auquel l'Ontario commence lentement à mettre fin.

Partisan de l'Accord du lac Meech et adhérent obligé de l'entente de libre-échange, le gouvernement Peterson peut revendiquer par ailleurs, en début de second mandat, un bilan plutôt positif dans les domaines constitutionnel, linguistique et économique. Forcé dorénavant de faire son deuil du marché protégé canadien, l'Ontario n'en demeure pas moins le principal pivot infrastructurel du Canada. Le défi du libre-échange devrait toutefois inciter cette province, dans l'avenir, à intensifier la collaboration interrégionale—et en particulier l'axe Québec/Queen's Park—afin de mieux parer aux effets potentiellement dommageables du libre-échange dans certains secteurs de l'économie des provinces. Au reste, la "révolution entrepreneuriale" façon québécoise apparaît pour Stevenson une mesure de réajustement économique difficilement applicable à l'Ontario. En revanche le gouvernement Peterson, soucieux de renouer avec le "leadership constructif" de l'ère Robarts, pourrait éventuellement s'associer à Ottawa en vue d'élaborer une stratégie globale de développement pour le Canada de demain.

ONTARIO ISOLATED?

In his column in the *Toronto Star* of 14 January 1989, Don Braid asserted that "Quebec and the West have become the true insiders" in Canada, having finally succeeded in achieving the objectives of Premiers Lougheed and Lévesque "to wreck Ontario's influence and limit Ottawa's authority." Braid concluded that Ontario is now the outsider in Canadian federalism as a result of the notwithstanding clause in the charter of rights, the distinct society clause in Meech Lake, "the dismantling of the national energy policy and the move to world oil prices" which provided Alberta with a guarantee against price setting by Ontario," and, "most important, the free trade deal" which "begins to free both the West and Quebec from dependence on Ontario markets and products."[1]

Eight months earlier, on 26 April 1988, Tom Courchene in his Robarts Lecture at York University entitled, "What Does Ontario Want," provocatively concluded that Ontario, in its economic policies at least, had backed itself into a corner in opposition to the federal government, its sister provinces, the business community and the new world economic order and in doing so, had forsaken the balancing and statesmanlike role it had traditionally played in the federation as exemplified by Robarts' Confederation of Tomorrow Conference in 1967.[2] He expressed concern that the Ontario and federal governments might be on a collision course and suggested that "a central government conforming more to a confederal than to a federal mold will surely tend to ensure that Ontarians begin progressively to articulate their interests through Queen's Park" which would not likely be in the interests of the country as a whole.[3] His hope was that it might be opportune for another "Confederation of Tomorrow" conference, this time built around the question "what does Ontario want?" It is apparent from his paper that Courchene believes that Ontario should be emulating Quebec in many aspects of the entrepreneurial revolution that has been fostered by successive Quebec governments in the 1980s.

The premise of this paper is that while Braid and Courchene have identified some major shifts in the balance of the Canadian federation in the late 1980s, the isolation of Ontario and the supposed break from its past traditions which they portray is overdrawn. Nevertheless, Courchene's stimulating analysis, which aroused considerable interest at Queen's Park, and his call for a reassessment of Ontario's role and of the role of the federal government in supplying the glue holding the federation together, is timely particularly in light of the free trade agreement and the Meech Lake Accord, whether or not the latter is finally adopted. This paper, therefore, is directed in considerable part to addressing some of the points in Courchene's thesis.

The year 1988 was an unsettling one for Ontario in the Canadian federation. Although the Liberals under David Peterson had won a solid majority in the election of September 1987, and although the government retained a high level of support in the public opinion polls, the legislative sittings were marred by fractious debates on Sunday shopping, automobile insurance, housing and trade-related issues. By year-end the government was facing growing media criticism that it was not exhibiting a clear sense of direction and was reacting to, rather than leading, events. This was in sharp contrast to the 1985-87 minority government period, when the implementation of most elements of the 1985 political accord between the Liberals and the NDP gave rise to a public impression of an activist, reforming government with a clear mission. Although economic conditions remained buoyant as the province experienced its sixth successive year of growth, the boom in Toronto and southwestern Ontario was accompanied by a sharp increase in inflationary pressure.

On the intergovernmental scene, the year 1988 in Ontario was dominated by an exhaustive four-month set of public hearings of the Select Committee on Constitutional Reform, whose report led to the adoption in June by the Legislature of the Meech Lake constitutional package, a continuation of the close relationship between Premiers Peterson and Bourassa in spite of some policy differences between the two provinces, a rather tense relationship with the federal government sharpened by the federal election campaign and differences over fiscal issues and the trade agreement with the United States, and increasing dissatisfaction on the part of leaders in other provinces that the buoyant conditions in Ontario were not shared across the country.

Ontario's economic growth in the 1980s stood in sharp contrast to the 1970s. Then its economic performance was consistently worse than that of the rest of the country, and this had led it to ally itself with the federal government in support of strong federal action to restore fiscal and economic balance in the country, in particular through energy policy. Since the recession of 1981-82, Ontario's economy has grown by an average (1983 to 1988) of 5.9 per cent per annum as opposed to 4.3 per cent in the country as a whole, and by 1988 its average unemployment rate was 5.0 per cent, as compared to the national average of 7.8 per cent. Ontario's share of immigration to Canada returned to over 50 per cent, and the province, especially the Toronto area, became once again a mecca for migrants from the rest of the country. As a result, by the end of 1988, annual consumer price index increases in Toronto approached 7 per cent, as opposed to a national figure of well under 5 per cent. The expansion also led to sharp increases in expenditure demands on the provincial government, as housing shortages became acute, transportation and other infrastructure facilities became overloaded and badly in need of new investment, and as those who did not share in the increased prosperity placed new pressures on social programs.

The booming conditions in Ontario, and in the Toronto area in particular, made it easier for leaders in other parts of the country to call for federal action to divert economic activity away from Ontario, and for even federal politicians to engage in rhetoric which, to some Ontario ears, sounded like a federal attempt to discriminate against Ontario in federal investment and other economic decisions.[4] The debate over the establishment, through federal action, of international banking centres in Vancouver and Montreal but not Toronto, took on some of the regional overtones of the CF-18 maintenance contract that had so disturbed interregional amity in the previous two years. Throughout 1988, cries were heard from the other regions that the Bank of Canada's high interest policy was a policy designed to deal with pressures generated in Ontario and that it was causing their regions untold harm. The Ontario government was pilloried in business and financial circles for not following their universal advice for reductions in expenditures instead of responding to the expenditure demands caused in large part by economic growth. Certain federal government spokespeople accused the Ontario government of undermining federal attempts to improve relations with the United States and with the provinces, to reduce the role of government in the economy, to reform the tax system, and to encourage regional economic balance in Canada.[5]

Premier Peterson and some of his cabinet colleagues were equally unsparing in their criticism of the federal government's handling of the trade agreement and what to the Ontario government seemed to amount to an abandonment of many aspects of Canada's ability to act in its national interest. Criticism of the federal government from Queen's Park, echoed in many other provincial capitals, also focused on federal-provincial financing issues. The province charged that the federal government was solving its deficit crisis in part by cutting its commitments to provincial governments through limitations on the growth of Established Programs Financing transfers for health care and post-secondary education which "will reduce Ontario's revenue by almost $1 billion in 1988-89 alone,"[6] by cutting transfers for manpower training, by delaying funding for child-care programs, and by not renegotiating regional development or housing agreements. Added to this was a concern that the federal government was not making expenditures in areas of great concern to the province such as VIA Rail and the Toronto airport. Some policy and political advisors at Queen's Park were suspicious that the federal government's policy of "national reconciliation" implied catering to the concerns of other parts of the country who were only united in their envy or distrust of Ontario.

During 1988 it appeared that while Premier Peterson had succeeded, in spite of policy differences, in developing good personal relations and lines of communication with most of his fellow premiers, relations remained awkward at best with the prime minister and most of his colleagues. The accommodation that had been arrived at over the four post-war decades by provincial Conservative governments with mainly Liberal federal governments, based on a calculation that they were both appealing to essentially the same electorates, had not developed since the Mulroney and Peterson accessions to power in 1984 and 1985.[7] The first experience of a provincial Liberal government working with a federal Conservative government since 1935 was not an easy one. The federal cabinet, which tended to operate on many issues regionally, lacked a strong minister from Ontario with a regional mandate, while at Queen's Park a number of political advisors had cut their teeth while working for federal Liberal governments fighting federal Conservatives in Ottawa.

ONTARIO'S DEFINING CHARACTERISTICS: COMMENTARY ON COURCHENE

Tom Courchene, in his Robarts Lecture, argues that Ontario, in recent years, has been acting as a destabilizing influence in the Canadian federation. He characterizes traditional Ontario opinion as centralist, secure in the knowledge that the federal government, in devising national policies, must take Ontario interests into account. He suggests that until recently Ontario governments have not been leaders in social reform but have conservatively adapted programs initially developed by others to meet changing needs. On federal-provincial issues, until the 1970s, he concludes that "Ontario over the post-war period was quite sensitive of its economic preeminence in the federation and managed cleverly, even graciously, to carve out compromises within the federation where failure to do so would have impinged on its own interests."[8] He classes the Confederation of Tomorrow Conference in this category along with Ontario's support of equalization, federal regional development programs, and the principle of allowing Quebec to opt out of certain federal programs within provincial jurisdiction. Courchene draws a parallel between Ontario in Canada up to the 1970s and Saudi Arabia within the OPEC cartel. He argues that this comfortable position had become unstuck by the late 1970s and Ontario was cornered into an "Ontario-first" position whereby it attempted to impose its own vision and self-interest on the rest of Canada.

He suggests that the prime cause of this transformation was the energy boom of the 1970s which threatened Ontario's economic and fiscal preeminence. He says that the resulting support by Ontario for the divisive policies of the post-1980 Trudeau regime, such as the national energy policy and the unilateral constitutional initiative, set the stage for the alignment of most of the rest of the country against Ontario in the free trade debate. He agrees with Don Braid by concluding that "the free trade agreement is every bit as much about Ontarian hegemony as it is about continentalism."[9] He cites lack of enthusiasm by the rest of the country to Ontario proposals to break down interprovincial non-tariff barriers as further evidence of the gap between Ontario's agenda and that of the other regions.

Courchene says that the Peterson government has also isolated itself because it, at least in its first term, adopted a social policy agenda outside the context of an integrated socio-economic framework, while the rest of the country was on an economic policy agenda. He contrasts Ontario with Quebec, which he says has been much more outward- and forward-looking in its economic and social policies. He suggests that government policies and the spirit of entre-preneurship in Quebec are both preparing that province much better for the requirements of global economic challenges than is the case in Ontario. In the conclusion to his paper, Courchene foresees an explosive situation in Canada if Ontario were seen to be the cause of a rejection of the trade agreement, and a rapid requirement for Ontario to adopt an economic agenda if the trade agreement proceeds. He speculates that if the federal government and Ontario continue to act at cross purposes on economic policy, Ontario will be tempted into a go-it-alone approach which could upset the balance of the federation and produce a result diametrically opposed to the centralist views of most Ontarians.

Before commenting in more detail on Courchene's thesis and putting forward some alternative views on Ontario's current situation in the federation, it might be useful to review some of the traditional roles Ontario has played in the Canadian federal system, or, as Courchene has described them, the "defining characteristics" of the province.[10] He lists seven: first, Ontario's political and economic weight means that "national policy had frequently had little choice but to be cast in a pro-Ontario light"; second, "since Ontario could generally count on the federal government furthering the province's interests, Ontario has been (and still is) in favour of a strong central government"; third, "Ontarians tended to direct their political activities and loyalties toward the federal rather than the provincial government"; fourth, "the management of the big levers of economic stabilization has always kept a close eye on the Ontario economy"; fifth, Ontarians and their government would rather protect their own interests by blocking the action of other governments than by acquiring further provin-cial powers; sixth, "Ontario's interests were more in the direction of freeing internal trade than in freeing international trade"; and seventh, "Ontario was never a leader in social policy" because of its basic conservatism, its relative immunity from the worst results of business cycles and because of a realization that "Ontario and its taxpayers would end up paying for the lion's share of extending any new social policy initiatives beyond the province." He admits there are other cultural and social dimensions to Ontario's place in the country, but he restricts himself to these seven, which tend to fit his argument about

Ontario's isolation and, as he admits, in part because the economist in him suggests that the province is not driven by altruism!

While not denying the validity of the general thrust of Courchene's "defining characteristics", I believe he may be too much of an economic determinist and that there are other ways of explaining Ontario's place in the federation. Richard Simeon, for example, in his contribution on Ontario in Confederation in *Government and Politics of Ontario*,[11] points out that over time Ontario's stance has varied from strong support of provincial rights to a strong defence of federal power. A century ago Premier Mowat, in alliance with the premier of Quebec and others, strongly supported free trade with the United States in opposition to Macdonald's national policy. As Ramsay Cook said in his introduction to the Destiny Canada conference at York University in 1977: "Ontario, under Sir Oliver Mowat, invented the theory of provincial autonomy."[12] In this century the bitter battles waged against the federal government by Premiers Hepburn and Drew undermined several major federal government policies. Ontario has often in the past appeared to be isolated from other provinces. A decade ago Desmond Morton said: "What unites us in Canada is a range of limited Canadas viewed by people from various regions of the country—except for Ontarians, who, with an enraging arrogance, always assume that they can speak for all of Canada." (Courchene implies that the General Motors syndrome, where what was good for Ontario was good for Canada, is now a dead letter.) And yet, just as Courchene urges Ontario to take up again the national role played by Premier Robarts, there are always voices in Canada pressing Ontario governments to act as "an alternative federal government."[13]

Courchene is correct that traditionally, Ontarians more than the residents of any other province, identify themselves as Canadians rather than with their province, and that recently they have been the most centralist of Canadians. This lack of provincial identification affects all sectors of Ontario society. I recall two national conferences on the future of the country at the Universities of Toronto and York in 1977 in the period prior to the Quebec referendum which heard eloquent regional spokesmen from the Atlantic, the West and Quebec but whose Ontario spokesmen spoke solely on nation-wide concerns. This national identification of Ontarians makes it difficult for any Ontario government to persist for long in a national debate with what is perceived to be a parochial "province-first" approach. More so than in other provinces, the national identification and Canadian nationalism of Ontarians has contained an element of anti-Americanism, or at least a conscious rejection of some of the supposed American frontier virtues. The cultural establishment of English Canada centred in Toronto, along with the labour unions, led the fight against the trade agreement and the creeping Americanism it said would accompany it. Ontarians more generally have not developed the same uninhibited north-south relationship with the border cities of the Great Lakes "rust belt" that some other regions of the country have with their immediate neighbours to the south.

The diversity of Ontario, as a microcosm of Canada, also means that the decision-making process in the provincial government normally involves a constant search for balance and compromise among competing interests. These approximate many of the trade-offs federal governments are forced to make. Thus, resource-based northern Ontario reacts to Toronto much as does western to central Canada, rural southern Ontario (and Ontario has the largest agricultural output of any province) has very different priorities from urban Ontario, the business and cultural communities are in basic opposition on the trade issue, and the francophone and multicultural elements of Ontario society have different aspirations. This search for compromise makes the single-minded pursuit of a specific provincial interest in federal-provincial negotiations difficult to sustain. It differentiates Ontario, for example, from Alberta and its pursuit of control over its oil and natural gas resources, Newfoundland and its fishery, or Quebec and its constant decentralizing pressure in order to maintain essential control over its French-speaking society. The diversity of Ontario society also makes highly unlikely (in spite of Courchene's desires) a parallel in Ontario to Quebec's entrepreneurial revolution of the 1980s which resulted, for example, in almost all sectors of Quebec society becoming fervent supporters of the trade agreement.

Ontario has also been called "a citizen society" with a "civic culture" where "the politics of affluence is the politics of equilibrium between tradition and reform."[14] By and large the population more than in other provinces has trusted its political representatives to act on their behalf to deal with issues as they arise, provide good government services, deliver economic prosperity to at least a substantial majority, and play a constructive role on the national scene. Whether the government's motivation is self-interest (as Courchene suggests) or altruism, there has normally been non-partisan support from the public when the province's political leaders play a constructive role in trying to "knit together the diverse interests of Canadians."[15]

Courchene lists as one of his defining characteristics Ontario's tradition of being a follower, rather than a leader, in social policy. While this may be true with regard to some of the major social policy reforms initiated by Saskatchewan in the early post-war period or Quebec more recently, Ontario has been a leader, as Courchene acknowledges, in many sectoral areas as befits the first province to face many of the problems of an increasingly complex society. Thus in areas like workers' compensation, public housing, anti-discrimination programs, legal aid, pension reform and education curricula, other provinces have tended to look to Ontario as an innovator. I have some difficulty with Courchene's assertion that Ontario eschewed a social policy leadership role because of concern for the impact on federal-provincial fiscal arrangements, which in my experience was normally a very secondary concern to policy-makers in Ontario.

The fact that Ontarians do not tend to look to Queen's Park as the embodiment of provincial interest, in sharp contrast to Quebec and some other provinces, means that the bulk of Ontario's impact on federal decision-making is not through the provincial government. The stereotype of a Queen's Park-Ottawa axis or a Queen's Park-Bay Street axis has generally been overdrawn in other parts of the country. What does happen is that many national organizations and businesses with headquarters in Ontario have always been crucial influences on federal policies. Their impact has not been directed to promoting policies and programs that are specific to Ontario as a geographic entity, but to policies and programs based either on an Ontario-centred view of the country or on compromises among competing interests that do not reflect the perceived interests of more single-minded provinces. This has at times allowed Ontario governments rather smugly to avoid creating waves in the Canadian federation on the assumption that the federal government would be forced anyway into decisions that protected and promoted Ontario interests. This assumption, as Courchene notes, has been shaken, however, since the election of the Conservatives in Ottawa in 1984 and the Liberals in Queen's Park in 1985 and their subsequent failure to find a tacit political accommodation.

ONTARIO IN 1988

Courchene's analysis also refers to the political change that took place in Ontario in 1985. Whereas in Quebec the election of the Liberals in 1985 represented a shift to the right on the political spectrum (although, as he notes, the PQ government had set the stage for the entrepreneurial revolution there), the election of the Liberals in Ontario in the same year represented a shift to the left. Its social agenda was determined in considerable part by the accord with the NDP as well as by Liberal criticism, while in opposition, that the Tories had neglected social issues. It would have been highly unrealistic to expect that such a government would adopt as a basic thrust a sharp diminution of the role of the provincial government along the lines of the Quebec Liberal program. On the other hand, I think it is becoming apparent that the post-1987 Ontario Liberal government is moving towards a more "economic" agenda, although not necessarily in Courchene's favoured directions.

The "catastrophe" Courchene feared in April 1988 of Ontario votes blocking the free trade agreement did not come about, although more seats in Ontario in the November election went to candidates opposing the trade agreement than to supporters. The stage is now set for Ontario and other governments to collaborate with each other and the various sectors of the economy to take advantage of the opportunities and protect against some of the downsides of free trade. Mr. Peterson disappointed some of his supporters but eased the concerns of others when he said, after the passage of the trade agreement: "when you have lemons, you have to make lemonade."[16] This pragmatic response largely defused the major issue which in 1988 had caused a sharp rift between the provincial government and the business community, and which on the national front had isolated it from the federal government, Quebec and most of the other provinces.

Even though media criticism and legislative debate focused on short-term issues, by the end of 1988 a longer-term, more "economic" agenda was beginning to surface from Queen's Park. During 1988, the first two reports of the Premier's Council, "Competing in the Global Economy" were given wide distribution. The Council, which had been established in 1986, was comprised of the premier and his key economic ministers along with a number of leaders of the province's business, labour and academic communities. The reports made a number of recommendations to improve the competitive efficiency of the economy in the context of global competition (with or without a trade agreement with the United States), including greater assistance for industrial research and development, exporting firms, risk-taking entrepreneurs, and worker adjustment. Some of the Council's research was based on successful Quebec programs to aid entrepreneurs. The Council's recommendations, which implied a more interventionist industrial strategy than that of the federal government, quickly (in spite of some recommendations that were too vague to be implementable) formed a framework for provincial economic policy with several recommendations for assistance for technological development becoming 1988 provincial budget initiatives. The Council reports were read widely in other governments. The federal Centres of Excellence program announced in 1988 was modelled in large part on a provincial program initiated in 1987 on the Council's recommendation. Thus the work of the Council, by the end of 1988, was beginning to remove the spirit of isolation or even confrontation on economic issues between the provincial government, the business community, and other governments.

In 1988 fiscal pressures were beginning to force the provincial government into constraints designed to curb the unsustainable spending patterns that had their origins in the minority government period. While booming revenues and discretionary tax increases permitted a reduction in the deficit, Ontario moved during the period of Liberal government from virtually the lowest per capita spender among the provinces to a position close to the national average. As a result its tax rates by 1988 approximated those of Quebec for the first time in many years.

A second council chaired by the Premier began work during 1988, this one to recommend ways of achieving long-term health objectives and at the same time regaining control of health expenditures, which for 1988-89 accounted for one-third of the budget. A task force on the social assistance structure of the province reported during 1988, recommending large initial expenditure increases with the promise in the longer term of a greater integration between social assistance payments and work incentives. Although the prescriptions in the "social agenda" were not the same as that followed by Quebec and praised by Courchene, the province was beginning to bring its social agenda into a broader socio-economic framework.

By the beginning of 1989, therefore, Ontario's agenda did not appear to be as off-side in relation to that of the federal government, Quebec, most of the other provinces, and the business community as Courchene claimed it was in April 1988. With the exaggerated rhetoric of the trade debate during the federal election campaign behind them, governments on both sides of the issue were able to look more clinically at the problems and opportunities the agreement posed. It was even possible for the federal government and Ontario at the end of the year to work out an agreement on pricing policy and support for the Ontario wine industry, under threat of retaliatory action by the United States if the existing provincial pricing discrimination remained. The fall of 1988 also saw the first of what could be several interprovincial agreements to reduce or eliminate provincial purchasing preferences and other non-tariff barriers. Finally, now that barriers were coming down between Canada and the United States, Ontario's traditional priority of an internal Canadian common market was being addressed! By the end of the year, it also appeared that the sharp differences between Quebec, the federal government, and Ontario on the deregulation of financial institutions were narrowing as some of the walls between the four pillars of the financial sector began to crumble, albeit in fits and starts. Ontario and the federal government were still at odds on federal financial cutbacks affecting provincial finances, but on this issue Ontario was at one with its sister provinces. Economic forecasts for 1989 and 1990 pointed to a slowdown in economic growth with Ontario's growth rate projected to fall below the Canadian average for the first time since the 1981-82 recession. By early 1989, therefore, the prospects were for a decline in interregional tensions hitherto triggered by inflationary growth in southern Ontario.

On the constitutional and linguistic front, Ontario's actions in 1988 appeared to conform more closely to the model of constructive leadership that both Courchene and Premier Peterson have attributed to John Robarts. From January to June the Select Committee on Constitutional Reform conducted the most exhaustive inquiry into constitutional matters in Ontario's history, receiving 288 submissions and hearing constitutional experts, interest groups and ordinary citizens from all parts of Ontario and many other parts of the country. The Committee found, both among the supporters and opponents of the Meech Lake Accord, an eloquent attachment to the country and a sympathetic desire to find an accommodation that would reconcile conflicting views of the federal system and Quebec's role in it. The all-party committee unanimously recommended adoption of the constitutional amendments agreed on by the first ministers at Meech Lake and the Langevin Block in 1987 (albeit with a minority report from the Conservative members urging a court reference on the impact of the amendments on Charter rights). The Committee also recommended the establishment by the Ontario Legislature of a standing committee on constitutional and intergovernmental affairs and a more open process for future amendments, an Ontario commitment to promote the rights of Franco-Ontarians as well as early action to deal with aboriginal self-government, the participation of the territories in nominations to the Senate and the Supreme Court, and an elaboration of the constitutional definition of the fundamental characteristics of the country.[17]

The debate in the full Legislature on the committee report on 28 June and 29 June displayed a remarkable all-party commitment to the traditional bridge-building role of Ontario in Confederation and particularly the historic relationship between Ontario and Quebec.[18] A reading of the debate reveals a conscious rejection by most participants of the more centralist vision of Canada represented by the *Toronto Star*, many Toronto-based elites and important elements of the Liberal Party itself, and reveals support for "the idea of pluralism and accommodation captured in the Meech Lake Accord,"[19] as the Liberal member for Durham Centre put it. In adopting both the committee report and the constitutional amendments by votes of 112 to 8, the Legislature committed itself to taking an active role in dealing with many of the concerns expressed by opponents of the Accord during the committee hearings and which were also prominent in the reluctance of the governments of New Brunswick and Manitoba to support the amendments. In his contribution to the debate, the Premier proposed not only the establishment of the standing committee which would discuss future proposals for constitutional change, but also an annual state of the federation debate in the Legislature and the calling of a "public non-governmental conference on the process of constitutional reform and the priorities Ontario and all Canadian governments should pursue."[20] Courchene's call for another conference on the confederation of tomorrow was taken up only two months after he made the proposal!

Courchene as a supporter of Meech Lake, praises Peterson for the role he played in its adoption in spite of the opposition to the Accord in Ontario and the fact that it "does not square well with Ontario's 'defining characteristics'."[21] In Courchene's view, which I share, "Meech Lake is the logical culmination of the Confederation of Tomorrow process,"[22] a process which included along the way the report of the federal Pépin-Robarts Task Force on Canadian Unity. By the end of 1988, Premier Peterson, buttressed by the select committee report, was being looked on by both the Prime Minister and the Premier of Quebec as a key figure in the increasingly difficult campaign to secure the adoption of the accord by the two remaining provinces.

Peterson continued his bridge-building role with Quebec in 1988 as he conferred regularly with Premier Bourassa, most notably at a joint meeting immediately following the federal election held in Toronto on 24 November, at which the two leaders vowed to put their differences on the trade agreement behind them.[23] During the year, ministers and civil servants of the two provinces met frequently to compare experiences in policy and program development, Ontario MPPs visited Quebec, journalists from the two provinces participated in exchanges and tourism between the two provinces increased substantially. In spite of those activities, however, a reading of the press in the two provinces would quickly reveal continuing evidence that two solitudes was still all too accurate a description of the preoccupations of much of the population of the two provinces.

In language policy, Ontario was also playing a constructive role. As the Commissioner of Official Languages put it: "There is also cause for rejoicing in Ontario, where the French Language Services Act comes into force in 1989" and "Ontario continued its linguistic nation building."[24] A massive effort continued during the year within the government to ensure that government services would be available in both languages by 1989 as prescribed in the omnibus legislation. In the education sphere, the first French-language school boards were established in the province in December and the government committed itself to the establishment of the first French language college of applied arts and technology. The momentum appeared to be established for the constitutional entrenchment of official language minority rights sometime after 1989, in spite of the linguistic storm that erupted in the country at the end of the year in response to the Supreme Court ruling on the language of signs in Quebec and the Quebec government's response to it. There was a palpable sense of frustration in various circles in Ontario, however, at the perception that Quebec appeared to be reducing its commitment to the protection of minority language rights just as break- throughs were occurring in Ontario.

At the end of 1988, therefore, the Ontario government was:

- less in a position of isolation from its business community and most of the other governments in Canada on the major economic issue of the day as a result of adoption by Canada of the trade agreement;

- still more concerned with social issues than the market-oriented governments in Ottawa and Quebec but moving towards more of an economic agenda;
- starting to come to grips with a series of longer-term problems and opportunities relating to the overall competitiveness of the economy;
- facing a series of wrenching economic adjustments resulting from the implementation of the trade agreement and a possible recession;
- still carrying on an uneasy relationship with a federal government which the provincial government rightly or wrongly saw as more oriented to other regions of the country and less committed to some of the actions and symbols of nationhood important to many Ontarians;
- dealing with a series of expenditure pressures largely resulting from boom conditions at a time when the federal government was seen to be reducing its willingness to pay its share;
- aware of vocal opposition from many opinion leaders in the province, particularly from within the Liberal party, to both the free trade agreement and the Meech Lake Accord, on the grounds that they would severely weaken the country's capacity to withstand powerful forces of Americanization;
- soldiering on with attempts to forge stronger bonds between Ontario and Quebec in the face of occasional indifference or even lingering hostility in some quarters in both provinces;
- maintaining strong support for the Meech Lake Accord while not discovering a route to avoid the impasse; and
- preparing the way for legislative, and eventually, constitutional entrenchment of a range of official language minority rights in the province.

THE FUTURE: COLLABORATION OR "GO IT ALONE"

Courchene's hypothesis is that Quebecers have emerged from the internal debates of recent years "with a new confidence and awareness of who they are in relation to themselves, their province and their country," and that westerners now "have a better awareness in terms of their economic (free trade) and political (triple E Senate) agenda, both of which constrain the influence of the centre", while Ontarians have emerged "more confused about who they are and more divided in terms of what they want."[25] He does not analyze where the people of the Atlantic provinces are, perhaps because in 1988 their opinion leaders were demonstrating a little volatility on the free trade and Meech Lake issues! He describes the dilemma before Ontario as one of either accepting the demands of a more market-oriented economic order in a free trade context and a more decentralized and collaborative political order in the spirit of Meech Lake, or continuing with an agenda based more on social priorities and government intervention which could lead to a destabilizing "Ontario-first" approach and yet which would not restore the strong central government traditionally desired by Ontario elites.

The actual developments that have taken place in Ontario and in the Canadian federation since April 1988 have, I think, demonstrated that Courchene has put the dilemma facing Ontario too strongly. If the past is any indicator, Ontario is too complex a society and there is not enough identity between the population and the provincial government for any sharp ideological choices to be made (at least by Liberal or Conservative governments) which could permanently fly in the face of traditional public attitudes or large sectors of the population. The "isolation" of the province which he outlined is gradually diminishing, both because of the trade decision and the regionally self-correcting elements of the business cycle. It is likely, even without a change of government in Ottawa, that the inherent forces working on both the federal and Ontario governments will result, over time, in both governments adopting a closer set of perspectives than they have had over the last four years. While the warmth of federal-Ontario relations may be cyclical, as Simeon says, and while economic changes have undercut Ontario's traditional economic pre-eminence, isolation of Ontario is unlikely to be a permanent feature.

In spite of my view that he has overstated Ontario's dilemma, I believe Courchene poses some probing questions that should be addressed seriously in any reassessment, at least in the short run, by the province of its role in the federation. Any such reassessment must take account of a number of new factors that may make it more difficult for Ontario to assure that its interests will be satisfied by the normal operations of the federal system.

For example, Ontario's future relations with the federal government must take stock of the fact that the federal government is now less able to take strong economic nationalist measures such as those often supported in the past by Ontario. The current federal government is also less willing, for both fiscal and ideological reasons, to strengthen nation-building public sector ventures like the CBC and VIA Rail. After all, it was elected on a platform that, on the surface at least, is on a different wavelength from the Ontario government on some major philosophic issues such as the most appropriate role for government in the economy.

In terms of economic factors, such a reassessment must also be cognizant of economic flows that will be increasingly determined by market forces and which will be more north-south in direction, of a rapidly-changing environment where there will be winners and losers both between and within Canadian economic regions, of global economic pressures that will put great strains on the continued viability of key sectors of the Ontario economy such as the automotive industry, and of a requirement for rapid public and private adaptation to a more knowledge-based economy and an aging population.

Ontario's role vis-à-vis the other parts of the country will also face new challenges. The accommodation between Quebec and the rest of the country remains fragile, especially in the event of a failure to ratify the Meech Lake Accord. Quebec itself is confidently pursuing its own agenda, freed from some of the traditional constraints, real and perceived, on public and private sector action imposed by the federal government in Ottawa and by the business leadership of Toronto. On the other hand, with the adoption of the trade agreement, one of the psychological causes of resentment of Ontario in Quebec and the rest of the country has been removed. The trade agreement and the likely result of future negotiations with the United States on subsidies will weaken the capacity of both the federal and provincial governments to take steps that have in the past alleviated regional or sectoral grievances or promoted public-private sector collaboration in trade and industrial expansion. Overall, the immediate challenge must take account of a weakening, according to many observers, of a commitment across the country to make the accommodations constantly needed to preserve the Canadian federal system.

The Ontario government in the past has on various occasions reviewed its approach to intergovernmental relations and its role in Confederation. Such reviews have never ended up with a rigid blueprint built around a specific set of objectives, strategies and tactics to maximize Ontario's interests in an overall sense. More typically they have concluded that a variety of strategies are required, according to the issue and circumstances. They have generally involved flexibility on constitutional matters,[26] tough bargaining on financial issues, improving the effectiveness of intergovernmental machinery, building alliances and consensus where several governments have similar interests, allying Ontario's interest with the national interest and dealing bilaterally where the interest is specific to Ontario. Pragmatism, balance and a sectoral approach have normally characterized Ontario's actions and an aggressive "Ontario first" stance has been consciously avoided. In spite of the best of intentions, however, Ontario has on occasion sounded smug and insensitive when it has not taken the trouble to analyze in advance the impact of its position on other parts of the country.

I doubt, therefore, that the province is really faced with as stark a choice as Courchene poses, or that if it were, it would consciously choose black or white. In a sense Courchene is looking at the country as a whole rather than just Ontario's role in it, and his analysis tends to be with the perspective of a market economist viewing Canadian "welfare" in terms of potential per capita GNP.

This in the past has not been the overriding perspective of Canadian and Ontario decision-makers, and certainly not the emotional perspective of most Canadian nationalists. Nevertheless, I believe there would be agreement that the global context has sufficiently changed and the trade agreement and "the spirit of Meech Lake," if it survives, have sufficiently changed the Canadian environment that a serious reconsideration by both the province and the federal government of their relations with each other and of Ontario's role in the federation is appropriate. Let me suggest a few approaches in the spirit of Courchene's admonition that the province regain the statesmanlike mantle of the Robarts years (which Courchene has romanticized!) and avoid becoming isolated:

- more consciously emulate Robarts' tactics, as Courchene says, to "manage Ontario's privileged position to ensure that Canada's interests coincide with Ontario's interests,"[27] in other words, to get the federal and Ontario agendas closer together and less inhibited by partisan differences;

- as a corollary, develop a more constructive working relationship with the federal government both politically and bureaucratically, building on the many interest group, sectoral and professional common interests that have not always been exploited;

- maintain and build stronger and deeper Ontario-Quebec linkages on the principle that Ontario's role is still important in keeping Quebecers attached to Canada and on the premise that Ontario and Quebec, as each other's largest customer and most logical point of comparison, have much to learn from each other, many psychological barriers to overcome, and many profitable opportunities for joint endeavours;

- build better relationships and deeper understandings with the other regions of the country that have suffered in the years of differences over energy, the constitution, and trade (Courchene suggests that Ontario buy western coal for Ontario Hydro, a proposal that has foundered in the past because of transportation costs and may founder in the future for environmental reasons!);

- use the consensus-building exercise within the province, e.g., the Premier's two councils, centres of excellence, etc., as building blocks for national endeavours to meet external and future challenges;

- accept less grudgingly a federal role to ensure regional balance in the country which, in good times in Ontario, may seem like an anti-Ontario approach;

- do not hesitate to think and propose in national terms, on the premise that Ontarians have little sense of Ontario loyalty but want to see the country functioning well; avoid Ontario-first and parochial approaches. The Ontario public has consistently supported its government when it is seen to be acting constructively on the national scene;

- recognize clearly and forthrightly that the days of a protected Canadian market supplied primarily by Ontario are over and that the test of industrial and economic policy will increasingly be global competitiveness;

- assume a more decentralized and collaborative approach to the country's decision-making in the spirit of the trade agreement and Meech Lake, on the assumption that whether or not Meech Lake is adopted, it still represents an accommodation close to the only kind that will permit a constitutional reconciliation with Quebec. Do not (even if there were to be political changes in Ottawa) fight for a recentralization in the style of the early 1980s that would rekindle past interregional confrontations; and

- act on the recommendations of the Select Committee on Constitutional Reform to open up the constitutional and intergovernmental relations processes and provide opportunity for more public and legislative involvement.

These suggestions, some of which are already accepted or being implemented, will not, in my opinion, lead to restoring a more constructive balance between Ontario and the federal system if there is not also some change in the approach of the federal government to Ontario as a government and a region.

I would suggest to the federal government, for example, that as part of its theme of "national reconciliation" it build in a greater emphasis on reconciliation with some of the non-business sector elites of Ontario. The trade debate made it very clear that English-Canadians, particularly in Ontario, were very concerned about maintaining the symbols, institutions, programs, and east-west linkages that distinguish them from Americans. I would suggest that it is important to be conscious that Ontario's "civic" culture, supporting national language legislation, equalization and regional development programs, is all part of the "civic" virtue of nation-building. If a strong sense develops in Ontario, as it did in 1988, that the federal government was prepared to sacrifice important elements of its capacity to "nation build" in the interests of closer market relations with the United States, some of the "civic" spirit in Ontario could dissipate. To counter this, I would suggest that the federal government be more creative in deliberately encouraging and building, in collaboration with

Ontario and other provinces, east-west institutions and linkages to balance some of the north-south pressures generated by the trade agreement.

I believe a healthy relationship depends on the federal government bending over backwards to achieve collaborative approaches (although it does take two to tango) to the major economic decisions requiring actions by both governments such as tax reform. The deregulation of financial institutions, the subsidies negotiations with the United States and work-force adaptation are other areas requiring collaboration, just to name a few. Federal-Ontario relationships would be assisted by an explicit recognition that Canadian prosperity depends on an effectively-operating infrastructure in its major centre. The whole country suffers, for example, when its major airport is a national disgrace. Finally, I would suggest that if decisions in Ottawa are to be controlled in part by strong regional ministers, there should be a minister or ministers from Ontario mandated to work with the provincial government on Ontario concerns.

Some of these suggestions are being followed, but the principles behind them need constant reaffirmation. The Mulroney government's objective of "national reconciliation" has in general greatly improved the tone of federal-provincial relations in comparison to the early 1980s." Richard Simeon points out, however, "to the extent that free trade ends up conferring its benefits and costs unequally on different regions, it could well fuel the politics of regional jealousy....one wonders whether it will be possible to sustain a commitment to regional redistribution and equalization in the absence of economic ties among regions. Thus free trade could exacerbate regional differences, while reducing the capacity of the federal government to reduce them."[28] Simeon suggests that there is a dialectical relationship between the Macdonald or more centralist view of Canadian federalism and the Laurier, or more accommodative, or collaborative version. While the Laurier view has been in the ascendancy in the Mulroney period, the danger is that crucial elements in the nation-building process may suffer. But as Simeon says "a commitment to cooperative federalism and policy innovation are not necessarily incompatible."[29]

In light of the increasingly global nature of the challenges facing Canada, and the increasing recognition in all societies that attempts to centralize action and planning stifle creativity, there is great scope for Ontario and the federal government to take the lead in working on projects involving the process of "thinking globally, acting locally" that the future may call for. In this respect, I was struck by a recent presentation by Pierre Pettigrew, entitled "Rethinking Ottawa", in which he makes the point that the federal government seems "too small to help solve big questions and too big to tend to Canada's immediate preoccupations."[30] Pettigrew suggests that for the sake of Canada's ability to succeed in a world of global multinationals, the federal government should be actively establishing institutions that will act in partnership with business to further Canadian economic objectives, using Quebec's "market nationalism" as a model. He concludes that the federal government has naively assumed that market forces will act in the interests of the whole country and has abdicated from some of its indispensable economic policy responsibilities.

It seems to me that Pettigrew's prescription applies equally to Ontario, and in this respect he and Courchene join forces to suggest that Ontario could take lessons from Quebec's economic policy approach. The key is to do it in collaboration with the federal government and Quebec, and not in isolation.

If Ontario were to follow the "go it alone" approach, and act more like some of the other provinces in pursuit of provincial interest, the results could be very damaging to the sometimes fragile consensus that now holds the country together. As noted earlier, Courchene compares Ontario's role in Confederation to that of Saudi Arabia in the OPEC cartel, the dominant force in the association which must exercise self-restraint if the alliance is to hold together. Let me suggest another parallel, which may have as much political, if not economic, relevance. I recently visited Yugoslavia where Serbia, the "Ontario" of that federation, as the largest republic and within which the national capital is situated, has recently decided that it has had enough of what it deems to be a series of reductions of its previously pre-eminent role in the Yugoslav federation, reductions which its leaders had previously accepted in the interests of preserving a fragile regional and ethnic balance in the country's governing structures. Serbia's attempts, under a new charismatic leader, to regain greater authority in the federation, have aroused great concern in other republics such as Croatia and Slovenia as well as in the Albanian-speaking minority, and the federal balance dependent on Serbian self-restraint is in danger of breaking apart.

Another aspect of contemporary Yugoslav federalism fits rather chillingly into Courchene's pessimistic scenario. As recent federal governments and the Communist party of Yugoslavia accepted a greater degree of decentralization in the country's political structures and a more market-oriented economy, they not only found Serbia unwilling to continue its traditional self-restraint, but also found the federal government was losing its capacity to act in areas that heretofore had been exclusively federal. Yugoslavs increasingly began to identify with their particular ethnic origins. The country-wide symbols and loyalties of the Tito era weakened sharply, the willingness to share among regions declined, and the federal government found it had lost many of the tools necessary to cope with a national economic crisis.

We can avoid this fate, it seems to me, only if Canada and Ontario work together to face the global challenges to both province and country. This, it seems to me, would be the true legacy of John Robarts, the ultimate pragmatist dedicated to making his province and the country work.

Notes

1. *Toronto Star*, 14 January 1989.
2. The 1988 Robarts Lecture, York University, Toronto, 26 April 1988.
3. Ibid., p. 54.
4. See for example Carol Goar's column in the *Toronto Star* of 3 December 1988, where she cites bitter "anti-Ontario barbs coming out of Quebec in the final stages of the federal election campaign," particularly on the part of the Hons. Lucien and Benoit Bouchard.
5. See Hyman Solomon's column in *The Financial Post* of 20 June 1988, where Solomon quotes Stanley Hartt, who had just resigned from his post as federal deputy minister of Finance as saying "There seems to be a thing going there, where if the feds say white, Ontario says black. In the old days, Ontario was a leader. It is the most populous and wealthy province, and served as a central block to the national structure. But those days appear over. Now there's a negativism and small-time approach to their outlook."
6. *1988 Ontario Budget Statement*, the Hon. Robert F. Nixon, 20 April 1988, p. 13.
7. As Jeffrey Simpson put it: "For nearly 42 years, from 1943 to 1985, the Conservatives had governed Ontario like basset hounds, ears alert to every whisper of change in public opinion, noses alive to the smells of danger and political opportunity, barking at the federal government when necessary, licking Ottawa's hand when required..." Jeff Simpson, *The Spoils of Power—The Politics of Patronage* (Toronto: Collins, 1988), p. 217.
8. Courchene, "What Does Ontario Want?", p. 26.
9. Ibid., p. 38.
10. Ibid., pp. 20-25.
11. Donald C. Macdonald (ed.) *Government and Politics of Ontario* (Scarborough, Ont: Nelson Canada, 1985), pp. 133-58.
12. *Destiny Canada Final Report*, Toronto: York University, June 1977, p. 16.
13. Courchene, "What Does Ontario Want?", p. 28. See also George Radwanski in *The Financial Times*, 12 February 1979. "At least as important... was...the new-found willingness of Davis, for whatever reasons, to participate in the constitutional debate, not just as the parochial voice for Ontario, but as a spokesman for broader national interests. His acceptance of this traditional role of Ontario premiers was long overdue, and it could be a highly significant and beneficial development if it lasts."
14. François-Pierre Gingras in an essay on Ontario in David J. Bellamy, Jon H. Pammett and Donald C. Rowat (eds.) *The Provincial Political Systems*, (Toronto: Methuen, 1976).

15. Ibid.
16. *Toronto Globe and Mail*, 2 February 1989.
17. Ontario, Select Committee on Constitutional Reform, *Report on the Constitutional Amendment, 1987* (Toronto: Government of Ontario, 1988).
18. Ontario, Legislative Assembly, *Hansard* official report of debates, 28 and 29 June 1988.
19. Ibid., p. 4784.
20. Ibid., p. 4857.
21. Courchene, "What Does Ontario Want?", p. 42.
22. Ibid., p. 2.
23. See, for example, Denis Lessard in *La Presse*, 24 November 1988, "M. Peterson confiait à son entourage qu'il voulait absolument éviter le type de relations Ontario-Québec du début des années 1980, un retour au temps de Bill Davis et René Lévesque."
24. *Commissioner of Official Languages*—Annual Report 1988, April 1989, p. iii and p. 219.
25. Courchene, "What Does Ontario Want?", p. 47.
26. See the various reports of the government's two Advisory Committees on Confederation which were in existence from 1965 to 1972 and from 1977 to 1981.
27. Ibid., p. 29.
28. Richard Simeon, "National Reconciliation: The Mulroney Government and Federalism," in Andrew Gollner and Daniel Salée (eds.) *Canada under Mulroney: An End of Term Report* (Montreal: Véhicule Press, 1988), pp. 35-36.
29. Ibid., p. 44.
30. Pierre S. Pettigrew, *Rethinking Ottawa*, contribution to panel discussion on the state of the federation, Council for Canadian Unity, Ottawa, 19 May 1989.

FOUR

Manitoba: Stuck in the Middle

Paul G. Thomas

D'ordinaire peu porté aux coups d'éclat en matière de relations intergouvernementales, le Manitoba a pourtant retenu l'attention au pays, en 1988-89, eu égard à la menace que la législature manitobaine fait peser sur l'avenir de l'Accord du lac Meech.

Ferme défenseur de l'Accord au départ, le gouvernement conservateur de Gary Filmon a néanmoins fait volte-face sur cette question peu après que le gouvernement Bourassa se soit prévalu de la clause nonobstant dans le but de se soustraire—en partie—au jugement de la Cour suprême sur l'affichage commercial.

Contre un adversaire libéral qui pourfend sans relâche l'Accord, le gouvernement Filmon a décidé—réélection oblige—de composer avec l'opinion publique, majoritairement anti-Lac Meech, et donc d'user d'une procédure dilatoire au plan législatif qui pourrait compromettre la ratification de l'Accord dans cette province.

L'auteur de l'article signale au passage les incohérences de Filmon lorsque, entre autres, celui-ci stigmatise l'emploi de la clause dérogatoire par le Québec alors que lui-même s'en faisait l'ardent promoteur quelques années plus tôt.

Thomas dresse également un profil économique du Manitoba; province relativement "démunie" dont l'économie, essoufflée pour l'heure, nécessite une prompte diversification de ses secteurs d'activités, le Manitoba a toujours été redevable à Ottawa de ses paiements de péréquation ainsi que de l'aide accordée pour divers projets de développement. Cependant, l'affaire des CF-18 et des CF-5 combinée à la récente réduction des transferts fédéraux au Manitoba ont eu pour effet de brouiller le bon-ententisme traditionnel entre les deux ordres de gouvernement, tout en précipitant éventuellement la crise actuelle autour du Lac Meech.

INTRODUCTION

Events in Manitoba during 1988 attracted more national attention than usual. In a province better known for its relative political stability and predictability, there was plenty of political excitement and many of the developments had national significance.

Two years into its second term, the New Democratic Party administration led by Premier Howard Pawley was defeated in the Legislature when a disgruntled government backbencher voted against the budget. In the ensuing provincial election, a minority Progressive Conservative government led by Premier Gary Filmon took office, even though the party secured fewer seats than it started with. Many saw the real winner in the election as Sharon Carstairs, the energetic leader of the Liberal Party, which staged a remarkable political comeback. After two decades of political decline, the Liberals elected 20 MLAs and became the official opposition.

Among other impacts, this realignment of political forces within the province made the Meech Lake Accord the dominant issue of provincial politics during the latter part of the year. In December, three days after praising the Accord when introducing the legislative resolution to adopt it, Premier Filmon withdrew his support. This followed upon Premier Bourassa's response to the Supreme Court's decision on Quebec's sign laws, a response which in Mr. Filmon's view cast doubt on that province's commitment to minority language rights. For a time the New Democrats sat on the fence. Mr. Pawley had been one of the signatories to the Accord, but there was significant opposition to it within his party. Having replaced Mr. Pawley as leader prior to the election, Mr. Gary Doer waited to declare the provincial NDP's opposition to the Accord until after the federal election campaign in part so as not to undermine the national party's efforts to win seats in Quebec. What had changed after the Mulroney victory was the certainty that the Free Trade Agreement would proceed. Reversal of the party's stand on the Meech Lake Accord was justified, Mr. Doer explained, because the decentralizing implications of the Accord would weaken the national government's capacity to manage the economic and social policy adjustments made necessary by free trade.

While both opposition parties had declared previously that the Meech Lake Accord was not a confidence matter that would call for the resignation of the government, the Filmon Conservatives were obviously in a precarious situation. Intense and not always gentle pressures from Ottawa to ratify the Accord compounded their political difficulties. When introducing the resolution to approve the Accord, Premier Filmon praised Prime Minister Mulroney for launching a new beginning in federal-provincial relations after the discord of the Trudeau years. Meech Lake was said to symbolize more harmonious and constructive federal-provincial dealings on constitutional and other matters. After the Accord was withdrawn from the Legislature, however, Manitoba's relations with Ottawa seemed to deteriorate rapidly and the opposition parties, both in Manitoba and Ottawa, accused the Mulroney government of using economic coercion to bring Manitoba into line on the Accord. Even as he was embarking to Ottawa to fight cutbacks resulting from the 1989 federal budget,

Premier Filmon was reluctant to draw any connections between Ottawa's actions and the province's stand on the Accord.

The withdrawal of $208 million (by a provincial estimate) in economic activity through federal budgetary decisions came at an inopportune time in terms of the provincial economy. After five years when Manitoba's economic performance surpassed that of most provinces, 1988 saw a dramatic slow down. The worst drought since the 1930s led to major declines in agricultural production and hydro power generation. In spite of significant gains in mining and manufacturing, overall the economy was stagnant during 1988. Although the provincial budgetary picture was brightened by higher than anticipated increases in federal transfer payments, largely in the form of higher equalization entitlements, this good fortune was not expected to last.

The Filmon government is committed to eliminating the provincial deficit, cutting taxes, reducing the role of government within the economy and preserving essential services. Its approach to promoting economic growth contrasts with the former NDP government's greater reliance upon public spending to stimulate the economy. The Progressive Conservatives are looking to increased private sector investment to lead the recovery and to create new jobs.

This article examines these and other developments in Manitoba over the past two years in terms of their impact on federal-provincial relations. The short-term agenda of the Filmon government will be dominated by considerations of political survival, at least until it sees the prospect of a majority government through another election. As the alternative government-in-waiting, the Liberals know that the longer the Filmon Conservatives stay in office and demonstrate reasonable competence, the more their own political momentum will subside. An early election could be devastating for the NDP who hold the balance of power since they are in no shape organizationally or financially to fight another election.

In these political circumstances, a variety of questions arise. How will the Meech Lake process be finalized within the province and what impact will Manitoba's decisions have on the national fate of the Accord? In terms of dealings with Ottawa in other areas (like agriculture, the environment, the fiscal arrangements, regional development and so on) how will Manitoba fare? Will the existence of an ideologically congenial government in Ottawa mean a more sympathetic hearing for Manitoba's case or will the past conflicts between the provincial and federal wings of the Progressive Conservative party come back to haunt the province? Many observers see the Liberals poised to take power in Manitoba. What would a Liberal victory signify on both the provincial and the national scene? Are we witnessing the redrawing of the electoral map in Manitoba to restore us to the pre-1969 days when the Liberals and Conservatives contested for power and the NDP was relegated to a third party status? Of necessity, answers to these sorts of questions must be tentative and therefore contentious at this point.

THE ECONOMY

In addition to being at the centre of Canada in geographical terms, Manitoba has represented the average, or close to the average, among the provinces in other important respects: population, wealth, natural resources, manufacturing and taxing capacity. Best described as "lower middle class" among the provinces, Manitoba is a so-called "have not" province which qualifies for federal equalization payments, a label many Manitobans would reject. They see themselves as less rich than Ontario, not as poor as the Atlantic provinces, and a little better off than Saskatchewan.

Manitoba's population was estimated at 1,083,600 on 1 April 1988, a modest increase of less than one per cent over the previous year. Average per capita income stood at $17,574.[1] Unemployment averaged 7.4 per cent during 1987. Manufacturing activity (at 12 per cent of Gross Domestic Product) is more than twice the relative size of manufacturing in Saskatchewan, and two thirds larger than in Alberta. Most of the manufacturing activity takes place in Winnipeg where nearly 60 per cent of the provincial population lives.[2] Even Winnipegers do not always realize the employment generated by manufacturing because there are not the huge factory complexes found in southern Ontario. The resource sector (agriculture, hydro electric power, minerals, and forestry) accounts for 14 per cent of the GDP, less than half the share in the other prairie provinces. As elsewhere, the service sector has been the fastest growing component in the Manitoba economy and now accounts for close to 70 per cent of the GDP.[3]

While Manitoba's diversified economy weathers the highs and lows of fluctuating economic cycles well, it lacks the dynamic sectors that stimulate strong and sustained growth. During the 1970s, Manitoba ranked ninth or tenth in interprovincial comparisons of all major economic performance indicators. High interest rates and adverse conditions in world food and metal markets were important factors in the poor performance. The restrictive fiscal policies of the Lyon administration after 1977 also contributed to the economic difficulties. When the NDP took over after 1981, it introduced a Jobs Fund ($200 million) to stimulate employment. There were also major increases in public investment through the Limestone hydro project and the redevelopment project in downtown Winnipeg. The availability of increased federal development dollars after 1983 assisted the recovery. Manitoba outperformed other provincial economies during the first half of the 1980s. However, this relatively good economic performance was fuelled mainly by strong public spending, which began to decline in 1988 when the major capital projects neared completion and the provincial Jobs Fund was being phased out. When the drought hit, the economy came to a virtual standstill. At less than one per cent, growth during 1988 was far below the forecast, job creation was below one per cent and unemployment rose at a time when the national trend was downward.[4] Forecasts for 1989 were mixed, with any recovery inhibited by federal budgetary actions which pulled hundreds of millions of dollars out of the provincial economy. As always, the economy remains vulnerable to weather conditions and to trends in export markets.

THE POLITICAL CULTURE

Manitoba's marginal economic status has been an important contributing factor to its political traditions.[5] While radical rhetoric has occasionally dominated political debate, the economic actions of governments have tended to be pragmatic and moderate. Small "c" conservatism has been the dominant philosophy for most of the province's history. A limited role for the state, a preference for small government, and a prudence with respect to public spending have been the prevailing norms, irrespective of the party in power. Only during the period of the Lyon government did the politics of ideological extremes prevail.

As the Manitoba party system moved during the early eighties towards increased polarization between the left and the right, there seemed no middle ground for the Liberals to occupy. The Liberal Party compounded its own problems by presenting a blurred image to the electorate through successive elections during the 1960s and the 1970s. From the mid-sixties onward the party went into a spiral of decline, falling from 19 seats in the Legislature and 33 per cent of the popular vote in the 1966 provincial election down to no seats and 7 per cent of the popular vote after the 1981 provincial election.[6] Just when Manitoba seemed to be following predictions about the emergence of a two-party system based on class and ideological differences, the Liberals staged a remarkable political comeback capturing 20 seats and the role of the official Opposition after the 1988 election. All three parties now seemed to be resolutely centrist in orientation, with only marginal differences among them. There have been differences in approaches to managing the economy, but these have not been as stark as the parties would have us believe. The future direction of Manitoba's party system is far from clear.

APPROACHES TO FEDERALISM

Irrespective of which party held power, Manitoba's approach to the federal system has usually changed very little. With the notable exception of the Lyon administration, successive Manitoba governments have supported a strong national government. A recurrent theme in Manitoba submissions to federal-provincial conferences has been that a strong provincial economy will require national leadership and financial support. The province has frequently sought cooperation with Ottawa in projects and programs of economic and social development. Whether out of economic necessity or an implicit philosophy of constitutional pragmatism, Manitoba has never been deeply offended by the so-called "intrusions" of the federal government into matters of exclusive provincial jurisdiction.

There have been periods of "fed bashing", most notably during the Lyon government when Manitoba adopted a very aggressive approach to combat the centralizing tendencies of the Trudeau regime. Another outbreak took place after the CF-18 decision when relations between the Pawley and Mulroney governments degenerated into verbal warfare. However, under so-called "normal" conditions, the relationship tends to be more harmonious. Typically, Manitoba has restricted its criticisms of national policies to those which have been developed unilaterally, applied paternalistically, terminated abruptly or have been perceived as unfair in terms of interprovincial equity. Historically Manitoba governments have defended a constitutional order which is flexible and adaptive to change. They have been sceptical of constitutional proposals which, though supposedly intended to protect provincial interests, could end up blocking or inhibiting joint actions by the two orders of government to solve practical problems. Manitoba governments have sought to be constructive in intergovernmental forums. Trying not to sound too vain, Manitoba has insisted that as an average province in economic terms, with a multilingual and multi-cultural population, and sitting in the middle of the country, it has a unique perspective to contribute to debates over the definition of the country.

The approach of past governments both reflects and reinforces the underlying attitudes of Manitobans in general. Manitobans have been strong supporters of national unity. Studies of political attitudes reveal that Manitobans have a higher identification with Canada as a whole than do respondents in the three provinces further west. Like respondents in all provinces, Manitobans see their provincial government as closer to them than the national government, but they are more supportive of the national government than people in the remainder of the West.[7] Support for western separatism has been least strong in Manitoba, always remaining very much a fringe element.

While Manitobans have been stronger supporters of national unity, they joined other western Canadians in rejecting in large measure the vision of a bilingual country promoted by the Trudeau government. Language reform, whether at the federal or the provincial level, has been a highly divisive issue and has earned the province considerable negative notoriety elsewhere in the country. During the French-language controversy of 1983-84, the Progressive Conservatives led by Sterling Lyon prior to December, 1983 and by Gary Filmon after that date, forced the Pawley government to withdraw a proposed constitutional amendment by walking out of the Legislature and allowing the bells to ring.[8] In addition to confirming the province as officially bilingual, the constitutional amendment would have provided for the translation of a limited number of past laws passed in English only and for the extension of French-language services by the provincial government. Majority public opinion was clearly on the side of the Tories in opposing the amendment and when the party's national leader lectured a provincial party gathering about the need for linguistic fairness, he was booed; an episode which Mr. Mulroney has apparently never forgotten. Eventually the Supreme Court ruled that Manitoba was forced to translate its laws and, as that time consuming and expensive task was undertaken, the ugly passions of the moment gradually subsided. Still, the language issue remains volatile. It is one example where extreme attitudes rather than moderation prevail. As is shown below, the debate over Meech Lake has brought together some strange linguistic bedfellows in opposition to its language provisions.

One of the problems Manitoba faces in its dealings with Ottawa, according to a senior provincial official, is the tendency by the national government to treat the West as a single political region with common interests.[9] Benefits bestowed on a given province in the West are seen and portrayed as benefitting the region as a whole. The problem was revealed in the CF-18 affair, an event which serves as a symbol to condense Manitoba's frustration at times with national decision-making. In October 1986, when the Mulroney government awarded the CF-18 maintenance contract to Montreal rather than to Winnipeg none of the other western provincial governments supported Manitoba. According to Michel Gratton, Mulroney's former press secretary, an announcement of the decision to favour Quebec over Manitoba was postponed several months to assist fellow Conservative Premier Grant Devine of Saskatchewan in his re-election bid.[10] Defending his actions, Mulroney pointed to the lower unemployment rate in Manitoba and the other forms of national generosity bestowed on the West. When Premier Pawley made a personal attack on Mulroney's honesty and trustworthiness, relations deteriorated badly. Mulroney ordered that Manitoba be kept in the dark on all federal announcements and that the Pawley government not be allowed to share any political credit for federal benefits. It took six months before a modicum of peace was restored.

Under the NDP during the 1980s, Manitoba frequently found itself the odd man out in the West. The Pawley government took a different policy stance from the other, conservatively-inclined governments of the region on the issues of free trade, the fiscal arrangements, the Crows Nest Pass freight rates, trucking deregulation and the Canada Health Act. Whereas the Lyon government had supported Alberta and Saskatchewan in their opposition to the National Energy Program and in their advocacy of a constitutional amendment (Sec. 92A) extending provincial control over natural resources, the Pawley government was more prepared to see national leadership on resource issues. As a consuming province of oil and natural gas, Manitoba's interests have diverged at times from those of the producing provinces, as reflected in a recent clash with Alberta.

During 1987 the Pawley government was involved in negotiations to buy the Inner City Gas (ICG) distribution system as a means of combatting excessive prices for natural gas negotiated by the company with Trans- Canada Pipelines of Alberta (TCPL). In addition, the government signed contracts with alternative Alberta suppliers at a better price and applied to the National Energy Board for access to the TCPL delivery system in order to move the cheaper gas to Manitoba. At this point, the Alberta Government threatened to block the export of gas where a breach of contract was involved and was successful in having the NEB deny the Manitoba application. Negotiations to buy the company were broken off by the Pawley government in January, 1988. This followed upon ICG securing a lower price from TCPL and some taxation complications arising with the proposed takeover. Not only did the episode cause tensions between the provinces, but the Pawley government was criticized by the opposition parties and by editorial writers for creating unnecessary confusion and spending public money on a botched takeover bid.

THE MEECH LAKE PROCESS

Given what was said above about Manitoba's support for national unity and its concern to be a constructive participant in intergovernmental affairs, why has the province ended up being one of the two remaining hold outs on the Meech Lake Accord? Three sets of factors appear to be at work. First, there are the short-term political developments and the interplay of partisan forces within Manitoba which delayed ratification of the Accord and allowed time for opposition to crystallize. Second, in a small political system like Manitoba's the policy views of the Premier take on added importance. The leadership approach taken first by Premier Pawley and then by his successor Premier Filmon have been key to the province's position. Nevertheless, party politics and political leadership operate within the parameters of political feasibility and acceptability. In this respect, the provisions of the Accord and their potential negative impact on significant segments of the Manitoba population have produced intense opposition to its passage, at least as presently worded.

Premier Pawley had been part of the agreement reached by the Premiers at their annual meeting in August 1986, that the priority in constitutional talks should be given to Quebec's five conditions for its acceptance of the 1982 constitutional package. Consideration of other constitutional issues, such as Senate reform and the fisheries, would be postponed pending completion of what became known as the "Quebec round". This agreement was confirmed in a communiqué by all first ministers at their November 1986, conference. During the ensuing winter and spring, a series of bilateral discussions were held across the country between federal and Quebec negotiators and their provincial counterparts in order to prepare first ministers for the meeting at Meech Lake to take place on 30 April 1987.

During the preliminary bilateral negotiations Manitoba raised a number of concerns, but Quebec's initial proposals had been expressed so vaguely that formulating precise objections was difficult. Quebec began by asking for its own veto over future constitutional amendments, but this was never acceptable to Ottawa or any of the other provinces, including Manitoba. Granting all provinces a veto over a longer list of constitutional matters was the eventual result of the Meech Lake negotiations, an outcome which caused some discomfort because Manitoba favoured a flexible constitution.

Manitoba also expressed concern about possible restrictions on the future use of the federal spending power. In a bid to attract support from the poorer provinces which had benefitted most in the past from federal spending in provincial fields, Quebec's representatives had linked the spending power proposal to a possible strengthening of the equalization provision (Sec. 36) of the 1982 constitution. Quebec suggested that the equalization formula should not be changed unilaterally by the federal government. Apparently this possibility was quickly rejected by the federal government, which in the fall of 1986 was renegotiating the Fiscal Arrangements Act with the provinces.

During these initial discussions, Manitoba had no problem with the principle of recognizing Quebec as a distinct society. Only when the actual wording of the distinct society clause was produced did anyone in the Manitoba government detect a potential conflict with the Charter of Rights and Freedoms.

According to several sources, Premier Pawley expected the Meech Lake meeting to be inconclusive. Going into the meeting, Pawley wanted to avoid being seen as the spoiler. Over the previous six months in the aftermath of the CF-18 decision, the government had raised a long list of complaints about federal actions and inactions and had been criticized for counterproductive "fed bashing". The Premier was reluctant to stage another fight on Meech Lake when free trade was pending and he was bound by party policy to oppose the Mulroney initiative.

At the meeting itself, Pawley felt alone in expressing reservations. He left the meeting feeling that there was a general agreement to proceed in certain directions, but he was not expecting to ratify a final constitutional text when the leaders reconvened at the Langevin building in June, 1987.

Initial reaction in Manitoba to the Meech Lake Accord was generally favourable. Some Franco-Manitobans were concerned that the obligation of the provincial and the federal governments to preserve, but not to promote, their continued linguistic identity would freeze the bilingual status quo. Aboriginal leaders were worried that the Accord might block their constitutional aspirations. At this point the opposition was limited and low key. The Pawley government proceeded to draft a list of amendments covering spending power, aboriginal government, multiculturalism, protection for the northern territories, and a commitment to public hearings before the constitutional revisions took effect. In an effort to avoid being a minority of one, Pawley held discussions with Premier Peterson of Ontario and they agreed to stand together in seeking changes to two clauses.[11] Peterson would make the case for amending the distinct society clause to recognize the fact of multiculturalism, while Pawley was to argue for changes to the spending power clause.

At the Langevin meeting, the Meech Lake draft was improved largely through the initiatives of Manitoba and Ontario. Proposals to place a provincial consent mechanism on the future use of the federal spending power, such as had been proposed in 1969 and 1979, were withdrawn at the insistence of Manitoba. Greater clarity in wording of the spending power provision was also introduced at the urging of Manitoba. Premier Pawley was prepared to live with the remaining ambiguity in Section 106A of the Accord (especially the words "national objectives" as opposed to the stricter "national standards") because he believed that future social democratic governments could use the flexibility to take different policy directions from other governments. However, some other members of the cabinet, caucus and the party were more wedded to the concept of minimum national standards. At the joint urging of Manitoba and Ontario, a non-derogation clause was included to protect the multicultural nature of Canadian society referred to in the Constitution Act of 1982. On the matter of aboriginal rights, the Manitoba position was flatly rejected. At four in the morning, Pawley sat on the back stairs with Peterson debating whether to jettison the Accord in its entirety. He recognized that some progress had been made. He wanted to demonstrate good will towards Quebec. And he recognized that by standing alone, he would block what was already being hailed as a great act of national reconciliation. In giving his assent, Pawley warned Prime Minister Mulroney that the public hearing process in Manitoba would not be a charade and that further amendments might have to be considered. While all the leaders present agreed to promote the Accord back in their own provinces, Mr. Pawley's commitment in this regard was more qualified than the others.

Back home the NDP government was situated precariously. In the 1986 provincial election, it had won 30 seats compared to 26 for the Progressive Conservatives and one for the Liberals. In the fall of 1987 a long serving MLA resigned from cabinet and announced his intention to leave the Legislature at the start of the 1988 session. Another backbencher, Mr. Jim Walding, was aptly described by a local journalist as a volcano waiting to erupt. He had served as an MLA since 1971, had been appointed Speaker during Mr. Pawley's first term, and had not been chosen for cabinet after the 1986 election. He made no effort to hide his discontent. While Premier Pawley was criticized later for ignoring the problem, he made several efforts to placate Walding, among other things choosing him to move adoption of the Throne Speech. Mr. Walding voted with the government on that occasion, although his contribution to the debate consisted of an attack on the government's mismanagement of the public automobile insurance scheme and its profligate spending habits. Following his throne speech performance, most experts expected Mr. Walding to torment his party's front bench for the remainder of the session, but ultimately to support the government.

The NDP government was in no hurry to adopt the Meech Lake Accord. Over the winter of 1987 and 1988 there was mounting criticism from within the party. In December 1987, 150 prominent New Democrats wrote an open letter to the Premier urging him to reject the Accord. In January 1988 at least 15 constituency associations passed resolutions critical of the Meech Lake Accord to be presented at the party's annual convention in March. While Pawley continued to support the Accord, he indicated in December 1987 that he would not introduce it at the start of the 1988 session, he would consider amendments based on the public hearings, and would perhaps allow a free vote to be held. He linked progress on Meech Lake to greater provincial input to the free trade talks then being conducted by the Mulroney government. Ontario refused to join Manitoba in using Meech Lake to fight free trade, arguing that they were two separate issues.[12]

At the annual party convention in March 1988, a compromise resolution was passed calling upon the NDP government to deal with the flaws in the Accord prior to legislative passage. The compromise was arranged to avoid embarrassment for both Pawley and the national party who had endorsed the Accord.[13] Those opposed to the Accord gained an opportunity to lobby for changes. Three days after the convention, on 8 March 1988, Jim Walding surprised nearly everyone by voting against the budget and the government fell. The final tally was 28 to 27.

The Pawley government resigned and an election was scheduled for 26 April 1988. Mr. Pawley also resigned as leader and was replaced by Gary Doer. The NDP started the election campaign well back, with perhaps only two or three seats being considered safe. Mr. Filmon's Conservatives held a comfortable lead and their campaign seemed to be premised on the avoidance of any blunders. The wild card was the Liberals, whose building momentum could scarcely be captured by the opinion polls. Turnout on election day was 76 per cent, the highest for several years. Many first time voters apparently opted for the Liberals. While the Tories won enough seats to form a minority government, their popular vote was actually lower than in 1986. They won 25 seats, one less than before. The Liberals won 20 seats, 19 of them in Winnipeg. As expected, the NDP came third with 23 per cent of the popular vote (down 18 points from 1986) and only 12 seats (down from 30).[14]

Table 4.1
Manitoba Provincial Election Results

Party		1986	1988
Liberal	Vote %	13.8	35.4
	Seats	1	20
NDP	Vote %	41.4	23.6
	Seats	29	12
Progressive Conservative	Vote %	40.4	38.3
	Seats	27	25

The Meech Lake Accord did not figure prominently in the election. According to a newspaper-sponsored poll, management of the economy was the most important issue and the Progressive Conservatives were clear winners over both the Liberals and the NDP in terms of who would do the best job.[15] Only 20 per cent of the respondents agreed that developing a provincial position on the Meech Lake Accord was important. Twenty-four per cent said that the Progressive Conservatives would do the best job, while the Liberals and the NDP each received the endorsement of 16 per cent of respondents on this issue. Despite the low prominence of the issue, Mrs. Carstairs, who was strongly opposed to the Accord, pronounced it "dead" on the morning after the election.

On 9 May 1988 Mr. Filmon and his 16-member cabinet were sworn in. Originally the new Premier indicated that the Accord was a low priority behind straightening out the economy and the government's finances. However, the government's Throne Speech presented on 21 July 1988 announced that a Meech Lake resolution would be introduced during that session. Opposition to the Accord was building. In June, the Winnipeg Chamber of Commerce had written to all MLAs urging them to reject the Accord.[16] Resentment over the distinct society clause for Quebec was growing, especially in rural Manitoba. In private, government MLAs were calling for a free vote on the issue and early in the session one of their number defected to the Liberals, citing discontent with the Accord, although his exclusion from the cabinet was judged by many to be the stronger motivation. There was press speculation that half of Filmon's 24-member caucus had serious concerns about the Accord, including several leading cabinet ministers. Late in November 1988, the Union of Manitoba Municipalities at its annual convention passed, by a 75 per cent majority, a resolution rejecting the Accord.[17]

On 15 December 1988, the Liberal Party unveiled in a discussion paper its official stand on the Accord. It criticized the flaws and ambiguities of the Accord and indicated that the party would insist on six amendments.[18] The list included: removal of the unanimity requirement for Senate reform and its replacement by the 7/50 formula; preservation of fundamental rights and freedoms against erosion through the Accord; clarification of the distinct society clause; the deletion of the provision allowing Quebec to claim a certain share of new immigrants; an amendment giving Parliament the right to decide what standards provinces must meet in order to qualify for compensation when they opt out of national shared-cost programs; and the inclusion of aboriginal self- government as an agenda item for future constitutional conferences.

On Friday, 16 December 1988 Premier Filmon began the process for ratification of the Meech Lake Accord by introducing into the Legislature a motion for approval. He described the Accord as a positive step.[19] It symbolized the end of a decade of federal-provincial discord under the former Trudeau government. The exclusion of Quebec from the constitutional deal of 1982 had produced a constitutional deadlock which meant that progress could not be made on other constitutional issues, such as Senate reform, the inclusion of property rights in the Charter and new ground rules for federal-provincial relations. He noted that the federal Parliament and eight provincial legislatures had already approved the Accord and quoted leaders from all parties (including Pawley and Broadbent) to the effect that the distinct society clause did not endanger the Charter and that the ability of Ottawa to sponsor new national initiatives would not be impaired by the spending power provision. Under the broadened requirements for unanimity respecting certain constitutional changes, Manitoba, he noted, became the equal of Ontario. He concluded by urging the Legislature to adopt the Meech Lake Accord as "a first step in the process of constitutional renewal."[20] Further, he asked the Legislature to consider passage of a companion resolution outlining solutions to other constitutional issues which the Accord failed to address, issues such as Senate reform, inclusion of property rights in the Charter, protection of women's rights and aboriginal concerns.

It was not clear from Mr. Filmon's remarks what sort of companion resolution or companion amendments he had in mind. The general approach of companion amendments was based on the recognition that direct amendment of the Accord was probably politically unacceptable. Addressing the concerns which had arisen by means of companion amendments would avoid the necessity for reopening the entire Accord. Amendments could deal with those concerns identified since the Accord was first signed. Adoption by the 11 other legislatures of such changes could be made a condition of Manitoba's ultimate assent to the Accord. A less politically demanding approach would be to adopt a set of companion amendments for consideration by other jurisdictions but not make Manitoba's approval contingent on their adoption. While the Liberal leader, Mrs. Carstairs, also spoke of the possibility of a parallel accord, it was doubtful that any approach which left Meech Lake intact would gain her party's support.

The weekend after the Accord was introduced in the Manitoba Legislature, Premier Bourassa invoked the notwithstanding clause to protect his new sign legislation that was to replace the previous Quebec legislation that had been ruled unconstitutional by the Supreme Court. The Quebec premier called Filmon to notify him of the decision and the Manitoba premier in turn warned Bourassa there would be an anti-Quebec backlash.[21] Overnight, Filmon decided to withdraw the Accord and this decision was confirmed after a meeting with his staff and then with his caucus on Monday morning. After consultation with the opposition leaders who supported his decision, the Premier rose at the afternoon sitting of the Legislature to announce the withdrawal. Quebec's action, he stated, violated "the spirit of Meech Lake" and left doubt as to their commitment to minority language rights. Filmon rejected public hearings at that time because they would probably provide a forum for ugly bigotry.

Many observers felt that Filmon had no choice but to halt the ratification process. According to a *Winnipeg Free Press* editorial, the Quebec action provided a convenient pretext, but the real reason for pulling the Accord was the growing wall of opposition to its adoption.[22] The editorial went on to suggest that Filmon would have a hard sell in convincing many Francophones of his devotion to minority language rights when he had fought the extension of their rights in Manitoba back in 1983-84. While Filmon had described the use of the notwithstanding clause as a tragedy, it was pointed out that he was part of the Lyon government which had fought for its inclusion back in 1981. Filmon's response was to argue that the clause should be used sparingly and never to abrogate minority rights indefinitely.

Early in 1989 Premier Filmon met several premiers in eastern Canada in order to explain his government's stand. There was press speculation that five provinces, including Manitoba, were working to develop a parallel accord to act as a caveat to the Meech Lake Accord in order to make the protection of aboriginal, women's and minority language rights paramount.[23] Apparently there was no substance to these reports.[24] Both Ottawa and Quebec had rejected the concept of a parallel accord. When the first ministers gathered in Ottawa on 27 February 1989, Mulroney and Filmon apparently got into a shouting match. The federal government seemed to be stepping up its pressure on Manitoba. Projects requiring federal financial support were delayed and there was speculation that Ottawa would not renew its economic development agreements with the province. Filmon insisted that he would not tolerate linking federal help to approval for the Accord and pointed out that his minority government was in no position to deliver the Accord because the two opposition parties were opposed.

On 3 March 1989 the Premier announced the creation of an all party task force to conduct public hearings and to provide advice to the government. The seven member task force (three Progressive Conservatives, two Liberals and one New Democrat) would be led by a non-voting chairman, Professor Wally Fox-Decent, a political scientist. The task force exercise would not eliminate the requirement for a subsequent legislative debate and further public hearings before a final decision on the Accord could be taken. The rules of Manitoba's Legislature require that constitutional amendments be debated initially for five days, during which period they take precedence over all other business. After the fifth day of debate, the amendments must be referred to a legislative committee for public hearings. Once the committee reports, a minimum five additional days of debate in the full Legislature are guaranteed if the parties wish to use them. Following this debate a vote would be taken. All of these procedures would follow after the Meech Lake Task Force reports to the Premier and once the motion to adopt the Meech Lake Accord is reintroduced into the Legislature. This led the *Winnipeg Free Press* to describe the task force "as nothing more than a procedure leading to a procedure."[25] Mr. Filmon indicated that he would not be outlining a government position to the task force.

From 6 April 1989 to 12 May 1989 the task force held 12 meetings (some of them lasting all day and into the evening) and heard approximately 300 presentations. Only individuals and organizations normally resident in Manitoba were heard in person; non-residents were permitted to file written submissions and 11 individuals and organizations took advantage of this opportunity. Approximately 90 per cent of the people who made presentations to the task force spoke against the Accord, with 40 per cent calling for outright rejection and another 50 per cent insisting on amendments before passage. Despite earlier fears, there were very few anti-Quebec sentiments expressed and approximately 20 per cent of the witnesses volunteered the opinion that it was important to gain Quebec's acceptance of the 1982 constitution.[26] Included in the ten per cent of the witnesses who spoke for the Accord was a contingent of national Conservative MPs and Senators from Manitoba, including Jake Epp, the senior minister in the Mulroney cabinet.

The opponents of the Accord can be divided into five groupings, although with some overlap. First, there were the social democrats and left-leaning liberals who were concerned about a weakening of the federal government's role in supporting greater equality of opportunity through the promotion of comparable national programs in all parts of the country. This coalition of interests focused its criticisms particularly on the spending power clause. They feared that the Accord entrenched a neo-conservative philosophy of less government and greater reliance on the market.

A second grouping involved individuals and organizations concerned about the impact of the distinct society clause on the rights protected by the Charter of Rights and Freedoms and the definitions of the Canadian community found in the 1982 constitution. Francophone, women's, multicultural and aboriginal groups feared that their position within Canadian society could be compromised by the wording.

Particularly at the hearings outside Winnipeg, there was a questioning of the perceived preferred status being granted to Quebec through the distinct society clause and the immigration provisions. Individuals, municipal associations and farm organizations rejected the idea that one part of Canada was more distinct than any other. With a few exceptions, the views were less anti-French and more an endorsement of a pluralistic, pan-Canadian identity. In a curious irony, former leaders of Grassroots Manitoba, which led the fight in 1983-84 against the extension of French language rights in Manitoba, joined now with the advocates of national bilingualism to denounce the distinct society clause—the former group because it recognized Quebec as distinctive and the latter group because they believed the Accord froze national bilingualism in its tracks.

A fourth group of witnesses expressed dismay that the Accord would likely block the constitutional aspirations of the two northern territories to achieve provincial status at some future date. The surprising number of people who took the time to express sympathy for the territories is probably related to the fact that Manitoba is itself a small, less affluent province. A sizeable native population also ensured that the future political development of the territories would be prominent. It was seen as closely tied to the issue of aboriginal self-government and the lack of progress on this topic during the proceeding five years. Native leaders expressed resentment that during the so-called "Quebec round" the issue had been put aside and was not even mentioned in the Accord.

A fifth group of witnesses was offended by the process by which the Meech Lake Accord was adopted. There were plenty of references, throughout the hearings, to 11 men sitting around the poker table deciding the country's future, to all night sessions, to the exclusion of advisers, to the lack of clear information about all the implications of the Accord, and to the insistence that amendments would be acceptable only if "egregious errors" could be found. For many Manitobans, the Meech Lake process symbolized the worst excesses of secrecy and lack of public consultation associated with so-called "executive federalism" and if the Accord was passed it seemed to them to promise only more of the same.

The Meech Lake Task Force was writing its report to the Premier during the summer with the expectation that it would not be made public until the Legislature resumed sitting in September. The chairman of the task force indicated a determination to search for an all-party consensus although complete agreement seemed unlikely. For the government, Premier Filmon has said several times that he still supports the Accord, but requires some assurances that minority rights will not be jeopardized and that other, unfinished constitutional business will be dealt with soon after ratification. For the Liberals, Mrs. Carstairs has been consistently opposed to the Accord as presently worded and has described a parallel accord as a device to allow certain politicians to save face. Unlike the Liberals, the NDP have to deal with the fact that their former leader signed the Accord. Their opposition has less credibility, therefore. They have tried to emphasize a nonpartisan approach towards amendments to the Accord.

Both opposition parties are likely to insist on the replacement of "national objectives" in the spending power clause with the words "national standards" and there may be a move to include some reference to the role of Parliament (as opposed to the cabinet) in setting such standards. Both are likely to push for the retention of the current amending formula for Senate reform; that is seven provinces with 50 per cent of the country's population. They both might advocate acceptance of the same formula for the admission of new provinces. Both will insist that the list of future constitutional meetings include one on aboriginal concerns. In terms of the distinct society clause, several options are apparently being explored. One is to make the clause part of the preamble meaning that it would not serve as an interpretative clause to determine the gray areas of the constitution. Another option is to amend the distinct society clause to make reference to aboriginal peoples, multiculturalism and the paramountcy of the Charter of Rights and Freedoms as part of the definition of Canadian society.

The two opposition parties will have to decide two tactical issues as well. One is at what stage in the proceedings in the Legislature they will seek to amend the Accord. Will they try to pre-empt the other party by proposing amendments at the debate stage or at the report/third reading stage after the committee hearings have been held? A second question is whether they will attempt to use the approach of companion amendments described earlier, which could be used to tie Manitoba's assent to the Accord to actions in other jurisdictions. It should be noted that there is all-party agreement that passage of the Accord is not a confidence issue that would lead to the fall of the government. There will be pressure, especially in the Progressive Conservative party, to allow a free vote on the issue. Many observers believe that no progress towards adoption of the Accord will be made until after the Quebec election generally assumed to be scheduled for this fall. Premier Bourassa, if he is re-elected, will then have to face the fact that Manitoba cannot agree to the Accord as written and, therefore, that there must be a search for a compromise.

THE BUDGETARY SITUATION

Since taking office the Filmon government has presented what can only be described as two "good news" budgets. They have reduced taxes, come close to eliminating the annual operating deficit, set aside a small amount of money for a financial rainy day, reduced the accumulated provincial debt for the first time in 20 years, avoided major cuts to social programs, and done all of this while there was plenty of talk about cutbacks in federal financial transfers.

When the NDP took office in 1981 the province's financial health was deteriorating. Instead of curtailing expenditures severely, the NDP government had increased retail sales taxes, tobacco and liquor taxes, and corporate income taxes. In 1982 they introduced a highly controversial payroll tax to help fund health and post-secondary education. The Pawley government blamed the tax increases on the federal government. It was a two pronged attack. First, Manitoba claimed with some justification, that reductions in federal transfers were unfair to the poor provinces; an argument that had earlier been made by the Lyon government. Second, the Pawley government condemned recent federal tax changes as having sacrificed fairness in the pursuit of economic growth. Like most other provinces, Manitoba collects its personal and corporate income taxes through a tax collection agreement with Ottawa, using the federal definition of taxable income. For the remainder of its term, the government hammered away at the concessions and loopholes in the federal income tax act, which meant that billions of dollars in foregone revenues were paid out indirectly to high income earners and large corporations. On one occasion the NDP government's budget included an estimate of the revenues lost to the province as a result of these tax expenditures.

According to its critics, the NDP government did not balance higher taxes with a serious effort at curtailing expenditures. Party ideology dictated that restraint be accomplished without major changes in the NDP's commitment to social spending. The government began slowly by marketing the need for restraint in an attempt to reduce expectations.[27] During the recession of the early 1980s the government pointed to public spending, especially the Jobs Fund, as necessary in maintaining levels of employment. Year-over-year increases in expenditures were gradually reduced, but only with difficulty as the Pawley government tried to avoid major program reductions or eliminations.

Even with higher taxes, the annual deficit rose, standing at over $500 million in some years, on a budget of about $3 billion in the mid-eighties. There was a growing consensus, even among New Democrats, that more had to be done to relieve the stress on the province's finances. A major report on taxation and expenditure options prepared for the Pawley government late in 1986 concluded that: "There is no magic in tax reform or in the field of taxation—no rabbits—no hats—and no magicians.—No remedy can be fashioned for Manitoba's fiscal difficulties that does not include both reform of taxation and reform of expenditure management".[28] The report rejected the radical restraint exercises undertaken in Saskatchewan and British Columbia.

Control over expenditure management was centralized in a strengthened Treasury Board. Yet in the 1987-88 fiscal year, expenditures rose by 8 per cent. The 1987 budget included a package of taxation increases totalling $227 million in new revenues. Sales, liquor, tobacco and the payroll tax were all increased, but the most contentious measure was a two per cent surcharge on net incomes. While the surcharge was intended to offset the lack of progressivity in the porous federal income-tax system, it was attacked by the business community as stifling entrepreneurial effort. Even with the tax increases, the deficit was forecast to be $415 million. By year end this figure had been cut to $306 million, largely because Manitoba received $620 million in equalization payments, which was $151 million more than budget estimates.[29]

In the 1988 budget proposal that led to their downfall, the NDP forecast expenditures growing by 8.3 per cent, almost twice the rate of inflation at the time. The projected deficit was $334 million.[30] Taxes were to be increased on liquor, tobacco and leaded gas. While there were no increases in personal income taxes or on small businesses, there were significant increases imposed on the mining sector whose profits had recently increased. The traditional non-confidence motion presented by the Progressive Conservatives condemned the government for the spending increases and the further tax grab. It was this motion that Mr. Walding supported on 8 March 1988 and on which the NDP government was defeated.

The newly-elected Filmon government presented a new budget on 8 August 1988. As promised during the campaign, the phasing out of the controversial payroll tax was begun. Increases in taxes on tobacco, liquor and fuel proposed in the NDP budget were maintained. The mining tax was increased by a lower amount than in the February budget. There were no increases in personal, corporate and sales taxes. Outside consultants were brought in to review the overall financial situation of the province. Forecasted spending was about $4.5 billion, slightly higher than the NDP estimate. Borrowing was down 16 per cent from the level of the previous year. The deficit for 1988-89 was projected to be $196 million, well below the figure ($334 million) presented in the NDP budget. The budget passed, with the Liberals as the official Opposition voting against it. Anxious not to precipitate another election, the NDP leader and the party's finance critic voted against the budget, but the rest of their members abstained.

The subsequent provincial budget presented on 5 June 1989, was described by many commentators as a pre-election document. The budget cut the personal tax rate to 52 per cent of basic federal tax from 54 per cent, although the surcharge on net incomes was not reduced. Tax reductions for each dependent child were raised to $250 from $50. The payroll tax was almost eliminated and there were the predictable increases in taxes on liquor, tobacco and fuel. Overall spending was forecast to increase 4.5 per cent to about $4.8 billion, but there were higher increases in the fields of health, the environment, child and family services and education.[31] With its reduced taxes on families and higher spending on social services, the budget seemed designed to appeal to the NDP which held the balance of power in the Legislature. The deficit was forecast to be a mere $87 million. It could have been eliminated entirely had the Filmon government not chosen to put $200 million aside in a fiscal stabilization fund. The fund was described as a "fiscal shock absorber" helping the province to avoid disruptions to programs or major tax increases when revenues fluctuated from one year to the next. To the opposition parties it was a "slush fund" for use before the Tories went back to the electorate to obtain a majority. The much improved financial picture was a short-term situation which resulted primarily from the tax increases imposed by the former administration, from higher mining taxes and from higher equalization payments from Ottawa. Revenues were up 12.5 per cent over the preceding fiscal year and equalization ($243 million in 1988-89) accounted for nearly half of the total.[32]

FEDERAL FINANCIAL TRANSFERS

The financial links between the province and the federal government are numerous: unconditional equalization payments; broad conditional grants for hospital insurance, medicare and post-secondary education; straight conditional grants such as the Canada Assistance Plan; and direct federal participation such as the Economic and Regional Development Agreements and the Western Diversification Fund. The array of financial transfers is both complex and bewildering, but there is no doubting their importance to Manitoba. During the decade from 1979-80 to 1988-89 federal transfers as a percentage of Manitoba revenues slipped from 42.6 per cent down to 32 per cent according to provincial estimates.[33]

About half the federal transfers to Manitoba are accounted for by equalization payments. In 1982 the formula for calculating equalization was modified over the protests of the provincial governments. Among the recipients, Manitoba was the hardest hit in terms of future equalization entitlements versus forecasts made under the old formula. Manitoba has always maintained that equalization, even though the legislation is controlled by Ottawa, is not a program like the others and changes should not be introduced unilaterally by the federal government. Manitoba was one of the provinces which fought hardest for the inclusion in the Constitution Act (1982) of the commitment to equalization. It also protested strongly the imposition after 1982 of a ceiling, equal to GNP growth, on total equalization entitlements. While the cap on equalization applies to total equalization payments and not to payments to particular provinces, and it has never been utilized to date, Manitoba believes it inappropriate to place financial restrictions on a program designed to ensure reasonably comparable levels of services throughout the country.

The other major transfer mechanism is Established Programs Financing (EPF), where Manitoba has again been a leading province in opposing reductions in federal contributions. EPF was adopted in 1977 and ever since has been surrounded with controversy. It involved a shift to block funding (cash plus tax transfers) divorced from actual provincial program expenditures in the fields of hospital insurance, medicare, and post- secondary education. There has been a battle of the balance sheets between the two orders of government over their respective contribution to the ongoing costs of these major programs. That dispute cannot be resolved. Suffice it to say that during the Pawley years Manitoba advocated a return to traditional cost sharing, but with more flexibility to operate programs based on prior agreement on objectives and clear program standards. The province protested strongly against the imposition since 1986 of ceilings on the growth of federal EPF contributions, the most recent of which was contained in the federal government's budget of April 1989. Manitoba estimated it would have to find $8 million more every year to make up for the reduced rate of growth in the EPF transfers. Of course, the national government has also set itself the task of reducing its deficit.

The April 1989 Wilson budget brought other bad news for Manitoba. Most dramatic was the closure in 1990 of two military bases operated by the Department of National Defence: CFB Portage La Prairie, and CFB Winnipeg. The first closure will represent a loss of $20 million annually to the local economy and the second another $20 million annually. The closure of the rural base was particularly disturbing. It led to a delegation of local official and all party leaders travelling to Ottawa to protest. The group was told by the federal Defence Minister that military spending should not be used for regional development purposes, even though the Manitoba delegation noted that a prison had moved into the Prime Minister's riding to invigorate the local economy.

Also announced in the Wilson budget was the decision not to put a high tech avionics package in the CF-5 jet fighters, a move which cost Bristol Aerospace Ltd. of Winnipeg up to $150 million in work. The anger in this case was caused by the fact that the CF-5 contract was the consolation prize given to Bristol Aerospace in 1986 when the CF-18 maintenance contract was awarded to another company against the recommendation of a bureaucratic task force which described the Bristol bid as technically better and less expensive. The Manitoba economy would also be hurt by the proposed VIA rail reductions, the elimination of a rail rehabilitation program, reduced commitments to crop insurance and, of course, the EPF cutbacks.

In criticizing the federal budget, Premier Filmon estimated that it pulled $20 million out of the provincial budget and $250 million out of the Manitoba economy. An unreleased study put the latter estimate at over $400 million. The Premier argued that if the cuts had been proportional to Manitoba's share of the GNP, the cuts in Manitoba would be $80 million less.[34] Manitoba's most senior federal cabinet minister, Mr. Jake Epp, denied that the province had been dealt with harshly. "This has nothing to do with the Meech Lake Accord and everything to do with a national agenda to get the deficit under control", he told the press.[35] He pointed out that Manitoba received more per capita in federal transfers than any other western province and that other projects, such as the Centre for Sustainable Development and the disease control laboratory, had been promised for Winnipeg.

REGIONAL DEVELOPMENT POLICY

During the summer of 1989, the Government of Manitoba was concerned that there would be deep reductions in the federal contributions towards economic development in the province. At stake was the future of the sub-agreements under the Canada-Manitoba Economic and Regional Development Agreement (1984) and the province's share of the Western Diversification Fund (WDF). Contrary to the pessimism of provincial officials, both elected and appointed officials in Ottawa insisted that there would be another round of ERDA sub-agreements. They also insist that, contrary to the alarms being sounded by provincial spokespersons, overall spending on regional development in the West would go up over the next five years, not down.

Manitoba was the first among the provinces in November 1983 to sign an Economic and Regional Development Agreement (ERDA) with the federal government. It was heralded at the time as representing "a new kind of federal-provincial cooperation, based on shared understanding of Manitoba's economy." There were very close working relations between Mr. Lloyd Axworthy, regional minister for Manitoba in the federal cabinet, and the Pawley administration. Their collaboration produced a steady flow of federal benefits, particularly to Winnipeg. On a per capita basis Manitoba had done very well under the first round of ERDA sub-agreements compared to other provinces.

Under the Manitoba ERDA there were nine sub-agreements to take effect in 1984 covering the following development activities: planning, transportation, the Port of Churchill, mining, urban bus manufacture, communications and cultural industries, the agri-food industry, and forestry. In total, these sub-agreements represented a commitment of close to $400 million, $240 million from Ottawa and $154 million from the province. An additional two agreements covering tourism ($30 million divided equally) and science and technology (where the agreement was to improve existing coordination) were signed in 1985. During 1986 the second Core Area Initiative (CAI) for the redevelopment of downtown Winnipeg was brought within the ERDA framework, with each of the three levels of government contributing $33 million. In summary, by the end of 1986 there were 12 sub-agreements in progress representing a total financial commitment of over $500 million.

Most of the original nine sub-agreements expired at the end of March 1989, although there was provision for committed funds to flow for a further 18 months. There were evaluation components built into some of the sub-agreements, but there was no requirement for an overall evaluation of the ERDA approach. Some federal ministers felt that Ottawa did not get full political credit for its contributions. Several days before the 1989 federal budget, there were accusations in the *Winnipeg Free Press* that Manitoba was guilty of using federal ERDA dollars to pad provincial spending accounts.[36] An anonymous federal official estimated that as much as $13 million had been diverted into provincial programs. He was quoted as saying that: "We know of a case where the provincial government decided to fund sexy projects on their own rather than put them through the ERDA agreement.... They get all the credit for the new program, while using the federal funds to do the not-so-sexy stuff."[37] For his part, the Minister for Western Diversification, Mr. Charles Mayer, who was from Manitoba, restricted his comments to the fact that ERDAs had lost their effectiveness because they no longer reflected the priorities of the two orders of government. Further, it was questionable why Ottawa should be spending in areas of primary provincial responsibility, like forestry management, especially if the provinces were not doing their fair share. Manitoba officials interviewed for this study suggested that Ottawa's charge about funnelling federal funds into provincial accounts was nonsense since the allocation of funds had been jointly agreed to. Manitoba's Finance Minister told the press that he was prepared to review the program, but the province opposed any cutback in Ottawa's contributions. The timing of Ottawa's complaint suggested to Manitoba's officials that it was a diversionary tactic to hide the fact that a new round of ERDA sub-agreements would involve far less federal financial support.

Early indications from Mr. Wilson's budget and contacts with federal officials indicated that less emphasis would be placed in the future on ERDAs and far more on the Western Diversification Fund (WDF). When the WDF was announced by Prime Minister Mulroney in August 1987, it reflected the national government's renewed commitment to the alleviation of regional disparities and, more particularly, to the diversification of the western region. The WDF involves a focus on new products, new markets and new technology. It was intended to lessen the West's traditional dependence on resource commodities that are subject to fluctuations in international markets and it was intended to offset reliance on imports. The WDF was described as $1.2 billion in new money for the West over the five-year period from 1987-92. Despite press reports about budgetary cutbacks in regional development spending, the target for WDP spending remains at the original level.

To administer the WDF, the Department of Western Diversification was set up in 1988 to coordinate federal programs in the region. Some of the existing ERDA agreements were transferred to the new department when the former Department of Regional Industrial Expansion was disbanded. The department provides grants and interest subsidies for projects that would not otherwise proceed in the proposed location, proposed scope or time. Consistent with the emphasis on diversification, only new businesses or expansions into unrelated business activity will be supported. There are also major project grants to deal with systemic or structural problems in the western economy. Part of the department's role is also to represent the West in the development of national policies and programs. With its headquarters in Edmonton, the department also operates a regional office in each of the other western provinces. Manitoba's office had 54 staff in 1988-89.

The WDF spending responds to proposals; expenditures are not based on a formula related to the per capita income in a province or the level of unemployment in a province as past DRIE approaches were. Bruce Rawson, the first Deputy Minister for the department, described the WDF approach as follows:

> Political masters introduced two key concepts in start-up instructions. They accepted the idea that judgement and not a slide rule would be required to operate the program and diversification was the goal, not straight forward business expansion or modernization.... Because we work from principles and not from a

detailed procedure manual, we need to have systems to ensure that all proposals are judged the same way.[38]

Given the discretion granted to officials of the WDF, it is perhaps not surprising that there were charges that Manitoba was not getting its "fair share" of project funding. Because the WDF spending is based on the flow of applications, the notion of provincial shares is really not appropriate. WDF officials in Manitoba insist that they have been aggressive in promoting awareness of the fund. As of June 1989, the breakdown of projects and the amounts committed for the four western provinces were as follows:[39]

British Columbia	—	390 projects	—	$105.6 m
Alberta	—	456 projects	—	$ 82.8 m
Saskatchewan	—	137 projects	—	$ 62.6 m
Manitoba	—	99 projects	—	$ 68.6 m

It was pointed out that the greater number of projects in B.C. and Alberta reflected the fact that those provinces had existing business development agreements with the federal government when WDF was announced. Manitoba was slower to generate project proposals, but its allocation on a per capita basis still compared favourably to B.C.

Manitoba now has the advantage of having one of its two cabinet ministers, Mr. Mayer, in charge of the WDF. Mr. Mayer has indicated that he wants to see WDF spending in his province used to offset the concentration of economic activity in Winnipeg. To date about 71 per cent of WDF spending in Manitoba has taken place or is committed to the Winnipeg area.[40] The federal approach will reinforce and complement the provincial government's promotion of rural development. A proposal for a rural development strategy has been submitted to Ottawa for cost sharing. There is a provincial cabinet committee on rural development and provincial departments have been asked to identify ways to decentralize their operations outside Winnipeg.

CONCLUSION

At the time of writing it appears likely that the Progressive Conservatives will maintain their hold on power during the remainder of 1989. The Filmon government has not encountered great difficulty in proceeding with its legislative program. Only a small number of bills have been withdrawn or modified because of combined pressure from the two opposition parties. It is impossible to know, of course, what actions the Conservatives have avoided taking because of their political vulnerability. To the general public the minority government seems to be running smoothly and with reasonable competence. For most people there is no obvious reason, therefore, why an early election is needed.

Given the further fact that the Conservatives have apparently fallen behind the Liberals in popular support, there is no rush to call an election.

The Liberals were seen as the real winners in the 1988 provincial election. However, with all 20 MLAs except their leader being freshmen, they have been upstaged at times by the smaller, but more experienced NDP contingent in the Legislature. All but one of the Liberal seats are in Winnipeg so that the party needs to build up its rural base of support. In the federal election of November 1988, the Liberals increased their representation from one to five of Manitoba's 14 seats, again all from Winnipeg. Their popularity received a further boost from the battering which Manitoba received through the federal budget of April 1989, the blame for which spilled over from the federal to the provincial Tories, in spite of protests by the latter. By early summer, there were press reports that the Liberals were ahead of the Conservatives by ten points.[41] However, the Liberals cannot cause an election by themselves.

So far it has been mainly the NDP which has kept the Conservatives in office by supporting the Filmon government on the Throne Speech and Budget votes. Many rank and file New Democrats have been uncomfortable with the informal and improbable coalition that has emerged. After all the Tories had been their main enemy for the past two decades. A minority of the NDP caucus members believes that the party cannot rebuild itself until the province has a taste of the Liberals in government. However, the leader's opinion, which has become the majority opinion in caucus, is that the electorate will punish any party which forces an early election. Besides, the NDP have been trailing badly in the polls, running below 20 per cent support over the last year, and the party has been in poor financial and organizational shape. The NDP may be expected to continue to support the Conservatives until the government presents a blatant challenge to NDP principles and policies. That would be a case of the Conservatives arranging their own defeat in order to win a majority government.

The longer term direction of the party system is unclear. The trend of the previous two decades towards a polarized two party system along class and ideological lines was interrupted by the 1988 provincial election and the re-emergence of the Liberals. After the 1986 election, there had been talk of the NDP having become the majority party in Manitoba based on a broad coalition of interests—working people, Francophones, the multicultural community, new Canadians, women, small business and the middle class. The Conservatives were narrower in their base of support and Mr. Filmon saw his main job as that of broadening the party's appeal to some of the groups which had attached themselves to the NDP. He had only limited success in this regard, but the Conservatives will probably continue to command 40 per cent of the vote, most of it in rural, southwestern Manitoba. To hold power over the longer term, they must add to their strength in Winnipeg where 31 of the 57 provincial seats will be located when the next redistribution is completed. The Liberals and the NDP will fight over the remaining 60 per cent of the vote.

For the immediate future, the biggest issue facing the Filmon government will be the Meech Lake Accord, something which was not a high priority for them when they took office. The Premier finds himself pressured on all sides—from Ottawa to adopt the Accord and from a wide range of groups within the province to reject or to amend it. The premier has held out the possibility of a parallel accord as a solution to his problem. Nothing is likely to happen on this front, however, until after the Quebec election. Mr. Filmon gained in the public's estimation and his party's support increased when he withdrew the Accord. If he could persuade Prime Minister Mulroney, Quebec and the other provinces to alter the Accord, it could catapult him into a majority government position. On the other hand, if he is ineffective in getting the other governments to address Manitoba's concerns there is always Mrs. Carstairs and the Liberals waiting in the wings.

Relations between the Filmon and Mulroney governments have gone from bad to worse over the last two years. Premier Filmon rejects the suggestion that Manitoba is being punished for its failure to approve the Meech Lake Accord, but some of the damage done to Manitoba through recent federal budgetary cutbacks, especially the defence base closures, appears to be disproportionate to that imposed on other provinces. Any second round of ERDA sub-agreements will make far less federal money available than previously. While higher equalization payments caused by the economic boom in Ontario enabled Manitoba to cut taxes and reduce its deficit, the provincial good luck is not likely to last. The 1989 Manitoba budget forecast the provincial deficit for 1990-91 going back up to the $250-290 million range from $87 million in the present year.[42] The Filmon government has expressed some support for Ottawa's efforts to deal with its deficit problems and it knows that transfers to the province cannot be excluded from that exercise. However, there will continue to be charges that the burdens of deficit reduction are not being distributed equitably. Over the last ten years there has been mounting public attention and concern about fair treatment for the province by Ottawa. It remains to be seen whether Manitoba will continue its traditional role of supporting a strong national government and striving to be a constructive presence in the federal system.

Notes

1.   The Conference Board of Canada, *Provincial Outlook, Executive Summary Spring, 1989*, p. 6.

2. E.J. Robertson, "Developing the West's Manufacturing Potential: The Role of Provincial Governments", *Canadian Public Policy*, vol. XI, July, 1985.

3. Hon. Clayton Manness, Minister of Finance, *The 1988 Provincial Budget*, Budget Paper A, "The Economic Context", p. 4.

4. Hon. Clayton Manness, Minister of Finance, *The 1989 Provincial Budget*, Budget Paper A, "Economic Performance and Prospects", p. 1.

5. See Rand Dyck, *Provincial Politics in Canada*, (Scarborough: Prentice-Hall, 1986) Chapter 7.

6. See Tom Peterson, "Manitoba, Ethnic and Class Politics" in Martin Robin (ed.), *Canadian Provincial Politics* (Scarborough: Prentice-Hall, 1978).

7. Richard Johnston, *Public Opinion and Public Policy in Canada* (Toronto: University of Toronto Press, 1985) pp. 50-53, and David Elkins, "The Sense of Place" in David J. Elkins and Richard Simeon (eds.) *Small Worlds: Provinces and Parties in Canadian Political Life* (Toronto: Methuen 1980) p. 10.

8. Bruce G. Pollard, "Minority Language Rights in Four Provinces" in Peter M. Leslie (ed.), *Canada: The State of the Federation, 1985* (Kingston: Institute of Intergovernmental Relations, 1985).

9. Interview with an anonymous senior intergovernmental official in the Government of Manitoba, 11 May 1989.

10. Michel Gratton, *"So What Are the Boys Saying?" An Inside Look at Brian Mulroney in Power* (Toronto: McGraw Hill, 1987) p. 195.

11. Gerald Friesen, "Manitoba and the Meech Lake Accord" in Roger Gibbins (ed.), *Meech Lake and Canada: Perspectives from the West* (Edmonton: Academic Printing and Publishing, 1988) pp. 51-62.

12. Gerald Flood, "Prime Minister urged to clarify Meech Lake" *The Winnipeg Free Press*, 28 December 1988. Also based on an interview with anonymous senior intergovernmental official of the Government of Manitoba, 11 May 1988.

13. Don Benham, "NDP Waffles on Meech Accord" *The Winnipeg Sun*, 6 March 1988.

14. *Report of the Chief Electoral Officer on the 34th Provincial General Election, April 26, 1988*, pp. 10-11.

15. Maria Bohuslawsky, P.C.'s, Liberals outshine NDP in key economic election issue" *The Winnipeg Free Press*, 16 March 1988 presented a report on a survey conducted by Angus Reid and Associates.

16. Patrick McKinley, "Chamber calls for help to axe Meech Lake" *The Winnipeg Free Press*, 18 June 1988.

17. Glen MacKenzie, "Rural vote against the Accord" *The Winnipeg Free Press*, 25 November 1988.

18. The Liberal Caucus of the Manitoba Legislature, *Discussion Paper on the Meech Lake Accord*, 15 December 1988 pp. 1-10.
19. Hon. Gary Filmon, "Meech Lake and Beyond", Speaking Notes on the 1987 Constitutional Accord, 16 December 1988.
20. Ibid., p. 5.
21. Donald Benham, "Man in the Middle" *The Winnipeg Sun*, 21 December 1988.
22. Editorial, "Don't seize the spirit" *The Winnipeg Free Press*, 29 December 1988.
23. John Douglas and Gerald Flood, "Parallel deal to Meech Lake pact in the works" *The Winnipeg Free Press*, 28 January 1989.
24. Interview with an anonymous senior intergovernmental official of the Government of Manitoba, 11 May 1989.
25. Editorial, "Mr. Filmon dodges again" *The Winnipeg Free Press*, 4 March 1989.
26. The author is grateful to the research staff of the Meech Lake Task Force for providing access to their preliminary analysis of the hearings.
27. J.R. Jones, "Phases of Recognition and Management of Financial Crisis in Public Organizations" *Canadian Public Administration* vol. 27, 1 Spring, 1984, pp. 48-65.
28. Michael B. Decter, "Managing Partner, The October Partnership", *Taxation—A Review and Recommendations for Reform*, November, 1986, p. 119.
29. Patrick McKinley, "Borrowing becomes a huge binge" *The Winnipeg Free Press*, 24 January 1988.
30. Hon. Eugene Kostyra, Minister of Finance, *The 1988 Manitoba Budget*, 26 February 1988, Financial Statistics, p. 1.
31. Hon. Clayton Manness, Minister of Finance, *The 1989 Manitoba Budget*, pp. 8-15.
32. Ibid., Budget Paper C, "The Fiscal Stabilization Fund", p. 2.
33. Ibid., Budget Paper B, "Financial Statistics", pp. 12-13.
34. Hon. Gary Filmon, Speaking Notes for the Response to the 1989 Federal Budget.
35. John Douglas, "Epp defends budget effect on Manitoba" *The Winnipeg Free Press*, 29 April 1989.
36. John Douglas, "Provinces accused of cram skimming" *The Winnipeg Free Press*, 25 April 1989.
37. Ibid.
38. Speech by Bruce Rawson, Deputy Minister, Western Diversification Department, 31 August 1988.

39. Interview with an anonymous official in the Western Diversification Office in Winnipeg, 9 June 1989.
40. John Douglas, "Mayer minds the West" *The Winnipeg Free Press*, 18 June 1989.
41. Frances Russell, "Improbable coalition sets up shop in Manitoba" *The Winnipeg Free Press*, 20 May 1989.
42. Hon. Clayton Manness, Minister of Finance, *The 1989 Manitoba Budget*, p. 26.

III

Focus on the Issues

FIVE

Federal-Provincial Fiscal Relations in the Wake of Deficit Reduction

Robin Boadway

Le dernier budget Wilson, en s'attelant à la réduction du déficit national, aura peut-être marqué du même coup un tournant majeur dans les relations fiscales fédérales-provinciales au Canada.

Depuis l'âge d'or de la centralisation fiscale fédérale durant la Seconde guerre mondiale jusqu'aux ententes de perception d'impôt conclues ensuite par Ottawa avec la plupart des provinces (hormis le Québec surtout), le régime fiscal canadien est parvenu graduellement, selon l'auteur, à un degré d'harmonisation assez singulier, comparé à ceux des autre fédérations existantes. Or, la situation budgétaire actuelle du gouvernement central menace cet équilibre fiscal. Ainsi, le fardeau financier occasionné par le paiement de sa dette accumulée pousse Ottawa à élargir son assiette fiscale afin de couvrir ses dépenses. C'est dans cette veine que s'inscrivent la récente réduction du taux d'augmentation des transferts fédéraux aux provinces ainsi que l'annonce, par le fédéral, de sa future taxe de vente "multi-stades" (ou T.P.S.). Mais, déjà, cette dernière initiative d'Ottawa est perçue par les provinces comme un empiètement inacceptable dans un champ d'imposition qui leur est traditionnellement dévolu pour une large part.

La réduction du déficit et des dépenses publiques du gouvernement fédéral, exigée par la réforme fiscale conservatrice, risque d'affecter éventuellement la répartition des champs d'imposition entre les deux paliers de gouvernement. Autre conséquence également-ment: l'avenir de la "mission" fondamentale du fédéral au chapitre de la péréquation. A cet égard, Boadway signale qu'Ottawa doit compter sur un espace fiscal approprié afin de satisfaire ses engagements envers les provinces, tel que prévu à l'article 36 de la Loi constitutionnelle de 1982. Au reste ce même article fournit au fédéral une justification presque illimitée de l'usage de son pouvoir de dépenser, une prérogative qu'Ottawa pourrait continuer à exercer dans certains domaines d'intervention publique de juridiction provinciale.

Somme toute l'auteur considère qu'à long terme, au Canada, la réforme fiscale sera un facteur moins déstabilisateur que l'action autonomiste des provinces en cette matière. D'après Boadway, l'objectif incessant de partage fiscal poursuivi par ces dernières menace d'affaiblir la capacité du fédéral de renforcer l'harmonisation fiscale interprovinciale.

INTRODUCTION

For much of the Post-War period, the Canadian confederation has enjoyed a relatively highly coordinated and harmonious system of federal-provincial fiscal relations. Yet, the structure of the system has remained largely unchanged since the mid-1970s. Some of it has survived more or less intact as it evolved out of the highly centralized arrangements put in place immediately after the War. This is so despite the fact that there has been a gradual and continuous change in the fiscal positions of the federal government relative to the provinces.[1] The cumulative effect of those changes is such as to make it opportune to consider whether the current system can survive in its present form into the future. Indeed, I would maintain that federal-provincial fiscal relations are at an important crossroads and the policy response over the medium term will have lasting effects on the fiscal roles and responsibilities of the two levels of government and hence on the shape of the country itself.

The federal budget of April 1989 contained measures that will affect the fiscal balance between the federal and provincial governments. The most obvious of these is the reduction in the rate of increase in federal transfers to the provinces under the Established Programs Financing (EPF) arrangements. This measure was taken primarily (or even solely) with the objective of federal deficit reduction in mind. Yet, I would argue, it will undoubtedly have longer term consequences for federal-provincial fiscal arrangements, consequences which appear not to have been fully recognized, at least in public discussion. It is not the only measure that will have an effect on federal-provincial fiscal relations. Some of the recent tax reforms will as well.

It will be the purpose of this paper to consider some of the longer term consequences of the sorts of measures which were contained in the federal budget as well as in the recent policy stance of the federal government. In pursuing such an evaluation, it is necessary to place the discussion into the current constitutional context. Recent constitutional changes have, in my opinion, altered significantly the respective fiscal responsibilities of the federal and provincial governments and, in particular, have imposed on the federal government certain obligations whose import has yet to be fully recognized. These changes in the economic balance of power have curiously gone unnoticed while policy discussions have focused on political and legal matters, such as the amending formula, the Charter of Rights and Freedoms, and other important issues.

I begin by setting the stage. The next section is intended to place the discussion of deficit reduction measures into an economic and constitutional context. A brief summary is given of the key features of the system of federal-provincial fiscal relations. Then, some stylized economic facts affecting the federal government budget options are presented. Finally, some of the important constitutional and economic policy changes with implications for federal-provincial fiscal relations are discussed. Subsequent sections consider current policy issues and options in light of these stylized facts and their implications for federal-provincial fiscal relations.

THE INSTITUTIONAL AND POLICY SETTING

Although it will be well known to most readers, it is useful to begin with a summary of the main components of the system of federal-provincial fiscal arrangements. The system can be characterized by the following four features.

i. Vertical Imbalance. The federal government collects relatively more tax revenues (i.e., occupies more "tax room") than it needs for its own purposes and transfers the balance to the provinces in a variety of forms. This feature of the fiscal system is of considerable importance for coordination and harmonization purposes as will be argued below. It is also a necessary consequence of a fiscal system in which there exist relatively large federal-provincial transfers.

ii. Horizontal Redistribution. The system of federal-provincial transfers includes as one of its key features a significant amount of redistribution among the recipient provinces. Less well off ("have-not") provinces receive relatively more from the federal government in transfers than their residents pay in taxes. This is true for virtually all the major transfer schemes discussed below. The extent of this interprovincial redistribution compares favourably with other federal countries.[2]

iii. Conditionality of Grants. Many of the important grants have included some element of conditionality in them. In other words, the federal government through the use of its spending power has imposed conditions on the use of grants with the intention of influencing the behaviour of the provinces in areas of exclusive provincial jurisdiction. The conditionality has often, but not always, been accompanied by cost-sharing provisions.

iv. Tax Harmonization. Both the federal and provincial governments collect a wide variety of taxes and some major tax fields are co-occupied by the two levels of government. For instance, both governments occupy the lucrative income tax fields, both individual and corporate. Other taxes have been occupied mainly by one level only. For instance, resource taxes are now virtually solely levied by the provinces, as are property taxes. Both levels of government use sales taxes, but at the moment they are on considerably different bases, the provinces using the retail level and the federal government using the manufacturing level. In the case of the co-occupied income tax fields, a considerable degree of tax harmonization has been achieved in the sense that common bases have been adhered to by the federal and most provincial governments for both the individual and the corporation income taxes. The system undoubtedly owes its existence to the Wartime Tax Rentals Agreements when the federal government was the sole occupant of the income tax fields and imposed a common income tax system across the country.[3] As yet, no comparable system of harmonization has emerged for any other tax source. Note that tax harmonization is a qualitative term referring to the degree of uniformity of the tax system across the federation. In the case of a co-occupied tax base, it ideally applies to both levels of government. The concept and purpose of tax harmonization will be discussed further below.

The primary instruments for achieving the above four outcomes are the major federal-provincial transfers and the Tax Collection Agreements. There are currently three major programs which account for the lion's share of federal-provincial transfers and which jointly contribute to the first three of the above characteristics. They are Equalization, EPF and the Canada Assistance Plan (CAP). It is rather important to recognize that these three programs jointly contribute to several objectives. The Equalization program is designed explicitly to be horizontally redistributive in the sense that it provides payments to have-not provinces according to how far their tax capacities fall short of the average for five provinces (British Columbia, Saskatchewan, Manitoba, Ontario and Quebec). However, it is not a purely redistributive scheme or a "net" scheme to use the term of economists. Such a scheme would finance payments to have-not provinces with revenues from have provinces with no additional financing required from the federal government. Instead, Equalization is a "gross" scheme since payments to have-not provinces are financed from general revenues. As such, it incorporates an element of vertical redistribution

The EPF system combines a number of the above features. It is an equal per capita transfer provided to all provinces by a combination of cash grants and tax transfers and financed out of federal general revenues. It is the largest form of transfers and contributes heavily to the vertical imbalance of the fiscal system. However, it is at the same time redistributive and conditional. Its redistributive aspects arise from the fact that the combination of general revenue financing and equal per capita grants imply that have-not provinces receive proportionately more per capita than have provinces.[4] Indeed, as has been pointed out elsewhere, in many ways it is potentially as effective an equalization device as the Equalization system itself.[5] EPF grants are also conditional. The Canada Health Act, like its predecessors the Hospital Services and Diagnostics Act and the Medical Insurance Act, provides for reduced cash payments to the provinces if the provincial health insurance programs do not fully satisfy certain criteria. The Act also provides for financial penalties in the event that health professionals are allowed to engage in extra billing of patients or user charges are imposed for the use of health services.

The third major transfer is CAP, which is a matching conditional grant based on provincial expenditures for social assistance and social services. As well as being conditional this program also contributes to the equalizing feature of the general system of grants in a way that is complementary with the Equalization program. One of the criticisms of the Equalization scheme is that it does not treat negative taxes (transfers) symmetrically with taxes in determining the tax capacity of provinces.[6] The CAP system effectively redistributes according to one component of negative taxes, i.e., welfare payments and therefore can be seen as making equalization more complete.

As mentioned, the fourth characteristic feature of the Canadian federal fiscal system is tax harmonization. Tax harmonization has a number of dimensions and admits of varying degrees, and, as such, it has tended to be used rather loosely in policy discussion. Broadly speaking it refers to the amount of similarity achieved in tax systems across jurisdictions. The jurisdictions can be different countries, as in the European Economic Community, or they can be provinces and the federal government, as in Canada. Tax harmonization can apply to the definition of tax bases; indeed, that is the most common use. Proposals for harmonizing income taxes in the EEC have concentrated on harmonizing corporate income tax bases. There are a number of economic advantages to harmonizing tax bases across jurisdictions when taxpayers can operate in more than one jurisdiction. The possibilities for inefficiencies in resource allocation arising from the use of selective tax measures are reduced as are opportunities for tax arbitrage, tax avoidance and relocation for tax purposes, all of which are wasteful. Finally, a common base simplifies the tax system and reduces compliance costs for taxpayers.

Tax harmonization can also apply to tax rates, either the rate structure or rate levels. For example, in the case of the income tax applying to persons, harmonization of the rate structure prevents tax structure changes being used competitively by different jurisdictions to attract high income persons or discourage low income persons. Uniformity in levels of tax rates reduces the possibility of inefficient allocations of resources across jurisdictions. In the case of different countries, the benefits of tax harmonization are usually reckoned in terms of the efficiency of investment allocation across countries since capital is relatively free to move from one place to another while labour is not. However, in a federation with a common market in both labour and capital, tax harmonization can have benefits in terms of eliminating possible inefficiencies in the allocation of labour across provinces as well as capital.

Tax harmonization in Canada is much further advanced in the income tax field than in other federations (or common markets) in which more than one income tax jurisdiction exists.[7] It is accomplished by the system of income Tax Collection Agreements negotiated by the federal government with each participating province under the authority of the Federal-Provincial Fiscal Arrangements and Federal Post-Secondary Education and Health Contribution Act. According to these Agreements, the federal government collects taxes on behalf of the provinces provided the provinces agree to adhere to the federal tax base and, in the case of the individual income tax, to the rate structure as well. Provinces are allowed to set their own rate levels by applying their chosen rate to federal taxes payable in the case of the individual income tax and to taxable income in the case of the corporation income tax. In addition, the federal government will administer "non-discriminatory tax credits" for the provinces in return for a small fee.[8] Quebec remains outside the Agreements for both income taxes and both Alberta and Ontario collect their own corporate taxes. Despite this, all provinces adhere to a virtually uniform base for the corporate tax, though Quebec's personal tax base deviates somewhat from the federal one. The result is a high degree of harmonization of income tax bases that results in an economical system of tax administration and minimizes tax distortions within the Canadian common market. Alas, such harmonization exists only for income taxes. The other major taxes, sales and excise taxes, resources taxes, and property taxes remain largely unharmonized.

Income tax rates are also harmonized to some extent. For the personal tax, all provinces but Quebec must adhere to the federal rate structure as a condition for joining the Tax Collection Agreements. For the corporate tax, a preferential tax rate applies to small businesses and to manufacturing and processing. These differential rates are actually administered through the base by means of a deduction. Participants to the Tax Collection Agreements who wish to apply differential rates must effectively do so in a similar way. Even non-participating provinces have applied similar differential rates to those used by the federal government. The setting of rate levels is decentralized to the provinces. Even here, some harmonization is achieved indirectly. Because of the Equalization and EPF schemes (as well as other redistributive transfers) the tax capacities of provinces are made more equal. Presumably tax rates would show much more divergence in the absence of these transfers than they do now.

By and large, the above system of federal-provincial finances has led to a situation in which the provinces have been facilitated in their ability to provide a relatively uniform standard of public services in their rather important areas of jurisdiction, which include virtually all health, welfare and education services. As well, the system of taxes, though not identical across provinces, is nonetheless quite uniform, both in the composition of the base and rate structure and in the rate levels across provinces. This has led to a fairly efficiently functioning common economic market within Canada. There are, however, some signs that that uniformity is gradually being eroded as more and more special measures are being administered within the Tax Collection Agreements. These include not only tax credits under the individual and corporate tax systems, but also a variety of rebates and surcharges. As well, and as discussed further below, the allowance of flat rates in some provinces violates the use of a common base which had been a key feature of the Tax Collection Agreements. Part of the thrust of this paper is that this gradual fragmentation of tax harmonization is a natural consequence of the growing share of the tax room occupied by the provinces.

In order to identify the tensions that may exist in the system in the near future, it is useful to present a few selective but illustrative facts which indicate some of the changes that have been taking place over time and the constraints that policy-makers face in addressing such concerns as the federal budget deficit.

The main concern facing the federal government is the stock of outstanding public debt and its annual increase, the budget deficit. The arithmetic of the debt and the deficit is deceptively simple. At the end of the current fiscal year (1988-89) the debt will amount to $320 billion, which is about 54 per cent of GDP.[9] This is up from about $81 billion, or 28 per cent of GDP, in 1980-81. According to the recent budget, the debt-to-GDP ratio will continue to grow over the next three years. From an economic point of view, this debt can be looked at as a repository for private wealth that would otherwise be held as productive capital or net foreign assets. This "crowding out" of real capital by the existence of the public debt results in lower rates of growth and productivity than would otherwise be the case.[10] In addition, it imposes a requirement to raise more taxes in the future, which themselves distort the economy and reduce its efficiency.

This large stock of debt implies sizeable debt servicing charges, whose magnitude obviously varies with the rate of interest. For 1988-89, debt service charges are $33.0 billion. As a percentage of budgetary expenditures (inclusive of debt service), this amounts to almost 25 per cent (or equivalently 33 per cent of non-debt expenditures). As a percentage of revenues, debt charges are almost 32 per cent and are expected to rise to 35 per cent in the coming fiscal year. This represents a significant additional tax burden for the economy to bear. Compare this with 1980-81 where debt charges were less than $11 billion, which was about 17 per cent of budgetary expenditures and 22 per cent of budgetary revenues. One must be somewhat careful in interpreting these figures for policy purpose since some of the interest charge represents a purely inflationary component. However, even correcting for inflation it is likely that interest costs are much higher as a proportion of federal revenue in 1988-89 compared with 1980-81 since real interest rates are much higher.

The stock of debt is the cumulative total of past deficits. For 1988-89, the deficit was $28.9 billion, expected to rise to $30.5 billion for the current year. This will, of course, add to the stock of debt in the subsequent year and to the debt charges. It is most useful to put this deficit in perspective by relating it to the major categories of spending in the budget. This will help to indicate the constraints faced by the government. For 1988-89, total budgetary expenditures of the federal government were $133 billion. This amount can be broken down into five major categories of comparable orders of magnitude as follows:

expenditures on goods and services	$27.3 billion (20.5 per cent)
transfers to persons	$30.0 billion (22.6 per cent)
transfers to other levels of government	$24.3 billion (18.3 per cent)
other transfers (including to firms)	$18.4 billion (13.8 per cent)
interest on the public debt	$33.0 billion (24.8 per cent)

These numbers might be compared not only with one another, but also with the size of the budget deficit of $28.9 billion. The options that these figures suggest for addressing the deficit will be returned to below.

The above figures are for the federal budget alone. In discussing the implications of budgetary policy for intergovernmental relations, it is also useful to present some simple facts about the relative size of the federal government compared with the provinces. From the above data, we see that federal spending for its own purposes (net of intergovernmental transfers) is $108.3 billion. Net of interest charges on the public debt, it is only $75.3 billion. For the same year, provincial and municipal spending is over $120 billion, of which about $80 billion is attributable to the provincial level alone. (For 1980-81, federal government expenditures net of intergovernmental grants were about $48 billion, compared with about $61 billion for the provinces and municipalities). Thus, expenditure responsibilities in the aggregate are higher at the provincial and local level combined than at the federal level and expenditures at the provincial level alone are comparable with those at the federal level.

The situation is somewhat different on the revenue side owing to the continuing importance of intergovernmental grants. For the year 1987-88, the federal government collected about 62 per cent of personal tax revenues and about 67 per cent of corporate tax revenues, while the provinces collected the rest. Twenty years ago, the corresponding proportions were 71 per cent and 77 per cent. For general sales taxes, on the other hand, the federal government collected about 48 per cent in 1987-88 compared with 56 per cent 20 years earlier. Thus, the federal share of the tax room of these major tax sources has been falling over the years as provinces assume greater and greater expenditure responsibilities. Of particular note is the fact that the federal government has been able to retain well over half of the income tax room, but has fallen below half in the general sales tax area.[11] As discussed further below, these numbers will continue to change into the future as provincial government expenditures grow in relative size. In addition, both federal deficit reduction policy and tax reform policies will influence the allocation of tax room in ways which may be largely irreversible.

The final dimension of the institutional setting to address is the constitutional one. The constitutional amendments enacted in the Constitution Act of 1982 have been discussed largely from the political and legal perspectives and the changes in those dimensions were obviously very important. However, the Act also included a number of amendments of economic significance whose consequences are likely to be felt only over a longer period of time. The devolution of authority and taxing power over non-renewable resources affects economic responsibilities within the federation, though it could be argued that they really only formalize what has been the practice in recent years. Various items in the Charter of Rights and Freedoms have potential economic significance, such as the equality provision and the mobility provision. But, from the point of view of federal-provincial fiscal relations, probably the most important and least discussed provisions are those found in Section 36 entitled "EQUALIZATION AND REGIONAL DISPARITIES."

Section 36 consists of two parts. According to Section 36(1), the federal and provincial governments are jointly committed to

a)   promoting equal opportunities for the well-being of Canadians;
b)   furthering economic development to reduce regional disparity in opportunities; and
c)   providing essential public services of reasonable quality to all Canadians.

Rather than simply enunciating permissible actions by governments, Section 36(1) actually imposes obligations on the two levels of governments. From the point of view of federal-provincial fiscal responsibilities, this section, especially 36(1)(a), elevates the pursuit of equity to a national objective thereby providing constitutional justification to actions of both levels of government which can be seen to have equity as an objective. As we discuss again below, this, along with part (c) it can be argued, provide explicit and powerful justification for the use of the spending power by the federal government, since it is possible to argue that it is almost always used with an equity objective in mind.

Section 36(2) imposes even further obligations on government, this time the federal government. It reads as follows:

> Parliament and the government of Canada are committed to the principle of making equalization payments to ensure that provincial governments have sufficient revenues to provide reasonably comparable levels of public services at reasonably comparable levels of taxation.

This obligation, which harks back to advice given by the Rowell-Sirois Royal Commission [1940], seems to be a very powerful one indeed. If interpreted literally, it would impose serious constraints on the role of the federal government in its fiscal relations with the provinces and has implications for not only the formal Equalization scheme, but also for other transfers as well.

It is not at all obvious what the legal implications of Section 36 will be. One noted constitutional expert, Peter Hogg, has suggested that because of its vagueness and political nature, Section 36(2) may not be justiciable. At most, it may represent a political obligation. At the same time, he argues that Section 36(1) may serve to support the federal use of the spending power in areas of exclusive provincial jurisdiction.[12] In any case, it is important that we judge the current deficit reduction exercise in the context of the constitutional obligations of Sections 36(1) and 36(2) alike, whether those obligations be of a judicial nature, or merely political ones.

What makes the extensive commitments of Section 36 particularly difficult for the federal government to fulfil is the fact that the sources of inequality and the instruments for dealing with it are not entirely within the direct control of the federal government. The federal government currently has little access to the tax source which is responsible for the greatest interprovincial disparities in tax capacity, viz., resource taxation. Indeed, the Mulroney Conservative government in its first term largely abandoned its claim to resource revenues at considerable revenue cost to itself by turning access to resource revenues over to the provinces. Furthermore, despite the shared responsibility for providing essential public services (Section 36(1)) and for enabling all provinces to provide comparable public services, the provision of some of the most important public services, particularly those that contribute to equity goals, lies within the exclusive jurisdiction of the provinces.

We turn now to a brief examination of the policy options currently facing the federal government in its quest to reduce the deficit.

CURRENT POLICY ISSUES AND OPTIONS FOR DEFICIT REDUCTION

As is obvious from the data presented above, one way to look at the problem of the federal deficit is essentially as a problem of the stock of debt accumulated in the past. Debt service charges (i.e., interest payments to holders of the debt) are larger than the deficit itself. In other words, tax revenues are more than enough to cover all non-interest expenditures of the government, including spending on goods and services as well as transfers to individuals and governments. Thus, it could be argued that from a long-run structural point of view, government expenditures are not out of line with tax revenues. If the debt were paid off, the government would be raising enough revenue by taxes to cover all expenditures.

The issue of whether or not to run down the debt is essentially a policy decision. In principle, the existing stock of debt could be carried and its carrying cost (interest) could be continually covered by taxes. As long as the stock of debt was not increased by further annual budget deficits, such a situation could go on indefinitely. The case for reducing the debt is based on two arguments. First, as already mentioned, many economists believe that public debt crowds out private capital and therefore reduces productivity and output in the economy. The magnitudes involved can be significant. Second, the requirement to finance the interest on the debt by taxes imposes a further drag on the economy since additional taxes mean higher marginal tax rates and lower incentives for productive activity. The case against reducing the debt is that to do so involves a redistribution against the current generations and in favour of future ones. That is, the long run gains from having a higher capital stock and lower tax distortions can only be achieved after considerable short run costs to the taxpaying generations at the time the debt is run down. Thus, the case for reducing the debt is not a clear cut one. It depends on how one trades off the above effects. It would certainly be a feasible option to, say, stabilize the existing stock of debt and aim not to increase it in the future. However, the government has opted to reduce the debt-to-GDP ratio over a period of time, and our discussion is predicated on that objective.

The running down of the stock of debt could be done in a variety of ways. Taxes could be temporarily raised, or expenditures could be reduced. Expenditure reductions could take several forms. There could be reduced spending on goods and services, reduced transfers to individuals (or firms), or reduced transfers to other levels of government. From a purely economic point of view, transfers to individuals are analogous to "negative" taxes rather than to expenditures on goods and services. Indeed, some economists have suggested that the government budget could more usefully be written by including only government expenditures on goods and services as expenditures and moving all transfers over to the revenue side of the budget (as negative items).[13] By this argument, reducing transfers would be equivalent to raising taxes as means for reducing the deficit, except that the distributive consequences may differ depending on how taxes were raised and transfers reduced. There might be an expectation that tax increases would tend to come more at the expense of the better off and transfer reductions at the expense of the worse off. However, that need not be the case. Some rationalization of the transfer system could be achieved by reducing the transfers accruing to those who do not rely on them (i.e., by restricting their universality). At the same time, reducing inter-governmental transfers would simply pass the deficit reduction problem onto the provinces. They would have to choose among increasing taxes, reducing expenditures on goods and services, and reducing transfers as responses.

Given that the deficit reflects interest costs alone, one could legitimately make the case that an appropriate way for a rational government to run down the stock of debt would be to increase taxes temporarily to pay off that debt and then reduce taxes as the debt is paid off. That would leave the government free to determine expenditure levels based on the need for those expenditures rather than on temporary deficit reduction criteria. Following the above reasoning, one could even interpret reduced transfers as equivalent to increased taxes and include them as temporary deficit reduction measures.

The argument against relying on tax increases to run down the stock of debt is the political economy one that so-called temporary tax increases are difficult to keep temporary. Once tax rates are increased, it is difficult to decrease them at a later date. From this perspective, the use by the federal government of temporary surcharges makes considerable sense from the pure visibility point of view. Presumably tax increases by surcharge stand a better chance of being temporary than do general rate increases. Furthermore, temporary surcharges have a considerable advantage for the federal government (and a corresponding disadvantage for the provinces) since they can be applied fully on federal taxes payable with no revenue implications for the provincial governments. Under these circumstances, they fully represent increases in the tax room occupied by the federal government. The provinces might legitimately take issue with the use of surcharges as running against the spirit of income tax harmonization. On the other hand, if the purpose of increased tax revenue is to run down the federal debt, it might seem sensible that this be done by a temporary increase in the tax room available to the federal government.

Many economists are of the uncompromising view that expenditure reductions are the appropriate way to reduce the government deficit.[14] This seems to me not to be a necessary consequence of the economic principles involved. Instead it reflects more a view about the size of government than about the size of the deficit.

From the point of view of federal-provincial fiscal relations, the most important consequence that deficit reduction will have is its effect on the longer run division of tax room between the two levels of government and, equiv-alently, on the magnitude of vertical redistribution through federal-provincial transfers. As discussed in the following section, given the underlying expenditure responsibilities of the two levels of government, the division of tax room and the level of federal-provincial transfer payments are of considerable importance for the shape of federal-provincial fiscal relations. They have evolved in the past from a setting in which the federal government has assumed a prominent role. Recall that, even in the absence of a deficit problem, provincial tax room has gradually grown relative to that of the federal government. Yet, a sizeable amount of federal-provincial transfers have been maintained.

The effect of deficit reduction on the allocation of tax room depends significantly upon how the deficit reduction is achieved. As mentioned, if temporary tax increases are used, the gradual decay of federal tax room will be partially arrested, if only temporarily. This would be especially true if the tax increases came about via surcharges to which the provincial tax rates did not apply. These surcharges represent a pure increase in federal tax room.

Deficit reduction occurring through the expenditure side can have different consequences for the allocation of tax room depending upon the category of expenditures involved. Reductions in spending on goods and services or on transfers to individuals (or firms) reduce the size of the federal government with no effect on the division of tax room. Thus, relative to tax increases, this will result in less tax room for the federal government. Such will be the shorter run effect. Only to the extent that the change is permanent will it persist into the long run.

The more dramatic change in the allocation of tax room would result from reducing the deficit by cutting intergovernmental transfers. Given the relative magnitudes of the deficit and the size of these transfers, this category of government expenditures must be a very tempting target indeed. Recall that such transfers are close in magnitude to the size of the federal deficit. Relative to reducing the deficit by tax increases or by reductions in other government expenditures, this would result eventually in a significant transfer of tax room to the provinces. Indeed, depending on how the provinces respond, the tax room transfers could be as large as the fall in transfers themselves. This would be the case to the extent that the provinces responded by raising their own taxes to cover the revenue reduction rather than by reducing expenditures. The reallocation of tax room involved in reducing federal-provincial transfers would likely be irreversible in the longer run for all practical purposes. Furthermore, it would likely result in the provinces attaining at least a comparable share of income tax room as the federal government.

Not surprisingly, the federal government has used a combination of all of the above measures to attempt to reduce the deficit. By far the largest share seems to have been borne by tax increases, especially if one interprets that portion as including reductions in transfers to persons. There has been some arresting of the growth of particular categories of spending on goods and services (e.g., defense). As well, there has been reduction of one percentage point in the annual rate of growth of EPF transfers. This, on top of the natural evolution of the tax room allocation which has been occurring in the provinces' favour over the past several years serves to accelerate in a seemingly irreversible way the growing importance of the provinces as revenue raisers relative to the federal government.

This rearrangement of the tax room (as well as its consequences) will further be affected by the measures of tax reform currently in the process of being implemented by the federal government. Tax reform is being implemented in two phases. Phase I, which is largely complete, involves the income tax system. This phase can be roughly characterized as a combination of base broadening and rate reductions for both the individual and corporation income taxes, as well as some reallocation of the share of revenues from individual to corporation taxes. As such, it will have no great effect on the allocation of tax room since it is intended to be revenue-neutral. However, the reallocation from personal to corporate revenues could have some eroding effect on federal personal tax room depending on how the provinces respond. For example, there is some evidence that some provinces (e.g., Ontario) will, or have, increased their personal income tax rates in response to the federal reduction.

The tax reform will, of course, directly affect provincial income tax structures, at least for those that participate in the Tax Collection Agreements. All such provinces must abide by the federal income tax base. Although this will be of no immediate consequence for federal-provincial fiscal relations it could result in some strain in the Tax Collection Agreements depending on how the provinces perceive the reforms themselves. Provinces have for some time expressed some concern over the lack of control they have over tax policies within their own jurisdictions. The federal government retains effective unilateral control over the base and rate structure of the income taxes. Given the considerably lesser predominance of the federal government in the income tax fields compared with when the Tax Collection Agreements began, provinces may become less and less willing to accept sole federal authority over the determination of the income tax bases in the future. This is discussed further in the next section.

Phase II of the tax reform may, however, be of more direct consequence for federal-provincial fiscal relations. The most obvious reason is that the introduction of a federal multi-stage sales tax up to and including sales at the retail level effectively means that the two levels of government are co-occupying the retail sales tax field.[15] When the federal sales tax is introduced, the federal and various provincial sales taxes will differ considerably. In addition to being a multi-stage rather than a single-stage tax, the federal tax will be much more broadly-based and will include services, for example. At the same time, the federal tax will be purged of taxes on producer inputs, including those capital goods which have been captured in the manufacturers sales tax net. Provincial sales taxes, being single-stage, are unable easily to avoid taxing producer inputs entirely. Indeed, Ontario has claimed that the revenues it would gain by broadening the base under a multi-stage tax would be lost by eliminating the implicit tax on producer durables. Thus, to attain the same revenue it would have to keep the same sales tax rate. In addition, the rate structure and set of exemptions will differ considerably across jurisdictions and retailers will be faced with collecting two quite different taxes.

The economic case for harmonizing sales taxes will be very strong indeed. That would presumably have to be accomplished by the provinces adopting a form of tax similar to that of the federal government, an eventuality that the provinces are currently resisting. It is hard to imagine the two tax systems persisting indefinitely. A common multi-stage tax would preferably have a similar base across jurisdictions, though the rates and exemptions could differ somewhat. In designing a multi-stage tax, it is always desirable to have as little differentiation in the rates as possible for reasons which have been discussed by the federal government in its White Paper on sales tax reform. When many jurisdictions are involved, there are additional reasons for keeping down the number of different rates, particularly across jurisdictions. Some of the taxes levied at earlier stages in the production process in one jurisdiction end up being credited in other jurisdictions. Some mechanism is needed for ensuring that the credits end up being charged to the initial jurisdiction. The government suggested a clearing house mechanism for doing this involving the use of invoices recorded by sellers. Such a mechanism becomes more difficult to administer the more diversity there is across jurisdictions. In addition, cross-border shopping to reduce tax liabilities becomes more prevalent the greater are the differences in tax rates across jurisdictions. It is essentially for these reasons that the European Economic Community, as part of their process of VAT harmonization, has attempted to reduce the range of rates across countries.

A single collection authority would presumably be highly desirable, especially for the taxpayers. It would reduce the cost of compliance as well as of collection for the governments involved. This suggests that a form of Tax Collection Agreement for the sales tax would be appropriate. However, in one significant way a sales Tax Collection Agreement is likely to differ from the existing income Tax Collection Agreements. Given the existing occupation of the same base by the provinces and given that they have more than half of the sales tax room, it seems unlikely that they would be willing to turn over unilateral control of the tax base to the federal government. Nor would that be entirely necessary since, for the sales tax, a deviation from the base by a province (e.g., by a zero tax rate on a commodity) could be readily accommo-dated by the tax administrators. Whether this decentralization of tax base setting under a harmonized sales tax has spillover effects on the income tax agreements is an open question. The maintenance of a common base is essential for the income tax unlike the sales tax. However, whether that base must be unilaterally controlled by the federal government is another matter.

The second effect of Phase II on federal-provincial fiscal relations is some-what more subtle and speculative. The implementation of a general multi-stage sales tax on consumption opens up a major new tax source for the federal government which is complementary with the existing individual income tax.[16] Despite the fact that the sales tax initially only substitutes for revenue obtained from the existing manufacturers sales tax, it is quite likely that, once the tax is in place, the "tax mix" will change. That is, it will shift away from income (direct) taxation towards sales (indirect) taxation. Economists would probably generally applaud such a move, particularly the growing number who think consumption rather than income to be the more suitable object of taxation. This shift will increase the proportion of sales tax room occupied by the federal government, while at the same time reducing the income tax room. The federal government could soon end up with less than half the tax room of both types from such a change when combined with a reduction in federal transfers.

Thus, the combination of deficit reduction plus tax reform could result in a significant reallocation of income tax room in favour of the provinces. Pre-sumably this is not being done intentionally. Let us now finally turn to the consequences of such a change.

SOME CONSEQUENCES OF THE EVOLUTION OF TAX ROOM CHANGES FOR FEDERAL-PROVINCIAL FISCAL RELATIONS

The burden of the above discussion is that the existing system of federal-provincial fiscal relations was begun at a time when the federal government had a predominant fiscal role in the Canadian federation. Its expenditures were larger than those of the provinces and it occupied a high proportion of the tax room. Indeed, in the immediate post-war period, the federal government oc-cupied all of the income tax room. Things have evolved considerably since then. Provincial expenditure responsibilities have grown relative to those of the federal government largely owing to their constitutionally designated role in the health, education, and welfare areas. Now, provincial expenditures are comparable in size to the federal government and much larger if municipal expenditures are included. This trend is likely to continue in the future. None-theless, the federal government has continued to occupy more of the income tax room than the provinces and to maintain a large system of federal-provincial transfers. Of course, the two are interdependent. In the absence of such transfers, federal tax room would be correspondingly smaller. Depending on how the provinces would make up their absent transfer revenues, they could end up dominating the income tax fields in the same way that they dominate the sales tax field already.

This evolution of fiscal power to the provinces is likely to continue in the absence of structural changes. As implied by the discussion of the earlier sections, the reallocation of tax room would be accelerated by two current policy developments. The first is the response to the deficit (debt) problems of the government. To the extent that reductions in federal transfers to the provinces (e.g., EPF grants) are used to reduce the deficit, tax room will be shifted from the federal government to the provinces. Second, phase II of the current tax reform involving the institution of a multi-stage retail sales tax in place of the Manufacturers Sales Tax may well eventually lead to a change in the federal tax mix in favour of indirect taxation at the expense of direct taxation. To the extent that this occurs, it will further erode the predominant position of the federal government in the income tax fields, probably in an irreversible manner. The question is: what difference should it make if fiscal power evolves to the provinces? The remainder of this paper will be devoted to some speculative comments in response to that question.

Given the relatively large expenditure responsibilities of the provincial (and municipal) governments, the continued occupation of a significant proportion of tax room by the federal government of necessity entails a sizeable contribution by the federal government of transfers to the provinces. The maintenance of a dominant position by the federal government in the allocation of the tax room and thus in the transfer of funds to the provinces, is of critical importance for the shape of federal-provincial fiscal relations for a number of reasons. Here, we single out three reasons though there are undoubtedly others of importance, such as the implications for the ability of the federal government to conduct an effective stabilization (fiscal) policy. The three we single out are chosen for their relevance to the traditional fiscal-federalism arguments for grants. In the Canadian context they take on a particular relevance because of recent amendments to the constitution. Each of the three is considered in turn.

1. The Equalization Responsibility of the Federal Government

Equalization in one form or another has been a feature of the Canadian fiscal system since Confederation. The present system evolved out of the fiscal arrangements of the Second World War and continues to be one of the main components of federal-provincial fiscal relations. The principle of equalization has been carefully and systematically analyzed by economists. A considerable amount of agreement has been reached concerning the case for equalization and the form it should take.[17]

Simply put, the economic arguments are as follows. In a federal state, the efficient allocation of resources among the provinces and the equitable treatment of like persons regardless of residence both require that there be no advantages resulting from provincial fiscal activities which favour living in one province rather than another. The elimination of these so-called net fiscal benefits (NFBs) involves at least the equalization of differences in tax capacities (the ability to raise revenues at comparable tax rates). It could also involve eliminating differences in the need for or cost of providing similar public services. In short, the economic analysis provides support for the dictum that provinces should be able to provide equivalent public services at equivalent tax rates.

There are a variety of ways that this equalization could, in principle, be accomplished. One way would be for the federal government to administer a set of purely redistributive transfers from those provinces with higher than average NFBs to those with lower than average. This is referred to as a net scheme and involves no federal funds at all. It has the disadvantage that it requires payments from the above-average provinces into the scheme. Such a system has not been used in Canada, although it has in the Federal Republic of Germany.

The alternative is the gross system whereby the federal government makes payments to the provinces according to their tax capacities, and possibly need and cost factors. This is the system that has been used in Canada. In the limit, the gross system could achieve full equalization by the federal government collecting all the taxes on behalf of the provinces and turning enough grants over to each province so as to enable each province to provide equivalent levels of public services. The Australian system approaches this because of the predominance of the federal government in the most important tax fields (see Bird, 1985). Such a system has been characterized as replicating the financial arrangements of a unitary state, including the efficiency and equity properties thereof, while at the same time reaping the benefits of decentralized decision making in the federation. In other words, the provinces would have the potential to provide equivalent public services at equivalent tax rates if they so choose, but may choose not to.

Naturally, this extreme form of equalization does not exist in Canada. The Equalization system equalizes the "have-not" provinces up, but not to the national average. It does not equalize the "have" provinces down. At the same time it can be seen that the EPF system goes part way in the direction of the unitary state model outlined above and other grants, such as the CAP, augment equalization further. Thus, the practice of equalization works in the direction that would be advocated on the basis of economic arguments alone, but it is not complete.

As has been mentioned before the principle of equalization has now been included in the constitution by virtue of Section 36(2) of the Constitution Act, 1982. The wording of Section 36(2) is fully in line with the economic argument for equalization, though with somewhat more flexibility in interpretation. Nonetheless, it does impose an obligation on the federal government that, if interpreted as an economist might interpret it, involves an equalization system of a fairly wide-ranging sort. By committing the federal government to the principle of making equalization payments to enable the provinces to provide reasonably comparable levels of public services at reasonably comparable levels of taxation, it suggests at least three characteristics of equalization. First, the system must be a gross one since it requires the federal government to make payments to the provinces. Thus, for example, it might be difficult to affect equalization through the personal tax system by having differential federal tax rates across provinces. Second, it commits the federal government to equalizing the ability of provinces to raise revenues, that is, to equalize on the basis of tax capacities. That is what the current formal Equalization system does. Third, it requires some equalizing on the ability to provide public services that may differ across provinces by need or cost.

Once the potential extent of the obligation is recognized, it is apparent that the equalization committment involves more than the Equalization system per se. Other programs must be seen as contributing to the equalization objective. The EPF program does so directly and in a way which is complementary with Equalization. For example, the EPF program effectively equalizes all provinces towards the mean and not just the "have-nots". In the extreme, if all provincial funds were obtained as equal per capita transfers (the formula used by EPF), tax capacities would be fully equalized. The CAP program can be seen both as equalizing by need and cost, as well as incorporating an element of tax capacity that is missing from the Equalization scheme, i.e., negative tax liabilities.[18] In fact, almost any shared-cost grant program could be interpreted as contributing to the equalization objective.

The implications of the commitment of Section 36(2) are potentially far-reaching. If this Section is interpreted as has been suggested above, that is, as imposing at least a political obligation on the federal government, this necessarily implies a continuing system of federal-provincial transfers of considerable magnitude and the tax room required to finance them. This is clearly incompatible with treating federal-provincial transfers as deficit reduction instruments. This conclusion is further strengthened by the last two reasons for the importance of the federal government maintaining its share of the tax room, to which we now turn.

2. The Equity Obligations of the Federal Government

Just as a reduction in the tax room of the federal government would reduce the ability of the federal government to fulfill its equalization commitments under Section 36(2) of the Constitution Act, so it would make it more difficult to pursue the obligations outlined in Section 36(1). These obligations are every bit as far reaching as the equalization ones. Recall that Section 36(1) gives the federal government, along with the provinces, responsibility for pursuing equity. More precisely, it commits them jointly to equality of opportunity, regional development, and the provision of essential public services.

The fulfillment of these objectives is no simple task. Unlike with income redistribution objectives, it requires more than the use of tax-transfer policies, although this is certainly one useful instrument available to both governments for achieving equity. More generally, the pursuit of equity can be argued on economic grounds to require more than redistributive transfers. It also involves the provision of in-kind transfers and certain types of public services. This is recognized in the wording of Section 36(1) by the explicit inclusion of equality of opportunity and the provision of essential public services.

The difficulty faced by the federal government in achieving the objectives set out in Section 36(1) is that most of the expenditure instruments available for addressing equality of opportunity and for pursuing equity through the provision of essential public services are in the "exclusive" jurisdiction of the provincial governments. These include many expenditures in the categories of health, education and welfare. From an economic point of view, a good deal of public sector involvement in these areas can be motivated only by equity considerations. For example, on pure efficiency grounds health insurance could as well, if not better, be provided by the private sector. All of the economic efficiency problems of providing health insurance, such as moral hazard and adverse selection, plague public insurance as well. The public sector role in providing health insurance comes from an equity, or social insurance, objective.[19] Furthermore, this objective could be used to justify the conditions of universal and comprehensive access which are written into the Canada Health Act. The same could be said for public education. It fulfills essentially a redistributive, or an in-kind transfer, role. There is no particular efficiency reason why education could not be purely private. The same also applies to welfare services.

Since these categories of in-kind redistributive transfers are all in the jurisdiction of the provinces, the only way in which the federal government can use them as instruments for fulfilling their new-found constitutional obligations under Section 36(1) is by exercising the spending power. From an economic perspective, Section 36(1) provides ample, indeed almost limitless, justification for the use of the spending power in areas of health, education and welfare. The Meech Lake Accord provisions pale by comparison. As with Section 36(2) it is not altogether clear that this interpretation was foreseen when the amendments were being implemented. However, that danger always exists when constitutional provisions include actual obligations on governments rather than simply circumscribing powers.

The consequence of this equity obligation being imposed on the federal government (which, granted, may have de facto existed before) combined with the fact that some of it can only be exercised by the provinces implies that the use of the spending power must be retained. As with the equalization objective this requires that the federal government retain enough of the tax room to enable it to make the possibly large transfers to the provinces to allow for credible use of the spending power. The retention of a significant share of the tax room is necessary for this purpose.

3. The Enforcement of Tax Harmonization

Despite the considerable degree of decentralization of taxing authority in Canada the income tax system remains highly harmonized. All provinces except Quebec have signed Tax Collection Agreements for the individual income tax. While Alberta, Ontario, and Quebec, comprising over 3/4 of corporate income, do not belong to corporate Tax Collection Agreements they nevertheless maintain income tax bases that are nearly identical with the federal one. The agreements require the provinces to adhere to a common income tax base (i.e., the federal one). Each province can choose a rate to apply to basic federal tax in the case of the individual income tax and to taxable income in the case of the corporation tax. The federal and provincial taxes are jointly collected by Revenue Canada and payments are made to the provinces according to tax assessments on behalf of each of them. The federal government bears the cost of tax collection and of uncollected taxes, but keeps any interest earned. The federal government is also willing to administer for the provinces "nondiscriminatory" tax credits for a nominal fee, provided they are not too difficult to implement. (The federal government decides which ones to allow and does so with considerable discretion since the governing Act does not establish criteria.)

The corporate Tax Collection Agreements also allow for a common formula for allocating taxable income among provinces in cases where the same firm operates in more than one. The share of taxable income attributable to a province is the average of its share of the wage bill and its share of the revenues of the firm in the province. This is a significant feature of corporate tax harmonization which avoids many complexities of tax administration and planning found in other jurisdictions.

This system of income tax harmonization, which yields a common base and rate structure but different rate levels, is unique among federal countries. The system for corporate taxes is similar to that aspired to by the European Economic Community beyond 1992. However, harmonization is restricted to the income tax bases at the moment, although there is the prospect for sales tax harmonization now that the federal government is itself entering the retail sales tax field. Again, the system being proposed across jurisdictions in Canada, should the provinces agree to implement value added taxes, is similar to that in effect in the European Economic Community.

The origins of the Tax Collection Agreements can be accounted for by the financing arrangements put in place during World War II. Prior to that time provinces levied their own income taxes on very different bases, resulting in what the Rowell-Sirois Royal Commission [1940] referred to as a "tax jungle." The exigencies of wartime finance combined with the disarray of provincial finances led to the federal government, with the provinces' consent, "renting" the income tax fields from the provinces (along with succession duties). That is, the federal government alone collected income tax revenues at rates sufficiently high to satisfy its own revenue requirements and those of the provinces. The federal government made unconditional transfers of funds to the provinces to enable them to meet their expenditure responsibilities. Various options were available to the provinces for calculating their entitlements. Interestingly enough, the formulas allowed for some element of equalization among provinces.

When the Tax Collection Agreements finally replaced the tax rentals in 1962 it was natural enough to retain a common base for all participating governments. Prior to the Agreements the federal government set a common tax rate, collected the revenues, and turned over to the provinces their entitlements as a transfer. From a visibility point of view the federal government bore the burden of collecting all taxes. By devolving the setting of tax rates to the provinces, they would now be seen to be responsible for deciding their own tax rates. This, of course, led to diverging tax rates over time, but a common base was maintained.

As time has passed, the income tax bases among agreeing and non-agreeing provinces alike have remained remarkably similar. Even the rates have not diverged greatly. This is true despite the fact that income tax room, especially at the personal level, has gradually been reallocated in favour of the provinces. Undoubtedly, the lack of divergence in rates is partly attributable to the extensive set of federal-provincial equalizing transfers that have been put in place. It may also be partly due to elements of tax competition among provinces which prevents large divergences in rates.

In recent years, the Tax Collection Agreements have come under considerable and increasing, strain. At various times, several provinces have expressed discontent over the existing arrangements. One province, Alberta, has chosen to leave the Agreement, while others have seriously considered doing so.[20] The sources of discontent are several. Since the federal government controls unilaterally the choice of the base, provinces are precluded from using the base for policy purposes. This was the ostensible reason Alberta gave for leaving their corporation income Tax Collection Agreement, though they have not yet used base changes for policy purposes. Provinces must accept federal base changes, and have done so through many tax reforms over the years. Such base changes have both policy implications as well as revenue implications. Whether it would be possible for the determination of the base to be jointly influenced by the two levels of government is an open question. To some extent now there is presumably at least consultation between the federal and provincial governments before tax changes are introduced.

The provinces have also been concerned about the federal government control of the rate structure, especially for the individual income tax. Some have suggested (e.g., British Columbia and Ontario) that provinces be allowed to apply their rate structures to the common base.

Finally, there has been some concern over purely administrative matters. Some provinces have felt that the federal audit procedures have sometimes concentrated too little on matters of purely provincial concern, such as the auditing of provincial tax credits and of the allocation of taxable income across provinces. Given the confidentiality of the audit process, this is obviously difficult to substantiate. Alberta officials have claimed that the entire cost of their corporation income tax administration is covered by additional revenues gained from their own independent audit. Some provinces, especially Ontario, have also been unhappy with the lag that sometimes has occurred between the interim payments to them and the amount finally owing. Over the past several years, interim payments to the provinces under the individual income tax have tended to be considerably less than the final amount owing to the provinces on the basis of final assessments.

These concerns of the provinces for more discretion over their own tax structures have increased gradually over time as they have become more important in the income tax fields. The only outlet available for autonomous provincial actions, short of leaving the agreements altogether, has been to increase their use of tax credits. Provincial tax credits, rebates, and surcharges have increased dramatically in the 1980s resulting in a significant erosion of the harmonization of the income tax bases. Moreover, the acquiescence of the federal government in the administration of so-called "flat rate taxes" in Saskatchewan, Alberta, and Manitoba has opened the possibility for serious departures from tax harmonization. Flat taxes are taxes levied on individuals using a single rate rather than a progressive rate structure. In the case of provincial flat taxes, the bases used are net income in the case of Saskatchewan and Manitoba and taxable income in the case of Alberta. These taxes effectively allow the provinces to levy taxes on their own concept of income rather than on basic federal taxes. They influence the provincial rate structure and are, therefore, a violation of at least the spirit, if not the law, of the Tax Collection Agreements.

From an economics point of view, this erosion of the Tax Collection Agreements is unfortunate. Income tax harmonization fulfills a number of objectives. It reduces the possibility of wasteful tax competition among provinces. It reduces distortions in the allocation of resources among provinces. It reduces the incentives to engage in tax planning designed to shift taxable income to low tax jurisdictions. And, it significantly reduces compliance costs for taxpayers. Thus, tax harmonization is well worth protecting.

The original success of the existing Tax Collection Agreements was attributable to the fact that they were initiated at a time when the federal government had been the sole occupant of the income tax fields. It was, therefore, natural to retain the same tax bases for the provinces and to allow the federal government to exercise unilateral control over base changes in the future. As the provinces become more and more important in the income tax fields, the system is bound to become more and more strained. The growing number of tax credits, rebates, surcharges, and flat taxes are symptomatic of that. Policy changes of the federal government which accelerate the reallocation of tax room to the provinces should be seen in that light, especially ones that may result in the provinces reaching an equal share to that of the federal government. They ultimately weaken the ability of the federal government to enforce tax harmonization across provinces. At some point, the pressures for disharmony will become too strong to resist.

CONCLUSION

The arguments of this paper could be summarized as follows. The maintenance of a substantial degree of tax room by the federal government is of importance for two reasons. First, it facilitates the harmonization of those tax bases that the federal government co-occupies with the provinces. Second, it enables the federal government to continue to make the sorts of federal-provincial transfers that improve the efficiency and equity of the federal economy while at the same time retaining the benefits of decentralized provision of public services by the provinces. We have come to take these two things for granted given that they have been with us for most of the post-War period.

Circumstances have changed since the basic federal-provincial fiscal arrangements that are in place now were first introduced. First, the provinces have gradually become more and more important players in terms of their share of public sector expenditures and taxes. This is bound to place strains on a fiscal system which has depended on federal leadership and predominance. Second, the federal deficit has placed considerable strain on the federal finances, strain which could be partly relieved by reducing transfers to the provinces and accelerating the evolution of provincial economic strength. Third, the process of tax reform itself could lead to a change in tax mix at the federal level and possibly a further dilution of federal predominance in the income tax fields. These changes have been taking place without a great deal of discussion as to their implications for federal-provincial fiscal relations.

At the same time, constitutional changes have been taking place that could be regarded as centralizing from the point of view of federal-provincial fiscal relations. The combined effect of Sections 36(1) and 36(2) is to give explicit recognition to the federal government's interest in equity and the provision of essential public services, as well as to impose on the federal government an obligation to making equalizing transfers of a potentially wide ranging sort. Although there may be some uncertainty as to the legal obligation this imposes on the federal government, the existence of a political obligation seems clear. The combination of this obligation, whose fulfillment requires continuing and substantial federal-provincial transfers and the economic advantages of tax harmonization, both suggest that it would be short-sighted for the federal government to rely on economizing on federal-provincial transfers to help solve its current debt problem. Doing so would result in transferring further tax room to the provinces, probably permanently.

My own view, which may well differ from that of other economists, is as follows. The existing extent of federal-provincial transfers should be protected. So should the federal share of tax room under the income tax. This will assist in meeting the obligations of Section 36 and also in maintaining at least the existing degree of income tax harmonization. The federal government should also proceed with full awareness of the federal-provincial consequences in implementing the goods and services tax. From an economic point of view, the tax itself is a good one. However, whether or not the provinces join in the system in the short run it would seem to me to be sensible not to skew the allocation of tax room unduly in favour of indirect taxes at the federal level and away from direct ones. The existing system of income tax harmonization should be protected and, if possible, strengthened. Maintaining a large federal presence is a necessary condition for that. Harmonization of indirect taxes is less important. In addition, given that the federal government will not be able unilaterally to control the base in any case, it is not as important that federal tax room exceed provincial tax room.

Debt reduction remains an important objective. In my view, the appropriate way to achieve that is using tax measures, given the once and for all nature of the problem. Expenditure reductions, to the extent that they are desirable, should be viewed as fulfilling long-run structural objectives, such as getting the public sector-private sector mix in line.

Notes

1. When the term "provinces" is used in this paper, it will generally be taken to include the municipalities for fiscal purposes. In a real sense, the municipalities are the creatures of the provinces and that is so recognized by the constitution.

2. There are other federal countries, especially Australia and West Germany, that undertake policies with at least as great a degree of equalization among various regions as Canada. In the case of West Germany much of this is accomplished by redistribution among individuals, although there is a scheme for interstate equalization transfers. The Australian case is rather unique in the extent to which interstate redistribution is pursued. Much of this redistribution occurs as part of a very high degree of vertical redistribution from the federal government to the states. This is a result of the fact that the most lucrative tax fields are solely occupied by the federal government and the least by the states. Unlike Canada, tax fields tend to be separated by jurisdiction. For a full comparison of fiscal arrangements among jurisdictions in various federal countries, see Bird (1985, 1986).

3. The Wartime Rental Agreements also applied to estate taxes. The federal government turned over the estate tax field completely to the provinces with the tax reform of 1971. Now, only Quebec maintains an estate tax.

4. This statement presumes only that total tax liabilities rise with levels of income and that is compatible with a wide variety of tax structures, even regressive ones. Thus, the average tax rate (taxes as a proportion of income) could fall with income levels and yet total taxes could rise with incomes. Studies of tax incidence in Canada tend to show that the tax system as a whole is roughly proportional (e.g., Gillespie 1976) and this is certainly enough to make EPF redistributive.

5. See Boadway and Flatters (1982) and Economic Council of Canada (1982).

6. See, for example, the report of the Parliamentary Task Force on Federal-Provincial Fiscal Relations (1982), also called the Breau Report.

7. This is discussed further in Bird (1986).

8. The admissibility of the tax credits is determined by officials in the Department of Finance. Admissibility criteria have not been set down in the legislation governing the tax credit agreements. The criteria actually used are drawn from a memorandum issued by the Minister of Finance in 1981. Credits must be easy to administer, they must not discriminate against residents of other provinces and they must not disrupt the free flow of investment across provincial borders. These criteria admit of different interpretation in particular cases.

9. These figures and the ones that follow are taken, unless otherwise indicated, from *The Fiscal Plan: Controlling the Public Debt*, Department of Finance, Ottawa, 27 April 1989 and *The National Finances*, Canadian Tax Foundation, Toronto, various years.

10. There is some dispute among economists about the extent to which public borrowing crowds out private investment. There are those who hold that private savers recognize that public debt is essentially a transfer from younger to older generations, and who will, for altruistic reasons, increase their saving so as to leave a larger bequest to future generations to offset at least partly the effect of public debt on the stock of capital. This dispute is well documented in a highly readable form in the symposium published in the Spring 1989 issue of *The Journal of Economic Literature*.

11. It is worth remarking that the mix of direct and indirect taxes has changed very little over the past decade. The federal government obtains about 12 per cent of its revenues from general sales taxation and about half from income taxation. Within the income tax category, there has been a gradual increase in the proportion obtained from individual income taxes and a corresponding decrease in corporate tax revenues. One of the purposes of Phase I of the tax reform was to reverse the trend. The provinces have obtained about 11 per cent of their revenues from general sales taxes and close to 30 per cent from income taxes. The trends reported in the text cannot be attributed to changes in the tax mix by either level of government.

12. Hogg's view of Section 36(2) appears in the following passage: "This obligation is probably too vague, and too political, to be justiciable, but it suggests that equalization payments will continue into the foreseeable future." (Hogg (1985), p. 84). Further on, he says: "Section 36 of the Constitution Act, 1982, expressing a commitment to redressing regional disparities and to making equalization payments, also seems to reinforce by implication a broad interpretation of the spending power." (Hogg, 1985, p. 126).

13. For a summary of this view, see Boadway and Flatters (1989).

14. This is a characteristic feature, for example, of those economists associated with the C.D. Howe Institute.
15. From an economic perspective, a multi-stage tax on consumption expenditures is equivalent to a single-stage retail sales tax on final consumption purchases. This and other equivalences among taxes are discussed fully in Boadway and Mintz (1987).
16. It is complementary in the following sense. A fully general sales tax on consumption is equivalent to a proportional tax on income with saving exempt. It is also equivalent to a proportional payroll tax. It has been recognized that the Canadian income tax system is not too different from a tax on consumption owing to the fact that a large part of asset income is sheltered from tax. For a discussion of this, see Boadway, Bruce and Mintz (1987).
17. A summary statement of the principles may be found in Economic Council of Canada (1982). The technical economic arguments are outlined in Boadway and Flatters (1982).
18. One of the shortcomings of the Equalization system that was noted by the Breau Report (1981) was the fact that only positive tax liabilities entered the formula and not negative ones (transfers). To an economist, the two are symmetrical.
19. This theme is developed more fully in Boadway (1986).
20. At the same time, it should be said that Ontario has also considered joining a corporation income Tax Collection Agreement.

References

Bird, Richard M., "Federal Finance in Comparative Perspective," in T.J. Courchene, et al (eds.), *Ottawa and the Provinces: The Distribution of Money and Power* (Toronto: Ontario Economic Council, 1985) pp. 137-77.

Bird, Richard M., *Federal Finance in Comparative Perspective* (Toronto: Canadian Tax Foundation, 1986).

Boadway, Robin W., "The Economics of the System of Federal-Provincial Fiscal Arrangements," Report prepared as Expert Testimony for *Winterhaven Stables Ltd.* versus *The Attorney General of Canada*, November 1986.

Boadway, Robin W., Neil Bruce, and Jack M. Mintz, *Taxes on Capital Income in Canada: Analysis and Policy* (Toronto: Canadian Tax Foundation, 1987).

Boadway, Robin W. and Frank R. Flatters, *Equalization in a Federal State: An Economic Analysis* (Ottawa: Economic Council of Canada, 1982).

Boadway, Robin W. and Frank R. Flatters, "Tax Expenditures and Alternatives for Evaluating Government Activities Conducted Through the Tax System," in Neil Bruce (ed.), *Tax Expenditures and Government Policy* (Kingston: John Deutsch Institute for the Study of Economic Policy, 1989), forthcoming.

Boadway, Robin W. and Jack M. Mintz (eds.), *The Business Transfer Tax*, (Kingston: John Deutsch Institute for the Study of Economic Policy, 1987).

Canada, *Report of the Royal Commission on Dominion-Provincial Relations* (Ottawa: King's Printer, 1940), also referred to as the Rowell-Sirois Report.

Economic Council of Canada, *Financing Confederation* (Ottawa: Supply and Services Canada, 1982).

Gillespie, Irwin W., "On the Redistribution of Income in Canada," 24 Canadian Tax Journal (July-August 1976) pp. 417-50.

Hogg, Peter, *Constitutional Law of Canada* (2nd Edition) (Toronto: Carswell, 1985).

Parliamentary Task Force on Federal-Provincial Fiscal Relations, *Fiscal Federalism in Canada* (Ottawa: Supply and Services, 1981), also referred to as the Breau Report.

SIX

La politique linguistique au Canada: l'impasse?

Yvon Fontaine

Recently, Canada has witnessed a new wave of legislative, constitutional and other measures throughout the country which have attempted to clarify the status of both French and English languages in Canada.

Those measures fall into three categories: 1) repressive measures such as the linguistic laws passed by both Alberta and Saskatchewan which try to lessen rights and privileges previously granted to the linguistic minority; 2) progressive measures, such as the Official Language Act, that attempt to strengthen the status of official languages in Canada; 3) measures, that, following the example of both laws 101 and 178, attempt to respond to the aspirations of Quebec.

The author adopts, in the main, the dual sociocultural vision expressed in the Meech Lake Accord which recognizes, on the one hand, the existence of a Pan-Canadian linguistic duality and, on the other hand, a territorial reality characterized by two principal poles, in this case Quebec—recognized as a "distinct society"—and English Canada, each of the two including its own linguistic minority, respectively English and French. However, Fontaine considers that the Accord is somewhat imprecise over the "linguistic resolution" in Canada, particularly regarding the francophones outside Quebec.

The francophone community outside Quebec, while less formal than that in Quebec, is nonetheless a functional one. It takes the form of several community networks, more or less marked out from the territorial point of view. Francophones outside Quebec wish to live, therefore, in a specific francophone environment, typical of them. In this respect, New Brunswick has perhaps shown us the way with recent legislation recognizing the concept of linguistic community, acknowledging in particular the francophone minority of that province. Bilateral agreements between the federal government and certain provinces also aim to preserve francophone communities outside Quebec. Nevertheless, the future of francophone communities outside Quebec is not fully assured for all; it is important therefore that the Canadian Parliament constitutionally strengthen the protection of the Canadian duality.

Although the focus in this article is on the situation of francophone communities outside Quebec, the conditions for linguistic reconciliation within Quebec are also examined. Such a reconciliation will require the acceptance by Quebec anglophones of their status as a linguistic minority in Quebec.

INTRODUCTION

Depuis plus de deux ans on assiste au Canada à une nouvelle vague de mesures législatives, constitutionnelles et autres qui tentent de régir le statut de la langue française et de la langue anglaise au Canada et qui cherchent également à établir le statut des communautés francophones et des communautés anglophones du Canada.

La liste des mesures est imposante. Parmi les plus importantes il y a l'Accord du Lac Meech,[1] la Loi fédérale sur les langues officielles,[2] les lois linguistiques de la Saskatchewan[3] et de l'Alberta,[4] la Loi 178 au Québec.[5] Il y a une série de jugements de la Cour suprême du Canada qui ont précédé la plupart de ces mesures législatives et qui ont été à la base de l'introduction de celles-ci. Nous pensons à l'arrêt dans l'affaire Mercure,[6] et aux arrêts dans l'affaire Chaussure Brown[7] et dans l'affaire Singer.[8]

Rares sont les moments dans l'histoire du Canada où nous avons assisté à autant d'événements qui visent la question linguistique en si peu de temps et qui touchent presque toutes les régions du pays. Ces questions sont à l'avant-scène de l'actualité nationale sans relâche depuis deux ans.

Les mesures prises ont eu pour résultat d'accentuer les différences plutôt que d'harmoniser le dialogue entre les collectivités francophones et anglophones au Canada. Les sondages les plus récents sont révélateurs à ce sujet. Pourquoi en est-il ainsi?

Pour expliquer pareilles attitudes, il faut analyser de plus près les mesures auxquelles nous avons fait référence plus haut. Il est possible de les regrouper en trois catégories: les mesures répressives, les mesures progressives et les mesures qui visent à répondre aux aspirations du Québec. Ces dernières peuvent être qualifiées de répressives ou progressives selon le groupe linguistique auquel on appartient.

Les mesures répressives sont celles qui visent à réduire les droits et privilèges déjà consentis en faveur de la langue française ou anglaise. Les mesures progressives sont celles qui cherchent à renforcer le statut des langues officielles au Canada. Enfin, la troisième catégorie réunit les mesures qui cherchent à accorder au Québec les outils qu'il juge nécessaires pour affirmer sa francité dans le contexte fédéraliste canadien.

Certaines des mesures législatives sont carrément répressives. C'est le cas des lois linguistiques de la Saskatchewan et de l'Alberta. Alors que la Cour suprême a statué que l'article 110 de l'Acte des Territoires du Nord-Ouest était toujours applicable à la Saskatchewan et par extension à l'Alberta[9] et ainsi conférait à la langue française des droits comparables à ceux prévus par l'article 23 de la Loi sur le Manitoba[10] et par l'article 133 de la Loi constitutionnelle de 1867,[11] les législatures de la Saskatchewan et de l'Alberta ont abrogé ces droits, qui remontaient à plus de 75 ans. Bien que les lois linguistiques des provinces en question reconnaissent à la langue française certains droits, ceux-ci sont nettement moindres que ce que lui garantissait l'article 110 de l'Acte des Territoires du Nord-Ouest.

Certes les mesures répressives des législatures de la Saskatchewan et de l'Alberta ont suscité un débat dans l'opinion publique au Canada. Par leur nature répressive elles ont nui aux communautés francophones de ces provinces et ont assombri les espoirs que pouvaient entretenir les communautés francophones des provinces de l'Ouest de voir les provinces être plus généreuses à l'égard des communautés de langue française. Les mesures prises par ces deux provinces ont également été critiquées par les défenseurs du bilinguisme au Canada. Seul le premier ministre du Québec a jugé opportun d'applaudir l'initiative du gouvernement de la Saskatchewan au moment où celui-ci introduisait sa loi linguistique. Dans l'ensemble, toutefois, ces mesures n'ont pas suscité la révolte que l'on connaîtra par suite de l'adoption de la Loi 178. Même si plusieurs ont été saisis d'indignation, ceux qui croient à une solution qui amènera la coexistence pacifique des deux collectivités de langues officielles au Canada n'ont pas perdu l'espoir de voir leur rêve triompher.

Dans la catégorie des mesures progressives, nous plaçons la Loi sur les langues officielles du Canada.[12] A plusieurs égards, cette loi représente un véritable progrès par rapport à la Loi de 1969,[13] aussi bien pour les francophones du Québec que pour les communautés minoritaires de langues officielles.

Bien que le débat ayant entouré le processus de l'adoption de la Loi ait été long et parfois difficile,[14] il n'a fait que révéler que vingt ans de bilinguisme au Canada ne suffisent pas à éliminer la haine et les craintes que suscitent des mesures qui tendent à encourager l'épanouissement des langues officielles et des communautés qui les parlent. Comme ce fut le cas avec les lois linguistiques en Saskatchewan et en Alberta, le débat n'a pas eu pour effet d'ébranler l'opinion publique qui est favorable à une meilleure protection de la langue française au Canada. Les alliances traditionnelles se sont maintenues.

Les alliances ont commencé à s'effondrer avec l'adoption des mesures visant à réconcilier les aspirations du Québec avec le reste du Canada. Le débat entourant l'adoption de la Loi sur l'affichage[15] et celui portant sur l'Accord du Lac Meech[16] démontrent clairement que ces deux événements, plus que tous les autres, sont en train de modifier l'échiquier politique au Canada.

Autant ces mesures semblent répondre aux attentes du Québec, autant elles semblent inacceptables au Canada anglais. Le Canada anglais a rejeté presque à l'unanimité la Loi sur l'affichage adoptée au Québec, quoique les opinions soient plus partagées en ce qui concerne l'Accord du Lac Meech.

D'un côté, le Canada anglais se demande s'il sera jamais possible de satisfaire les aspirations du Québec, et le Québec par ailleurs se plaint de ne pas être
compris du Canada anglais. Pour certains, la situation devient frustrante et on
n'y voit pas de solution.[17]

Le paradoxe n'est-il pas que le malaise qui prévaut est davantage le résultat
d'un manque de dialogue qui entraîne une mauvaise compréhension, plutôt que
la mise en présence d'aspirations irréconciliables?

C'est certes le cas avec l'Accord du Lac Meech et, à un degré moindre, avec
la Loi sur l'affichage au Québec.

LE CAS DE L'ACCORD DU LAC MEECH

L'Accord du Lac Meech consacre deux visions du Canada. Il reconnaît le
principe de la dualité et institutionnalise la société distincte dans le cadre d'un
territoire précis, le Québec. Il enchâsse aussi la vision du Canada anglais selon
laquelle il n'y a de territoire que celui des individus. Dans le paragraphe 1a) de
l'article interprétatif,[18] c'est cette vision du Canada anglais qui a prévalu. En
vertu de ce paragraphe, la dualité canadienne se définit à partir de la reconnaissance de l'existence de personnes de langue française ou anglaise et non à partir
de l'existence de deux grandes collectivités, une francophone, l'autre anglophone. Aussi la langue reste un droit individuel.

Les visions du Canada que consacrent les deux premiers paragraphes de
l'article interprétatif seraient, de l'avis des détracteurs de l'Accord, tout à fait
contradictoires, si bien que le compromis va s'avérer impossible à réaliser dans
la pratique. L'exemple le plus souvent cité à l'appui de cette thèse serait la mise
en oeuvre de la dualité canadienne. D'une part, l'Accord reconnaît que la
dualité linguistique canadienne s'étend sur l'ensemble du territoire canadien,
mais par ailleurs c'est par le truchement de la reconnaissance du caractère
distinct dans le cadre d'un territoire précis, celui du Québec, que l'on confère
les structures et les moyens nécessaires à la mise en oeuvre de la dualité.[19] En
confinant la dualité à un cadre territorial, le projet même d'une dualité linguistique pan-canadienne serait voué à l'échec.

Voilà une analyse qui est fausse. Comme le prévoit l'Accord du Lac Meech,
la dualité est constituée de plusieurs réalités. Le Québec qui est très majoritairement francophone, le reste du territoire canadien qui est très majoritairement
anglophone, le Québec où sont présents les anglophones et le reste du territoire
canadien où sont aussi présents les francophones.

On reconnaît que le fait linguistique procède d'une division territoriale, le
Québec majoritairement francophone / le reste du Canada majoritairement
anglophone. Quoi de mieux qu'un espace territorial distinct pour assurer la
promotion et le respect de ces différences. C'est d'ailleurs ce que revendique

le Québec depuis 30 ans. Ce qui est important à retenir c'est que l'on s'inspire de la théorie personnaliste de la dualité pour définir la réalité qu'elle renferme mais on adopte la théorie territorialiste lorsque vient le temps de créer les structures et les moyens qui serviront à en assurer la promotion au Québec. L'affirmation de la dualité est un projet collectif.

Pour les autres composantes de la dualité, soit les communautés francophones hors Québec et la communauté anglophone du Québec, elles ont également besoin d'un espace qui leur permettra d'assurer la promotion et le respect de leur particularité, ce que l'Accord ne leur garantit pas.

Pourquoi? Simplement parce que l'Accord du Lac Meech est un projet inachevé. Plusieurs ne seront pas d'accord. Ils diront qu'il s'agissait d'une tâche impossible, puisque ces communautés n'ont pas de territoires propres, de là le besoin d'exprimer la dualité suivant la théorie de la personnalité.

C'est une erreur. Il est possible d'établir au Canada un aménagement linguistique qui tienne compte des besoins du Québec d'une part et qui tienne compte des besoins des autres communautés de langues officielles d'autre part. Prenons le cas des communautés francophones hors Québec pour illustrer notre point de vue. Il existe bel et bien un espace francophone hors Québec. Il s'agit d'un espace différent, fragmentaire et qui doit être cimenté.

Bien que cet espace francophone hors Québec était territorial au début, il l'est de moins en moins. A l'image des Québécois dont ils partagent beaucoup de traits culturels, les francophones hors Québec sont profondément unis par la langue et la culture. Cette homogénéité au niveau de la langue et de la culture a créé chez eux des liens de solidarité. Les francophones hors Québec se sont regroupés en communautés solides et ces communautés ont constitué pour longtemps le rôle principal de leur identité. Dans certaines régions du pays, où les proportions de francophones sont importantes, les communautés continuent de s'articuler autour d'un espace territorial, soit les paroisses traditionnelles, les municipalités, etc.

A cause de l'urbanisation, toutefois, les communautés francophones y sont de moins en moins confinées, occupant des lieux nouveaux et qui ne se distinguent plus que difficilement de ceux occupés par les anglophones. Ces communautés ne se défont pas pour autant. Leur implication politique de plus en plus forte, le développement des institutions francophones et leur visibilité rehaussée le montre bien. Les communautés francophones continuent d'exister à la faveur de nouveaux réseaux, certes plus diffus mais non moins réels. Et l'espace qu'occupent ces réseaux est un facteur premier de leur identité. L'espace francophone hors Québec ainsi compris fait ressortir que cet espace prend de plus en plus la forme d'un réseau de lieux à différentes échelles : que l'espace francophone hors Québec n'a pas le caractère formel de celui des Québécois mais qu'il est néanmoins fonctionnel. Il ne faut toutefois pas penser que les communautés francophones de l'extérieur du Québec peuvent et veulent vivre leur francophonie de la même façon et avec la même intensité que les francophones du Québec. Ce serait une erreur de taille. Le débat qui entoure la question de l'affichage au Québec se fait à partir d'une prémisse qui commet justement cette erreur. Il prend pour acquis que la collectivité anglophone au Québec devrait être en mesure de vivre aussi pleinement son anglophonie que les anglophones de l'extérieur du Québec.

L'avenir de la dualité canadienne au plan pan-canadien passe donc par la reconnaissance et le développement de la spécificité de l'espace francophone hors Québec et un plus grand contrôle de celui-ci par les communautés elles-mêmes.

Au Nouveau-Brunswick, cette reconnaissance a été confirmée par l'adoption en 1981 de la Loi sur l'égalité des communautés linguistiques.[20] Cette loi reconnaît explicitement l'existence de deux communautés linguistiques officielles au Nouveau-Brunswick et reconnaît l'égalité de ces deux communautés.[21] De plus, la loi prévoit que le gouvernement du Nouveau-Brunswick assure la protection de l'égalité des communautés en leur reconnaissant le droit à des institutions culturelles, pédagogiques et sociales distinctes.[22] Il se donne également le mandat—dans les mesures législatives qu'il propose et dans la répartition des ressources publiques et dans ses politiques et programmes—d'encourager, par des mesures positives, le développement culturel, économique, pédagogique et social de chacune des communautés linguistiques officielles.[23]

Ce qui est important de retenir ici, c'est la reconnaissance du droit à des institutions distinctes. C'est bien sûr la somme de ces institutions qui créera l'espace francophone auquel les communautés doivent aspirer.

Au niveau fédéral, quoique le Parlement ne soit pas allé aussi loin dans la reconnaissance du droit à un espace francophone, la loi de 1988 concernant le statut et l'usage des langues officielles du Canada[24] reconnaît l'existence des communautés minoritaires de langues officielles.[25] Pour la première fois, la reconnaissance ne concerne pas uniquement la langue mais englobe la notion de communauté.

Deux exemples suffiront à illustrer ceci.

Il y a d'abord l'article 41 de la loi qui prévoit que «le gouvernement fédéral s'engage à favoriser l'épanouissement des minorités francophones et anglophones du Canada et à appuyer leur développement...». Bien que la loi ne prévoit pas que cet engagement signifie l'obligation de créer un réseau d'institutions distinctes, les politiques de mise en oeuvre s'orientent dans ce sens.

Deuxièmement, la loi prévoit que—dans l'élaboration des règlements, pour déterminer les circonstances où les communications avec le public et la prestation des services devront être dispensées dans les deux langues en fonction du critère de la demande importante et dans le cas des services aux voyageurs,—le gouverneur-en-conseil tiendra compte de la population de la minorité de la région desservie, de la spécificité de cette minorité et de la proportion que celle-ci représente par rapport à la population totale de cette région.[26] Le critère de la spécificité de la minorité assure que ce n'est pas seulement le nombre absolu de francophones ou d'anglophones, selon le cas, dans un milieu, qui déterminera si les services seront disponibles dans les deux langues. Cela dépendra aussi de la structure de la communauté, de sa cohésion sociale. En d'autres mots, il faudra se demander si la communauté possède déjà un espace francophone au niveau des institutions communautaires.

Comme nous l'affirmions précédemment, les politiques de mise en oeuvre de l'engagement législatif du parlement fédéral d'appuyer le développement des communautés minoritaires de langues officielles semblent favoriser la création d'un réseau d'institutions distinctes.

Sous l'égide du programme de promotion des langues officielles,[27] le gouvernement fédéral a signé avec plusieurs provinces des ententes bilatérales établissant des mécanismes généraux de collaboration. Pour le moment, des ententes ont été signées avec quatre provinces et un territoire.[28] Le Fédéral a également signé une entente-cadre avec la communauté francophone de la Saskatchewan.[29] Une brève analyse de cette dernière entente servira à illustrer l'orientation de la politique linguistique dans le sens de la création d'un réseau d'institutions distinctes.

Premièrement, notons que les parties à l'Accord sont le gouvernement du Canada et la communauté francophone de la Saskatchewan. Deuxièmement, l'entente a pour objet d'identifier des domaines d'activités prioritaires de développement pour lesquels le gouvernement canadien consent à verser 17 millions de dollars sur cinq ans.[30] Les activités sont pour la plupart la création d'infrastructures communautaires (centres culturels communautaires, bibliothèques, programmes de formation d'artistes et réseaux de diffusion de produits culturels).[31]

Par ailleurs, dans une des ententes entre les gouvernements de la Saskatchewan et du Canada, celle portant sur le développement de l'enseignement dans la langue de la minorité francophone,[32] on y prévoit également des sommes considérables (10 millions sur 5 ans) pour la création d'infrastructures scolaires propres à la minorité francophone.[33] Plus important, la Saskatchewan consent à mettre en oeuvre un système de gestion et de contrôle des établissements scolaires de la minorité francophone qui comprendra le contrôle de l'administration financière, des programmes, du recrutement des enseignants et de la nomination des administrateurs scolaires.[34]

La même orientation se dégage de plus en plus suite à la reconduction récemment du Programme de langues officielles dans l'enseignement. Par l'entremise des ententes bilatérales, on assiste à la réalisation de projets importants pour l'établissement d'un réseau d'institutions scolaires.

Cette orientation dans la politique linguistique en faveur de la création d'un réseau d'institutions distinctes s'est reflétée dans deux mesures législatives récentes qui ont avorté lorsque le Parlement a été dissous à l'automne 1988. Il s'agit du projet C-144 sur la fourniture des services de garde pour les enfants[35] et du projet de loi C-136 sur la radiodiffusion.[36]

Concernant le premier, le préambule prévoit expressément que le développement des services de garde dans tout le pays doit se faire en tenant compte de la diversité culturelle et linguistique de la population canadienne. De plus, l'alinéa 4(1)g) stipule que tout accord de financement avec une province doit préciser les moyens par lesquels la province satisfera les besoins de sa minorité francophone et anglophone.

Pour ce qui est du projet de loi C-136, une série de dispositions importantes révèle l'intention du législateur canadien de créer des systèmes de radiodiffusion distincts de langue anglaise et de langue française.[37]

A titre d'illustration, prenons l'article 3 qui prévoit, entre autres:

- que les radiodiffusions de langues française et anglaise diffèrent quant à leurs conditions d'exploitation et, éventuellement quant à leurs besoins[38]
- qu'une gamme de services de radiodiffusion en français et en anglais doit être progressivement offerte à tous les Canadiens, au fur et à mesure de la disponibilité des moyens.[39]
- que la société Radio-Canada a le devoir d'offrir une programmation en français et en anglais, de manière à refléter la situation et les besoins particuliers des deux collectivités de langue officielle, y compris ceux des minorités de l'une ou l'autre langue.[40]

En faisant le bilan des mesures législatives et autres mesures gouvernementales qui reconnaissent et appuient le développement de cet espace francophone, nous avons volontairement omis de mentionner l'article 23 de la Charte des droits et libertés[41] qui garantit le droit à l'instruction dans la langue de la minorité. Il s'agit sans doute de la mesure qui est la plus importante à la fois parce qu'il s'agit d'une garantie constitutionnelle et aussi à cause de sa portée. Même si après 7 ans on n'en connaît pas encore la portée exacte, il confère le droit à l'instruction dans la langue de la minorité et lorsque le nombre le justifie, le droit à l'instruction dans des établissements d'enseignement de la minorité.

En plus de ces mesures gouvernementales qui sont orientées vers le maintien et le développement des grandes institutions, tels l'éducation, la radiodiffusion et les services gouvernementaux, les communautés ont développé, de leur propre initiative et avec leurs propres ressources une panoplie d'organisations sociales communautaires qui font partie de cette toile de fond qui est l'espace francophone hors Québec.

Si les propos qui précèdent portent à croire que l'avenir est assuré, ce n'est pas le cas. Ce que nous avons voulu démontrer, c'est la façon dont l'aménagement linguistique au Canada pourrait se faire pour qu'il puisse y avoir réconciliation entre les visions et les réalités en présence et pour que celui-ci réponde efficacement aux besoins et aspirations des communautés qui composent la dualité linguistique canadienne. Nous sommes encore loin d'avoir réalisé un tel aménagement linguistique.

Il faut des engagements plus fermes, plus structurés au plan constitutionnel et au plan législatif.

Au plan constitutionnel, il faut, en premier lieu, un engagement plus ferme en faveur de la dualité. Il convient d'imposer à l'État un devoir plus ferme que ce qui est prévu à l'Accord du Lac Meech. L'Accord qui vise à consacrer le principe de dualité a le mérite de définir un rôle vis-à-vis les collectivités linguistiques. Ce n'est pas suffisant pour des communautés qui n'ont aucun contrôle sur les institutions du pouvoir.

Toute tentative d'imposer à l'État un devoir accru, par rapport à ce qui est prévu à l'Accord, consisterait sans doute à modifier ce qui est proposé à l'article 2 de la Loi constitutionnelle de 1867. Cette approche est indiquée parce que l'article 2 constitue spécifiquement une clause d'interprétation qui remplit la même fonction qu'un préambule et qu'il comprend la définition de "rôles" un concept nouveau dans notre droit. Si cette disposition ne modifie pas directement les pouvoirs et compétences des deux niveaux de gouvernement, elle peut avoir une influence sur l'efficacité de l'exercice des compétences législatives. L'exercice légitime d'un pouvoir serait restreint par le devoir de protéger. Nous inspirant de cela, il est possible de songer à ajouter aux rôles un devoir positif d'agir de sorte que dans l'exercice légitime d'un pouvoir, le législateur soit contraint de tenir compte de la dualité canadienne.

En second lieu, lors de la réforme du Sénat, on devra tenir compte de cette caractéristique fondamentale du Canada qu'est la dualité. L'aspect dualiste nous apparaît comme un élément très important et même peut être aussi important que l'égalité des provinces.

Un Sénat dualiste devra garantir une juste représentation des différentes composantes de la dualité et toutes les mesures législatives qui auront un impact sur la dualité canadienne devraient être soumises à la règle de la double majorité, à savoir la majorité des sénateurs, d'une part, et la majorité des sénateurs francophones d'autre part. Il est bien évident qu'une telle réforme exige que l'on s'éloigne du principe de la représentation par population. C'est d'ailleurs déjà le cas avec le Sénat actuel et c'est aussi ce que propose les tenants du Sénat égal.

Sur le plan législatif, il faut viser à ce que toute la législation fédérale respecte le caractère dualiste canadien. La difficulté à l'heure actuelle, c'est l'étendue des rôles que se sont donnés les provinces et le Parlement canadien vis-à-vis la dualité canadienne. Avec un rôle de protection seulement, il est fort probable qu'il n'y a aucune obligation de légiférer à l'avantage des deux collectivités. Le rôle de protection est probablement plus restreint. Il imposerait tout au plus un devoir de non-discrimination ou de non-assimilation. C'est pour cette raison qu'il serait souhaitable que le Parlement se voit confier le rôle de protéger et de promouvoir la dualité canadienne au lieu du seul rôle de protéger. Pour bien voir l'impact que pourrait avoir sur la législation une obligation constitutionnelle de faire la promotion de la dualité, on n'a qu'à se référer au projet de la Loi sur la radiodiffusion, celui sur la fourniture des services de garde pour les enfants ainsi que la Loi sur les langues officielles auxquels nous avons fait allusion plus tôt.

LA LOI SUR L'AFFICHAGE

Depuis l'adoption de la Loi sur l'affichage au Québec, une véritable panoplie d'opinions ont été publiées dans les médias au Canada et à l'étranger. Cette mesure a provoqué l'indignation de la communauté anglophone du Québec et le Canada anglais a condamné le Québec.

Pourquoi un tel tollé général? L'affichage commercial dans la langue d'une communauté donnée est-il si importante pour la survie culturelle et linguistique de cette communauté qu'il justifie une pareille révolte? Si d'aucuns le prétendent, il y a des raisons plus plausibles. Deux raisons peuvent expliquer la réaction du Canada anglais à l'égard des mesures prises par le gouvernement du Québec. D'abord, sur le plan purement juridique, il y a beaucoup de légitimité dans un discours qui condamne une mesure législative ayant pour effet d'enfreindre un droit fondamental garanti par la Charte canadienne des droits et libertés. Il faut pouvoir apprécier à sa juste valeur l'importance que revêt dans la tradition anglo-saxonne le concept de droits fondamentaux qui servent à protéger l'individu contre les abus de l'État. Parmi ceux-ci se trouve la liberté d'expression qui, de l'avis de la Cour suprême du Canada, englobe le discours commercial.[42]

Pareil constat ne règle rien. La réplique c'est celle que l'on connaît et qui est au centre du débat depuis décembre 1988—la réconciliation des droits individuels avec les droits collectifs des francophones du Québec. Pour le Québec, il n'y a pas de réconciliation possible et dans le cas de l'affichage commercial les droits collectifs des francophones du Québec de vivre en français doivent avoir préséance sur le droit à l'affichage commercial dans la langue de son choix.[43]

Sans doute le sens profond des mesures prises par le gouvernement du Québec c'est que la Loi sur l'affichage vient confirmer la volonté politique du Québec de faire passer la collectivité anglophone d'un peuple majoritaire à un peuple minoritaire au Québec. C'est ce processus de "minorisation" de la collectivité anglophone du Québec qui avait été entamé avec l'adoption de la Loi 101 qui se confirme avec la Loi sur l'affichage. C'est justement ce processus de "minorisation" qui a indigné la collectivité anglophone québecoise et le reste du Canada anglais.

Pour qu'il y ait réconciliation des intérêts entre la collectivité francophone et la collectivité anglophone au Québec, il faudra que cette dernière accepte de devenir une minorité. Il ne s'agit pas pour elle de renoncer à sa culture et à sa langue. Mais, à l'instar des communautés francophones hors Québec, la collectivité anglophone du Québec devra redéfinir l'espace qu'elle souhaite occuper au Québec. Elle ne doit pas s'attendre à pouvoir évoluer dans une société qui lui permettra de vivre aussi pleinement en anglais que le font les anglophones d'ailleurs au Canada. Cette solution représente à la fois un sacrifice mais aussi un défi pour l'avenir. Un défi qui ne sera pas facile à relever dans le contexte actuel. Pour que les anglophones du Québec acceptent une politique qui conduit leur collectivité vers le statut de minorité, la majorité francophone devra les rassurer qu'ils ont leur place au Québec. Toute politique visant à franciser le Québec devra être accompagnée d'une politique qui définit la place de la collectivité anglophone. Pour y arriver, il faut faire place au dialogue. Les principaux intéressés devront être d'intelligence pour qu'une entente soit possible.

Notes

1. Modification constitutionnelle de 1987, constituant l'annexe de la résolution autorisant la modification de la Constitution du Canada, fait à Ottawa le 3 juin 1987.
2. S.C. 1988, ch. - 38.
3. Loi linguistique, L.S. 1988, ch. L-6.1.
4. Loi linguistique, S.A., 1988, ch. L-7.5.
5. Loi modifiant la Charte de la langue française, L.Q., 1988, ch. - 54.
6. Mercure c. P.G. Saskatchewan, [1988] 1 R.C.S. 234.
7. Chaussure Brown's Inc. c. Procureur général du Québec [1988] 2 R.C.S. 712.
8. Singer c. Procureur général du Québec [1988] 2 R.C.S. 790.
9. Supra, note 6.
10. Loi de 1870 sur le Manitoba, S.R.C. 1970, app. II, art. 23.

11. Loi constitutionnelle de 1867, 30 & 31 Vict, c. 3 (R.-U.) [S.R.C. 1970], Appendice II, no. 5. (mod. par la *Loi de 1982 sur le Canada*, 1982, c. 11 (R.-U.), annexe de la *Loi constitutionnelle de 1982*, no. 1), art. 133.
12. Supra, note 2. Le Conseil de la langue française au Québec et certains groupes tel le Mouvement Québec français ont exprimé un avis contraire.
13. Loi sur les langues officielles, S.R.C., c. 0-2.
14. Il a fallu plus d'un an entre le dépôt en 1ère lecture et l'adoption en 3e lecture du projet de loi C-72. Ce sont des députés d'arrière-banc du parti conservateur qui menèrent l'opposition au projet de loi contre leur propre gouvernement. Leurs détracteurs leur donnèrent le sobriquet "les dinosaures".
15. Supra, note 5.
16. Supra, note 1.
17. Voir J. Simpson, *Globe and Mail*, les 19 et 20 juin 1989.
18. Le paragraphe prévoit que:
   "(1) Toute interprétation de la Constitution du Canada doit concorder avec: a) la reconnaissance de ce que l'existence de Canadiens d'expression française, concentrés au Québec mais présents aussi dans le reste du pays, et de Canadiens d'expression anglaise, concentrés dans le reste du pays mais aussi présents au Québec, constitue une caractéristique fondamentale du Canada;"
19. Supra, note 1, paragraphe 2(1) b).
20. Loi reconnaissant l'égalité des deux communautés linguistiques officielles au Nouveau-Brunswick, S.R.N.B. ch., 0-1.
21. Id., article 1.
22. Id., article 2.
23. Id., article 3.
24. Supra, note 2.
25. Id., article 41.
26. Supra, note 2., article 33.
27. Il s'agit d'un programme relevant du Secrétariat d'Etat du Canada.
28. Le Nouveau-Brunswick, la Saskatchewan, l'Ile-du-Prince Edouard et l'Ontario ainsi que le Yukon.
29. Entente-cadre visant à appuyer le développement de la communauté fransaskoise, 28 juin 1988.
30. Id., article 4.
31. Id., article 3.1.
32. Entente auxiliaire Canada-Saskatchewan relative au développement de l'enseignement dans la langue de la minorité francophone et de l'enseignement du français langue seconde en Saskatchewan, 14 juin 1988.
33. Id., article 3.

34. Id., chapitre II, article 1.
35. Loi autorisant les contributions par le gouvernement fédéral à la fourniture de services de garde pour les enfants et modifiant le Régime d'assistance publique du Canada en conséquence, Projet C-144, Deuxième session, trente-troisième législature, 35-36, 37 Elisabeth II, 1986-87-88. Adopté en troisième lecture le 26 septembre 1988.
36. Loi concernant la radiodiffusion et modifiant certaines loi en conséquence et concernant la radiocommunication, Projet de loi C-136, Deuxième session, trente-troisième législature, 35-36-37, Elisabeth II, 1986-87-88.
37. Id., article 3 et 44.
38. Sous-alinéa 3) (1) k) (iii)
39. Alinéa 3(1) i)
40. Supra, note 40.
41. *Charte canadienne des droits et libertés*, Partie I de la *Loi constitutionnelle de 1982*, constituant l'annexe 13 de la *Loi de 1982 sur le Canada* (R.-U.).
42. Supra, note 7.
43. Voir les propos du premier ministre Bourassa rapportés dans le *Globe and Mail* du 22 décembre 1988, page A-1.

SEVEN

Compromise and Delay:
The Federal Strategy on Child Care

Derek P. J. Hum

Ce chapitre vise à faire le point sur la politique fédérale touchant les services de garde, élaborée par l'actuel gouvernement conservateur. Dévoilée officiellement en décembre 1987, la stratégie nationale en matière de garderie fit d'emblée, et de toutes parts, l'objet de récriminations. La loi C-144, qui devait cristalliser l'essentiel du programme conservateur, mourut au Sénat avec le déclenchement de l'élection fédérale en novembre 1988.

Le programme de garderie aura sévèrement fait les frais du dernier budget Wilson: financement coupé de plus du double, engagement différé d'Ottawa de créer de nouveaux espaces de garderie et non-reconduction probable de ce programme septennal. Nonobstant ces mesures d'austérité l'auteur estime que l'approche conservatrice s'avère, dans les circonstances, un habile compromis, étant donné les positions divergentes en présence.

En désavouant les propositions jugées trop libérales du Rapport Cooke favorable au principe de l'universalité des services de garde, le gouvernement conservateur s'aliénait du coup le lobby des garderies à but non-lucratif. Sympathique à l'option du "choix parental" permettant aux parents de s'occuper eux-mêmes de leur(s) enfant(s), le gouvernement Mulroney aura finalement pris le parti d'augmenter la déduction pour les frais de garde aux familles et ce, au mépris des objectifs initiaux de sa réforme fiscale.

La stratégie nationale de garde d'enfants n'a pas provoqué, jusqu'à présent, un tollé parmi les provinces en dépit du fait que le gouvernement conservateur compte plafonner dorénavant les fonds destinés aux programmes à frais partagés, provenant du Régime d'assistance publique du Canada. Au demeurant, dans l'optique d'un Lac Meech ratifié, un gouvernement conservateur atténuerait le risque d'un "opting-out" à outrance par une consultation préalable auprès des provinces.

Malgré l'absence d'un consensus national sur les services de garde, Hum considère que d'ici la prochaine élection, les conservateurs se doivent moralement de légiférer une bonne fois pour toutes sur la question.

INTRODUCTION

Social policy questions just will not go away for the Mulroney Conservative government. During its first term of office, the attempt to de-index Old Age Pensions met with angry resistance, and the suggestion to target Family Allowance benefits was seen as an unforgivable attack on universality, coming as it did after the Prime Minister's characterization of such programs as a sacred trust. Both initiatives were motivated by a desire to trim the deficit. While these two suggestions had expenditure restraint in mind, the federal national day- care policy would have expanded social spending. Yet the National Day Care Strategy fared no better; Bill C-144, the Canada Child Care Act, received third reading in the Commons on 26 September 1988 but died on the Senate order paper. In the first budget after re-election, Minister of Finance Michael Wilson announced that "the government is not in a position to proceed with (the Child Care strategy) at this time."[1] In any case, neither the deficit nor social programs figured prominently when the election was called for 21 November 1988.

The election campaign could not mask altogether the apprehension of Canadians concerning their social programs. Despite a valiant attempt by the Conservatives to persuade the electorate that "managing change" and "leadership" were the prime issues, the Liberals succeeded in focusing attention on the Canada-United States Free Trade Agreement. This was accomplished not by the opposition stating any new findings or arguments about intangible economic benefits; rather it was the spectre of damage or removal of Canada's social programs under the requirement of harmonization that drew even non-partisan judges, artists, writers, and academics into the political fray. Similarly, the Meech Lake Accord was not an election issue; all three political parties believed that opposition to the Accord meant electoral suicide in Quebec. Nonetheless, in addition to the coalescing objections surrounding the "distinct society" clause in the Accord, an equally strong reservation was developing around the spending power interpretation. Specifically, would Canada be able to maintain its national social programs if provinces are able to opt out and still receive "reasonable compensation" for provincial programs which are "compatible with the national objectives"? More to the point, would national programs be possible, or likely, in the future? The favourite example cited was a national child-care program.

This paper considers the rise and stall of the federal national child-care strategy, particularly Bill C-144. The next two sections describe recent events leading up to the introduction of the child care strategy, as well as outlining the major differences of views concerning program delivery. The contents of Bill C-144, the Canada Child Care Act, are then sketched. The final two sections discuss Bill C-144, and suggest why the federal strategy failed as a compromise response to the different sides.

PRELUDE TO THE NATIONAL CHILD-CARE STRATEGY

Although all major political parties remain committed to promoting better child care for Canadians, the National Child Care Strategy[2] announced on 3 December 1987 by the Honourable Jake Epp, then Minister of National Health and Welfare, was in large measure, a delayed reaction to the 1986 Report of the Task Force on Child Care (the Cooke Report).[3] The Task Force was established by the Federal Liberals in 1984 before their defeat, and when it reported in March, 1986, its recommendations proved unpalatable to many. Fortunately for the Conservatives, a special Committee on Child Care[4] had been established by the House of Commons in November 1985 to "examine and report on the child care needs of the Canadian family." This committee was chaired by Conservative Member of Parliament Shirley Martin, but included members of the NDP and Liberal parties as well. Its report was released in March 1987. Happily, the Conservative government could safely remain silent on the Cooke Report's recommendations upon its release. By waiting for the House of Common's Committee to conclude its examination of the same questions, the government could chart its course in private while appearing appropriately judicious in public.

What was so disquieting about the Cooke Report? The description of conditions and diagnosis present no difficulties. The Task Force found that most children needing care are looked after in unlicensed spaces; the costs of child care is often prohibitive for low-income earners; parental leave arrangements are inadequate; and there is much variation among provinces in such matters as day-care subsidies for working parents, availability of non-profit spaces, cost of service, and degree of public (non-commercial) provision.

Provinces vary widely in the number of licensed care spaces available (see Table 7.1 for details). For example, the percentage of children under 13 years of age in licensed day care ranges from a paltry 4 per cent in Newfoundland to 20 per cent in Alberta, thus most children are in informal arrangements. Cost of care also differs widely, varying from under $5000 to provide care for two pre-schoolers in New Brunswick to double that amount in Alberta. A more interesting point is the extent of commercial child-care spaces in the different provinces. Saskatchewan has virtually none (3 per cent of spaces), while Quebec (12 per cent) and Manitoba (20 per cent) have small fractions. On the other hand, Alberta (70 per cent), Ontario (43 per cent), British Columbia (58 per cent) and Newfoundland (64 per cent) have well over half their spaces commercially provided. The reasons for this variety are undoubtedly many and

Table 7.1
Interprovincial Comparisons of Child-Care Spaces, Costs, Expenditures and Attitudes: Selected Statistics

Province	(1) Number of Licensed Child-Care Spaces 1987	(2) % Children under 13 in Licensed Day Care 1987	(3) % Commercial Child-Care Spaces 1984	(4) Avg Child-Care cost for 2 pre-schoolers 1984	(5) Income limit for maximum subsidy under CAP, couple with 2 children 1987	(6) % Tax back rate of day-care subsidy 1987	(7) Total gov't per capita expenditures 1984-85	(8) Federal share (%) 1984-85	(9) Wants CAP to cost-share commercial day care 1985	(10) NGOs wish day care made universal 1985
B.C.	18,595	10	58	$7,190	$13,512	50	$80	48	yes	yes
Alberta	43,082	20	70	9,144	17,160	30-90	134	27	yes	no
Saskatchewan	5,720	7	3	7,580	20,880	25	86	54	no	no
Manitoba	10,526	14	20	6,869	16,345	25-50	124	43	no	yes
Ontario	94,018	12	43	7,010	23,340/34,164	100	118	47	yes	no
Quebec	58,425	12	12	6,950	15,550	26	142	29	no	no
New Brunswick	4,503	10	37	5,236	11,652	50	67	57	yes	no
Nova Scotia	5,397	11	38	6,010	11,960	50	80	58	yes	yes
P.E.I.	1,264	16	47	4,540	12,960	50	60	61	yes	yes
Newfoundland	1,318	4	64	6,380	10,044	50	45	60	yes	no
Yukon	240	--	--	6,600	15,480	50	85	54	yes	no
N.W.T.	475	--	--	10,560	--	100	57	72	no	no

Sources: Columns (1) and (2), National Council of Welfare (1988), *Child Care: A Better Alternative*, p. 4. Columns (3) (4) (7) and (8), *National Task Force on Child Care* (1986), pp. 50, 192, 199. Columns (5) and (6), *Special Parliamentary Committee on Child Care* (1987), pp. 29, 149. Columns (9) and (10), *Canada Assistance Plan, Task Force on Program Review* (1986), pp. 97-8.

complex. In the case of Manitoba, it was a matter of ideology with the NDP government who, it must be remembered, were in government for all but four of the last nineteen years during which the province's day-care system developed. With the recent election of the Conservatives under Premier Gary Filmon and the strength of the Liberals, day-care policy in Manitoba will undoubtedly move in a new direction.[5] Ideology, while clearly important in Manitoba, probably has a lot to do with the evolved situation in Quebec as well as Saskatchewan. The same might well be said for provinces having a high percentage of commercial spaces, especially Ontario and Alberta. Both provinces are noted for their greater commitment to private sector delivery, although some have argued that Alberta's stance respecting private delivery has more to do with efficiency and decentralization objectives.[6] Still, it is hard to ignore ideology since, in the case of Alberta, 70 per cent of day-care agencies are for-profit, even though operating allowances provided to for-profit day-care services are generally not cost-sharable under the Canada Assistance Program (hereafter "CAP"). Given the wide variety of circumstances, it is simply not possible to explain provincial differences easily.

In the face of this variety across provincial boundaries, reflecting differing child-care preferences among Canadians, it should not be surprising that the Cooke Report's policy recommendations were controversial. The Report proposed a long-term strategy involving free, universally-accessible supplementary child care for all children. Specifically, formal child care for all children up to the age of 12 was envisioned both for working and non-working parents. The Report also recommended against allowing further deduction by individuals for child- care expenses in favour of direct payments to service providers.[7] Finally, it called for a new cost-sharing formula; one whereby the federal government would fund a larger share of total program costs for child care in poorer regions.[8] The cost to the federal and provincial governments of the Cooke Report proposals was reckoned at $11.3 billion (in 1984 dollars) when eventually fully-funded in the year 2001. To put this in perspective, federal and provincial governments in fiscal year 1986-87 together spent less than $0.7 billion for child care through the Canada Assistance Plan and the Child Care Expense Deduction.[9] Niceties aside about timing, phasing in, and the like, the Cooke Report vision would entail an (eventual) sixteenfold increase in government support for child care. No small change!

In addition to the issue of cost to government of providing support for child care, the government found two other features of the Cooke Report unacceptable. The Cooke Report favoured the provision of child care by professional deliverers in licensed centres, preferably non-commercial. Furthermore, since child care would be freely available, the logic of a child-care expense deduction no longer exists. The underlying model is that of primary and secondary education, in which parents pay no fees to enroll their children in publicly-funded (non-commercial) schools staffed by professional teachers.

The House of Commons Report on Child Care stands in direct contrast to the Cooke Report and became in reality, the legitimating authority for the government's position. Very explicitly in the first chapter, it asserts that "the primary responsibility for child care must rest with the family. Parents are and will remain the principal givers of care...."[10] Calling this a "mixed approach, involving voluntary, commercial, and public resources...", the Committee unapologetically declares that this view is "reflected in every chapter of [its] report."[11] Elsewhere (in Chapter 2), the Committee reaffirms its approval of the principle of tax relief measures to deliver child care benefits to individuals.

The Cooke Report and the House of Commons Special Committee on Child Care Report are, therefore, poles apart. Nonetheless, competing visions are now up for public display, and some of the major policy questions starkly posed. Do we want to spend $11 billion or more on a child-care delivery system? And do we want to continue with federal and provincial tax offset measures to assist families with child-care needs? These questions are considered next.

MAJOR CONTENDING VIEWPOINTS

The matter of costs is important to any major social program initiative, especially when the federal government faces annual deficits in the order of $30 billion, growing national debt and a slowing economy. Other issues aside, the projected costs of the Cooke proposals at $11.3 billion were simply too high. Sticker-price shock was also accompanied by wariness over the soft nature of the calculations done by the Cooke Report and the suspicion that the Cooke numbers could be a lower boundary. Indeed, the Cooke Report's figures assumed that day-care workers' salaries would increase only moderately, and that women, even when given free day care, would not dramatically increase labour force participation rates. More recent and realistic calculations by independent research suggests that the Cooke proposals might actually be in the order of $20 to $25 billion, a figure that exceeds the amount spent on the entire elementary and secondary education system.[12] Whatever the "true, realistic" number, neither the economic climate nor government finances would allow the Cooke Report to be taken seriously. Besides, the Conservatives had other reservations concerning such matters as the role of commercial day care and whether or not non-working parents should receive tax assistance, and the like. Therefore the government was fortunate; it could not afford what it did not like, in any event.

The role of commercial child-care provision is principally an ideological debate, some arguing that the care of children, when not done by parents, should be undertaken by well-paid, professionally trained caregivers in centres meeting stipulated standards. For them, market supply is, axiomatically, incompatible with quality care-giving since profit is possible only at the expense of quality. Others, including the federal government, do not accept this. And, as noted, conditions vary greatly among provinces, as well as policy preferences. There is much difference of opinion among the provinces. In its consultations concerning the Canada Assistance Plan (CAP) the Task Force on Program Review[13] found only Saskatchewan, Manitoba, Quebec and the North West Territories not wanting CAP to cost-share commercial day care. Significantly, all three provinces have the smallest percentage of commercial care spaces— Saskatchewan (3 per cent), Manitoba (20 per cent) and Quebec (12 per cent). Ontario, which has the most licensed spaces of any province, provides 43 per cent on a commercial basis. In short, the federal government did not really need the data on provincial differences to tell them that the Canadian public itself was divided on this matter. Suggested alternatives to the Cooke Report view were being expressed in terms of offering more "parental choice"[14] or accommodating a "mixed market approach."[15] The latter phase was, as noted, the eventual catch phrase of the Conservative-dominated Special Parliamentary Committee on Child Care.

A similar fate met the Cooke Report suggestion to eliminate child-care expense deductions in the long run. The government would not contemplate removal of child-related tax relief for those parents choosing to stay at home to look after their children or using informal types of child care. In this, the government was again comforted by the Special Parliamentary Committee's recommendations.

The federal national strategy for child care evolved in part as reaction to the Cooke Report. While intuitive in the sense of appreciating that the Cooke Report was neither financially feasible nor politically acceptable, the Conservatives did have the Special Parliamentary Committee's Report as the counter-document. The views of that Report appeared more in tune with the Conservative Party's and Mr. Epp's inclinations. The National Strategy on Child Care that emerged was, therefore, an attempt at compromise.

BILL C-144 (CANADA CHILD CARE ACT)

The Mulroney Government announced its National Strategy on Child Care on 3 December 1987. It was a masterful compromise in the sense that virtually all positions were acknowledged and partially accommodated. By the same token, no single viewpoint prevailed.

The National Strategy on Child Care contained the three following components:

1. Tax assistance to families with young children through more generous deductions for child-care expenses, higher limits, and refundable child credits for parents who care for their children at home.
2. A special Initiatives Fund of $100 million over seven years to encourage "innovative responses to problems related to child care," including the "development of non-profit community-based child care services."[16]
3. A Canada Child Care Act (Bill C-144) to replace certain provisions in the CAP. The new arrangements would cover both non-profit and commercial child-care services, provide expanded cost-sharing for operating costs, and capital funding on an enriched 75 per cent (federal)—25 per cent (provincial) basis but for non-profit centres only.[17]

The cost-sharing portion is intended to create an estimated 200,000 new child-care spaces in Canada. The federal government was willing to spend $5.4 billion on child care over the next seven years. Taking into account the child-care expenses deduction as well as the refundable child-tax credit, the actual total for federal spending over the next seven years could amount to $8 billion, of which it is estimated that only one-half would be really "new money."[18]

A portion of the strategy, namely the increase in the child-care expense deduction and the refundable child-tax credit, was enacted for the 1988 tax year. The Child Care Special Initiatives Fund has been underway since 1 April 1988 and the federal government has so far approved 77 projects.[19] It was Bill C-144, the cost-sharing provisions, which died on the Senate Order Paper. Although the re-elected Mulroney government has pledged to meet its child-care objectives "before the end of its term of office", the Wilson budget of 27 April 1989 announced a deferral of its committment to create new child-care spaces, with a projected saving to the government of $175 million in 1989-90 and $195 million in 1990-91.[20]

FEDERAL CHILD-CARE POLICY: MIXED OR MIXED UP?

The federal Child Care policy, we suggest, was a compromise aimed at appeasing all possible positions. Less generously, it might be labelled a shotgun approach. By expanding both direct and tax expenditures, the government hoped to signal its concern for social and economic equality even as it must adopt a position of restraint with respect to other programs. By allowing both a refundable tax credit as well as more generous child-care expense deduction provisions, the government granted relief to those who care for children at home, or do not have receipts for informal arrangements, as well as those who use formal child care services; all of this in the name of "recogniz[ing] parental choice." Simply put, Bill C-144 gave something to everyone.

The Bill gave flexibility to the provinces with respect to accommodating non-profit and commercial child-care spaces; but it limited enriched capital funding for non-profit spaces only. It would also remove the entire question of child care from the stigma and welfare structure of the Canada Assistance Plan provisions, enabling future development as an institutional service for parents and children, and not as something to help "those in need or likelihood of need". Finally, the new Child Care Act held out prospects of federal funding for capital costs and innovative experimentation as well as more generous cost-sharing for poorer provinces. On the other hand, while current CAP arrangements are open-ended, Bill C-144 would, for the first time, place a financial ceiling on the federal contribution to child care, and there is no commitment beyond the seven years. By acknowledging the sharp differences of views among Canadians and provincial governments concerning such matters as whether child-care spaces should be provided under commercial or non-profit auspices, whether or not parents employing informal arrangements without receipts or simply choosing to remain at home caring for their children should benefit from tax relief, and whether all of the federal financial eggs should go towards expanding the supply of child-care spaces or, alternatively, to assist demand by lower income families, the federal strategy was truly a "mixed" approach.

This being so, the reflex criticisms from various quarters are predictable. Those wedded in various degrees to the vision of a comprehensive, universally accessible and publicly funded child-care network see the federal response as inadequate, with funds misdirected from creating the much needed child-care spaces. Further, the decision to increase the child care expense deduction in the face of tax reform to replace deductions with credits not only goes against the grain but actually represents logical inconsistency. On the other hand, there are others who see C-144 as limiting in terms of future financing since provinces attempting to expand spaces might find themselves without matching funds. The vexing issue of standards, what they will look like, how they might be established, etc., are all unclear at the moment.[21]

NATURE OF THE COMPROMISE AND REASONS FOR FAILURE

The present stance of the Conservative government towards child care is a compromise to be sure. But it is not entirely a compromise born of a desire merely to please all sides. Mindful of the different provincial positions respecting the role of commercial spaces and their different fiscal capacities, the federal strategy promised flexibility in cost-sharing as well as additional support for poorer provinces. In effect, equalization is built into the funding of child care. But the *quid pro quo* extracted by the federal government was a ceiling on its financial obligations with respect to child care. That is, the open-ended cost-sharing nature of CAP, as it applies to provincial child care expenditures is no longer totally open-ended, although CAP remains open-ended with respect to other areas. Whether one approves of this attempt to trade more "equalized" federal aid to provincially delivered child spaces, for less assured future cost-sharing, depends upon one's preference for open-ended versus block funding formulas.

A noteworthy feature of the federal child-care strategy is the extent to which it is a harbinger of a post "Meech Lake" Canada. Section 106A of the Accord deals with the right of provincial governments to receive reasonable compensation for opting out of national cost-shared programs if they carry on a program compatible with national objectives. Critics who base their opposition on the decentralizing thrust of the opting out clause often raise the example of child care as one national service which the Meech Lake Accord would make difficult. Even those who see Meech Lake as a potentially centralizing rather than a decentralizing contribution concede that the Accord "will limit the ability of the federal government, present or future, to impose a narrowly-conceived, national, day care program on the provinces."[22] And those who view Section 106A as centralizing in the more limited sense of entrenching and legitimating the federal government will seek to "minimize the number of provinces choosing to opt out of a scheme by allowing for considerable regional variation within the national program itself."[23] Both views would seem to suggest that, as Banting puts it, "the Accord would nudge new initiatives towards the model of the Canada Assistance Plan, with a general umbrella program containing relatively few precise conditions at the national level, and the specific form of each province's program being negotiated separately and set out in a subsidiary bilateral agreement."[24] Given this analysis it is no surprise that the federal strategy on child care builds upon the CAP model in its orientation of being all things to all provinces.

The federal child-care strategy is not consistent with the spirit of the Meech Lake Accord. Yet it is, at the same time, both more and less than a redesigned flexible CAP. It is more insofar as it removes assistance to parents requiring child-care assistance from the strictures of "welfare services" and the language of "need or likelihood of need". It is also more in its willingness to adopt a funding formula which takes account of the differing fiscal capacities and relative need for services in each province through variable cost-sharing.[25] But the national child-care strategy is also less that the CAP in the sense that it imposes funding ceilings. The Senate Subcommittee on Child Care had a curious logic on this point. It approves of the open-ended nature of the CAP. At the same time, it asserts that the aim of the national child-care initiative is to create a child-care system that does not yet exist, and that "this process of building a system is not necessarily inconsistent with funding ceilings."[26] Yet, just as provinces cannot predict the number of their citizens needing income assistance with any accuracy, how can the federal government be certain its funding ceilings are adequate for the pace of provincial development of child-care spaces and provincial requirements for spaces? It seems fair to conclude that the ceiling on federal transfers derive more from a concern to limit federal transfers to the provinces than any required design feature to accommodate either the spirit of the Meech Lake Accord or federal-provincial politics.

Another feature of the federal government's attempt at grand compromise has to do with constituencies other than provincial governments; namely women voters, working mothers, parents who use informal child care, and mothers who choose to remain at home with their children. The government clearly agrees with the Parliamentary Task Force that the prime responsibility for care of children lies with the parents rather than with the government. Health and Welfare Minister Jake Epp was absolutely clear on this position.[27] Yet the political momentum and call for national child-care policy is perhaps more driven by the need to accommodate working parents. Consequently, by extending tax assistance through the refundable child-tax credit in the name of a national child-care strategy, the federal government, in effect, is signalling several things. First, it would appear that working parents have no greater claim to consideration than parents in general, including those who choose to stay at home with their children, or those who employ informal day care and do not have receipts. Second, the federal government can remain agnostic on the issue of whether the child-care strategy is to address the needs of the working parent or the custodial requirements of the child. By accommodating all parents without distinction, the strategy is conveniently left standing as a matter of parental choice whether one chooses to work or not, and whether one chooses formal child care or not.

If, then, the federal strategy on child care appears to be the epitome of compromise, why did it have such a rough time? The answers, I believe, have less to do with fiscal restraint or the policy process, but are to be found in the attributes of the main contending stake-holders and the characterization of the policy itself.

There is no denying the Conservative government's resolve to reduce the federal deficit during their first term.[28] Child care is perhaps the one area in which spending would return political credit far in excess of any fiscal criticisms. Restraint cannot be the entire answer. As to process, it has been pointed out that "in important ways Canadian policy making consists of high-level negotiations among competing bureaucracies and between federal and provincial authorities. Settlements emerge at this stage, and the public phase of policy debates has little impact on the decisions."[29]

The circumstances appear to have been different on this occasion. First, during the recent election campaign, almost all debating time and effort, by governments and the public at large, was given over to the Canada-United States Free Trade Agreement and other electoral rhetoric that virtually drowned out child-care matters. Second, government at both levels had had countless task forces, commissions and reports available to help guide policy formation. There was no information vacuum on this issue. Similarly, the public at large, including non-governmental organizations and various advocacy groups, had ample access to the many forums discussing child care. Not much new remained to be said at this stage, as opposed to action. The time for process was over; the moment had come to put money on the table and legislation in the House. It is hard to conclude that the child-care policy failed for want of careful and wide discussion.

What led to the eleventh hour collapse of Bill C-144? The child-care strategy was the product of hours of thought and consideration. The government was certainly not taken by surprise. However, the federal compromise strategy miscalculated the strength of feelings and depth of passion among the combatant stake-holders. Those wanting a quality, universally available, professionally staffed, non-profit delivery network gave little quarter in their opposition to Bill C-144, going so far as to declare a preference for the status quo CAP instead of the new Bill. Nor was there less opposition from those who preferred informal care arrangements, or who believed that parents who remained at home with their children should not be disentitled to any child-related benefits. Both sides viewed the situation as zero-sum game, and as a result, adopted uncooperative stances towards each other and confrontational tactics towards the government. This, then, was less a federal-provincial conflict than a radical difference of vision about child-care auspices. It is ironic that the Canada Assistance Plan model is, perhaps, the most amenable to further expansion or change. Both sides viewed their opposition's failure as a necessary condition of their own success, making accommodation appear undesirable.

A distinction is possible in characterizing development concerning social reform. The contrast is between the "big bang" or comprehensive reform strategy, and the "incremental" process typified by a steady series of smaller changes. One perceptive commentator, after reviewing income security progress in Canada and the United States during the last two decades, has suggested that Canadians like to debate reform within the big bang format but prefer instead to bring about changes gradually.[30] Here then is one possible clue to the failure of the Mulroney government child-care Bill to complete its mission. Gauged against the strong opposing views concerning both principles and delivery design of a national child-care system, Bill C-144 portends too dramatic a change to the status quo, acknowledged as unsatisfactory, but still preferable to legislation too vague as to standards and too uncertain as to future funding. Add to this the very real apprehension of those unconvinced that a national child care policy is anything but a political response to working women as opposed to a response to a parenting issue, one should not be surprised that national consensus is absent. Since little in the way of new facts or understanding is likely to arise before the end of the second term, the Mulroney government must make good its promise to reintroduce the issue of a national child-care strategy. Passage of a new Bill to create additional child-care spaces is largely a matter of federal will more than any potent blocking coalition. But look for the government to give itself a bigger lead time running up to the next election.

Notes

1. The Budget Speech, document dated 27 April 1989 for delivery in the House of Commons by the Hon. Michael Wilson, Minister of Finance. p.7. Details were made known on national television the evening before.
2. Health and Welfare Canada, *National Strategy on Child Care*, 3 December 1987, including News Release and statements by the Hon. Jake Epp, Minister of National Health and Welfare, the Hon. Benoit Bouchard, Minister of Employment and Immigration, and the Hon. Barbara McDougall, Minister Responsible for the Status of Women.
3. Status of Women Canada, *Report of the Task Force on Child Care* (Ottawa: Supply and Services Canada, 1986), commonly referred to as the Cooke Report.
4. Canada, *Sharing the Responsibility*, Report of the Special Committee on Child Care (Ottawa: Supply and Services Canada, March 1987).
5. D. Bracken, P. Hudson, and G. Selinger, "Day Care in Manitoba and the 1988 Provincial Election: The Potential for Change", *Nouvelle Pratiques Sociale*,1988, vol. 1, no. 1.
6. J. Hornick, R. Thomlison, and L. Nesbitt, "Alberta", in J. Ismael and Y. Vaillancourt (eds.) *Privatization and Provincial Social Services in Canada* (Edmonton: University of Alberta Press, 1988).
7. The Cooke Report, p. 297.
8. Ibid., p.293.
9. National Council of Welfare, *Child Care: A Better Alternative*, (Ottawa: Supply and Services, 1988) p.6.
10. Canada, *Sharing the Responsibility*, p.9.
11. Ibid., p. 10.
12. M. Krashinsky, "The Cooke Report on Child Care: A Critique", *Canadian Public Policy/ Analyse de Politiques*, vol XIII, no. 3.

13. *Service to the Public: Canada Assistance Plan*, A Study Team Report to the Task Force on Program Review (Ottawa: Minister of Supply and Services, 1986), commonly referred to as the Nielsen Task Force Report.

14. K. Ross, "Parents' Choice", *Policy Options*, 1986, vol. 7, no. 7.

15. H. Stevens, and D. Hum, "Contra Cooke: A Mixed Market Approach to Child Care", *Policy Options*, 1986, Vol. 7 No.9.

16. This flexible fund is available for programs addressing child-care problems related to shift-work, native groups, children with special needs, development of non-profit community-based child-care services, etc. The fund is not part of the Canada Child Care Act. The Act only requires that provinces commit themselves to according special priority to children from "low and modest income families", not necessarily native children or children with special needs.

17. Bill C-144, Canada Child Care Act, as passed by the House of Commons on 26 September 1988, Second Session, Thirty-third Parliament. The Bill received First Reading on 25 July 1988 and Second Reading on 24 August 1988.

18. National Council of Welfare, *Child Care: A Better Alternative*, op. cit., p.15.

19. Budget Papers, Tabled in the House of Commons 27 April 1989. p. 14.

20. Ibid., p. 14.

21. National Council of Welfare, *Child Care*, p.26. The National Council of Welfare goes so far as to recommend that the federal government be empowered to accept or reject the child-care standards of provincial governments and to withhold funds from governments that have unacceptably low standards. The proposed Act merely requires that provinces describe in an appendix to the agreement the Standards established for child-care services by the provincial authority (section 1 (h) iii). The appendix may be amended by the province providing the Minister with the required text changes. (section 2b).

22. T. Courchene, "Meech Lake and Socio-Economic Policy", *Canadian Public Policy/Analyse de Politiques*, XIV Supplement, September 1988. p. s73.

23. K. Banting, "Federalism, Social Reform and the Spending Power", *Canadian Public Policy/Analyse de Politiques*, XIV Supplement, September 1988, p. s87.

24. K. Banting, *The Welfare State and Canadian Federalism*, Second Edition (Kingston and Montreal: McGill-Queen's University Press, 1987) p. 200.

25. I have argued at length for the CAP to incorporate equalization features in cost-sharing for specific services. I will not repeat myself here. See D.

Hum, *Federalism and the Poor: A Review of the Canada Assistance Plan* (Toronto: Ontario Economic Council, 1983).

26. Report of the Subcommittee on Child Care, Senate *Debates*, 12 July 1988. p. 21.

27. "I am enough of a traditionalist to believe that the best people to do it (provide child care) are the parents." Jake Epp in *Winnipeg Free Press*, "Epp rejects view day care centres better for children" 14 January 1987, p. 11.

28. National Council of Welfare, *Social Spending and the next budget*, (Ottawa: Minister of Supply and Services, April 1989).

29. C. Leman, *The Collapse of Welfare Reform: Political Institutions, Policy and the Poor in Canada and the United States* (Cambridge, Mass.: The MIT Press, 1980) p. 199.

30. Ibid.

EIGHT

The New Environmental Law

Alastair R. Lucas

Au Canada et à l'étranger, la question environnementale s'avère d'ores et déjà incontournable. Dans cette optique A.R. Lucas aborde la facette juridique du dossier, particulièrement au regard du contexte canadien.

Les premières législations adoptées au Canada en matière environnementale remontent au début des années '70. Ces lois, émanant des deux paliers de gouvernement, visaient avant tout au contrôle des déchets dans l'air, l'eau et sur la terre. A la fin de cette décennie émergea une seconde génération de lois qui, dès lors, mirent davantage l'emphase sur la protection de l'environnement. On commença donc à articuler une stratégie à long terme qui puisse tenir compte, tout spécialement, des effets persistants de certaines substances toxiques.

A cet égard, l'escalade mondiale des désastres écologiques justifie la nécessité d'une concertation internationale en vue d'harmoniser l'ensemble des actions engagées par les Etats concernés. En contrepoint s'impose aussi le concept du développement soutenable, *tel que prôné par les Nations-Unies et endossé par le Canada, en vertu duquel croissance économique et respect des écosystèmes doivent aller de pair.*

Par ailleurs, au Canada, de récentes décisions judiciaires—telle l'affaire Crown Zellerbach—ont amené le gouvernement fédéral à repenser ses politiques d'évaluation environnementale. Il reste à savoir maintenant si la nouvelle loi fédérale sur l'environnement sera le ferment d'une coopération fédérale-provinciale améliorée ou bien le prétexte à d'éventuelles disputes sur le sujet entre Ottawa et les provinces.

En définitive, l'auteur souhaite la création future d'une charte canadienne de l'environnement qui permettrait d'enchâsser l'impératif du développement soutenable au Canada.

INTRODUCTION

In January 1988 over 250 lawyers and other professionals gathered in Toronto for a conference on environmental law. The previous week a competing commercial conference organizer had drawn double that number to its Toronto environmental law seminar. Similar events have been held in other major

Canadian cities. Law schools have reported unprecedented demand for environmental law courses and published environmental law materials are selling briskly.

As recently as the mid-1980s professional interest in environmental law was largely confined to a few academics, public interest lawyers, and personally committed practitioners. Law professors patiently explained to eager first year students fresh out of environmental management programs that opportunities to practice environmental law were extremely limited. One could teach; one could work for a public interest group; one could work for government in a few roles. As corporate counsel for natural resource development and manufacturing corporations, one could expect to encounter some environmental law issues. But one could not expect to survive as a pin-striped, brief case-toting private practitioner of environmental law. Now, this appears to have changed, or at least there is a very large gleam in the eyes of many Canadian lawyers who consider environmental law to be a major area for new practice development. Similarly, environmental consultants and in house industry and government environmental professionals consider a broader and sounder knowledge of environmental legal principles and trends to be increasingly important in their work.

What is the reason for this sudden, intense interest in environmental law? Is it merely a matter of greater competition in law and related professions so that even small crumbs of potential new business are hotly contested? Or is all of this entrepreneurial heat a consequence of more pervasive, more fundamental developments in environmental law? In this paper it is argued that the latter assessment is correct. Moreover, it is suggested that many signs point to even more significant environmental law reforms, as Canada, along with other nations, comes to grips with legal changes necessary to ensure the environmental sustainability of all economic development decisions and actions.

A SECOND GENERATION OF ENVIRONMENTAL LAWS

A major reason for this burgeoning interest in environmental law is the recent flurry of legislative activity that has produced a new comprehensive federal environmental statute,[1] and new statutes or major environmental statute amendments in many of the provinces.[2] This legislation is a response to the increasingly apparent inadequacies of the first generation of environmental statutes.

WASTE CONTROL LAWS

This first generation of environmental statutes includes the basic air, water and land pollution statutes enacted by Canada, and by the provinces in the early 1970s.[3] One category of these statutes is those that established separate environment departments for the first time.[4] The essential object of these Acts was control of waste that was being deposited on land or discharged into water or air. Regulatory systems were established to identify waste sources, to bring these sources under permit, then by means of permit terms or conditions, to control the quality and quantity of waste discharged.[5] Failure to comply with these requirements was made an offence punishable upon summary conviction by modest fines.[6] Waste discharge likely to cause harm to human life or health or to the environment upon which human life depends, was often established as a general offence.[7]

These statutes were clean-up laws, designed to minimize discharge of human and industrial waste into the environment. The underlying assumption was that the natural environment, with its air, water and land components, could, through careful management, be used to dispose of, dilute and cleanse the waste produced by human activity. It was a matter of measuring, then carefully and fairly allocating this environmental assimilative capacity.

It was recognized by governments and their advisors that civil legal actions, designed to resolve disputes between private parties and compensate persons damaged, were an ineffective legal tool for general systematic control of environmentally harmful waste discharge.[8] It was also recognized that existing statute law, such as the common nuisance provision of the Criminal Code,[9] public health statutes[10] and miscellaneous provisions scattered through natural resource development statutes[11] were not equal to the task of comprehensive environmental control.

Waste control statutes include comprehensive environmental statutes such as the Ontario Environmental Protection Act,[12] and the Quebec Environment Quality Act,[13] which deal with air, water and land pollution from the base of comprehensive definitions of "pollution", "contaminant" and "environment", and single resource statutes such as the Alberta Clean Air,[14] Clean Water,[15] and Land Surface Conservation and Reclamation Acts,[16] which covered much of the same ground but established a separate regulatory system for each environmental medium. Federal first generation environmental statutes include the Clean Air Act,[17] The Canada Water Act,[18] and the Fisheries Act Pollution Amendments and Industry Regulations.[19] Gaps were filled[20] and Acts were fine-tuned through development of regulations, policies and procedures during the late 1970s and early 1980s.

These environmental laws were administered by environment departments, that were largely technical agencies, staffed by the scientific and engineering experts necessary to implement the permit schemes and develop "safe" standards for waste discharge. Initially a great deal of effort was expended simply to bring all waste sources under permit.

SECOND GENERATION ENVIRONMENTAL LAWS

A second generation of environmental statutes is now emerging. These laws are a response to overwhelming evidence that the waste control approach, while significant, is only one aspect of an effective environmental protection regime.[21] A central objective of these new laws is control of persistent toxic substances. These materials either accumulate in the environment to produce conditions dangerous to the natural environment, or are simply so toxic and so persistent that even small amounts create serious danger over large periods of time. Such small dose toxicity and slow decomposition characteristics make the established assimilative waste regulation approach unsuitable for dealing effectively with toxic substances.

The new laws thus recognize that environmental protection is a long term process that must address potential intergenerational effects of environmental damage.[22] Because new scientific knowledge about the toxicity of particular substances is continually developing, the laws must be flexible and include the means for identification and effective regulation of new contaminants. The approach is preventive, but also anticipatory.

Also reflected in these second generation statutes is that fact that toxic substances respect no boundaries—provincial or international.[23] The second generation environmental laws are consequently outward looking, and international in their development, implementation and administration. Provincial laws must reflect interprovincial and federal-provincial understandings and commitments, and must also, if they are to contribute to the solution of the global problem, reflect current international conditions and Canada's international obligations. Federal laws such as CEPA must clearly implement specific international environmental commitments and must also be consistent with current international thinking about global environmental protection.

Another characteristic of the new environmental statutes is that enforcement provisions are far more sophisticated than the simple offence sections of the clean-up legislation. There is greater flexibility to permit the regulators a choice of appropriate enforcement tools, ranging from expeditious tickets for minor offenses, to serious indictable criminal offenses for actions that endanger life or health, mandatory administrative orders and civil legal actions.[24] Negotiation techniques may be used in appropriate circumstances and provision is made for citizen involvement in regulatory processes, particularly in enforcement.

The serious criminal offenses which carry large fines and even potential imprisonment,[25] have caught the attention of the corporate sector. Interest is particularly keen, when these offenses are combined with officer and director liability provisions that may render corporate officials personally liable for environmental offenses and subject to fine or imprisonment even if they merely acquiesced or failed to make appropriate inquiries into activity that resulted in serious environmental harm.[26] The clear message is that environmental offenses are serious crimes, and that nothing short of demonstrating that all reasonable care was taken in the circumstances will excuse corporate employees and even officers and directors. This has provided strong incentives for corporations to review or audit their compliance with environmental requirements, take any necessary corrective action, and prepare and implement environmental protection policies and plans so that environmentally damaging actions can be avoided.[27]

SOURCES OF LAW REFORM PRESSURE

CANADIAN PUBLIC OPINION

These environmental law developments are by no means a matter of technical law reform. They are propelled by a number of powerful forces that are rippling through Canadian society. The most important factor is a very high level of public consciousness about environmental problems. This public awareness increased through the 1970s and early 1980s so that environmental protection is now consistently rated high in Canadian public opinion polls on priority issues.[28]

More effective formal and informal environmental education appears to be a contributing factor. A series of regional environmental disasters and controversies ranging from the Chernobyl nuclear plant incident to ozone layer holes, the Saint-Basile-le-Grand PCB fire, the Valdez oil spill, and the Canadian toxic waste-tainted fuel scandal, have kept environment in the public eye. Physical evidence of lake acidification and forest damage that can, with increasing confidence, be attributed to acid rain, is before the public.[29] So are the weather conditions that many scientists are now prepared to attribute to global warming caused by a "greenhouse effect" produced by fossil fuel burning and forest clearing.[30] Even aboriginal rights issues, that emphasize preservation of land from resource development, have contributed to public awareness of potential environmental damage.[31]

Surveys have shown that members of the public are not only concerned about environmental quality, but that they are willing to pay for environment protection.[32] Public interest environmental groups report unprecedented public support for their activities. Even the attitudes of the business community towards environmental protection appear to be changing. The traditional defensive posture, and technical mitigative response to environmental issues is giving way to corporate environmental policies and codes of practice.[33] Business leaders such as Ian Smyth, President of the Canadian Petroleum Association, and Roy Aiken of Inco Limited have embraced the goal of environmentally sustainable economic development.[34]

Law and policy developments at the international level have also contributed to the pressure for Canadian environmental law reform. Canada has been a leading participant in a number of international initiatives built on the 1972 Stockholm Declaration[35] and on earlier precedents for managing global common resources concerning ocean fisheries[36] and international rivers.[37] These include the Third United Nations Convention on the Law of the Sea,[38] the Convention for the Prevention of Marine Pollution by Dumping of Wastes and Other Matter (London Dumping Convention)[39] and the 1985 Vienna Convention for the Protection of the Ozone Layer.[40] The Canadian concept of a 100 mile offshore pollution prevention zone enacted by the 1970 Arctic Waters Pollution Prevention Act[41] has proven significant in the evolution of international marine pollution law. Canadian representatives played an important role in developing positions and negotiating the 1987 Montreal Protocol to the Ozone Layer Convention concerning control of chloroflurocarbon and halon emissions.[42]

Development of international legal norms and institutional arrangements has also been assisted by the United Nations Environment Program (UNEP) which was a consequence of the 1972 Stockholm conference. UNEP's first director was a Canadian, Maurice Strong. The International Law Commission has also worked to develop and refine principles to govern the use of shared water resources.[43] The United Nations World Commission on Environment and Development,[44] chaired by Norwegian Prime Minister Gro Harlem Brundtland, has been a particularly powerful influence on Canadian environmental law and policy. The concept of environmentally compatible economic development recommended by the Brundtland Commission has been embraced by Canadian environment ministers and officials, particularly at the federal level.

In the Brundtland Report, sustainable development is defined as, "development that meets the needs of the present without compromising the ability of future generations to meet their own needs."[45] Though the Commission endorses continued economic growth,[46] it recognizes the priority of meeting the essential needs of the world's poor, thus implying a massive redistribution of wealth. Another key idea inherent in the sustainable development concept is that the state of technology and social organization imposes real limitations on the environment's ability to meet present and future needs. There will be no easy technological fix.

The Brundtland Report also spells out the institutional and legal system deficiencies that stand in the way of sustainable development. Environmental protection and resource management agencies, says the Commission, have made notable gains in research, in technical definition and understanding of issues and in raising public awareness. Environmental laws have induced the development of new control technologies, processes and products.[47] But there is a serious deficiency, namely:

> *"[M]ost of these agencies have been confined by their own mandates to focusing almost exclusively on the effects.* Today, the sources of these effects must be tackled. While these existing environmental protection policies and agencies must be maintained and even strengthened, governments now need to take a much broader view of environmental problems and policies.[48]

This suggests that:

> "[E]nvironmental regulation must move beyond the usual menu of safety regulations, zoning laws, and pollution control enactments; environmental objectives must be built into taxation, prior approval procedures for investment and technology choice, foreign trade incentives, and all components of development policy.[49]

Environmental requirements, the Commission concluded, can no longer be left to separate environmental agencies. They must be built into the decisions of central governmental agencies and key sectoral ministries concerned with economic development. These are the agencies in a position to directly influence the nature of the impacts of economic activity on the natural environment.

Following the Brundtland Commission's May 1986 visit to Canada, the Canadian Council of Resource and Environment Ministers established a National Task Force on Environment and Economy with representatives from government, industry and public interest groups. In its September 1987 Report[50] the Task Force endorsed the Brundtland Commission's sustainable development concept and made a series of 42 recommendations for actions by Canadian governments, industry, trade associations and environmental groups to establish the means for moving towards sustainable development. These include establishment of national and provincial round tables representing the various stake-holders to provide continuing advice and liaison.[51] In June 1988 Canada sponsored a major international conference on the atmosphere,[52] that produced, among other things, recommendations for development of a law of the atmosphere. Other developments consistent with sustainability include the Department of Energy, Mines and Resources June 1988 "Commitment to the Environment"[53] and Environment Canada's proposal to legislate and broaden the Federal Environmental Assessment and Review Process.

LEGAL SYSTEM DEVELOPMENTS

Apart from the second generation environmental legislation, several recent doctrinal developments have considerable potential for increasing the effectiveness of Canadian environmental law. These developments have occurred in the Constitutional law field and in the area of administrative law judicial review principles. In constitutional law, federal jurisdiction over environmental protection appears to have expanded. More generally, the Canadian Charter of Rights and Freedoms has arguably induced the courts to intervene more freely to review environmentally significant government decisions.

In Administrative law, relaxation of common law status to sue requirements has permitted individuals and public interest groups to attack more effectively environmental decisions through judicial review proceedings. Decreased judicial reluctance to review ministerial and even cabinet decisions has increased the potential for setting aside even top level government decisions that adversely affect the environment.

EXTENDED FEDERAL ENVIRONMENTAL JURISDICTION

In *Regina* v. *Crown Zellerbach*,[54] the Supreme Court of Canada upheld the application of the dumping at sea prohibitions of the federal Ocean Dumping Control Act[55] within the boundaries of the province of British Columbia. The significance of the decision lies in the fact that the provisions were held valid, not on the basis of one of the enumerated federal powers, such as Fisheries or Navigation and Shipping, but on the general Peace, Order and Good Government (POGG) power.

The specific issue was the validity of section 4(1) of the Act which prohibited, except in accordance with the terms and conditions of a permit under the Act, the dumping of any substance in the sea. "The sea" was defined in the Act to include the territorial sea and fishing zones of Canada, and "The internal waters of Canada other than inland waters." This latter category included marine waters within provincial boundaries.

Crown Zellerbach was charged under section 4(1) after its employees dredged wood waste from the bed of a coastal cove and deposited the waste further offshore, in order to facilitate log storage in the cove. Though the company held no permit under the Act, there was no evidence to suggest that the wood waste dumped caused harm to marine life or to navigation.

The Supreme Court reversed the lower court decisions and held the provisions valid as dealing with a matter of national concern under the POGG power. Le Dain J. for the majority, in a 4-3 decision, found that marine pollution is a matter of national concern because of its predominantly extra-provincial and international character and implications. It is, he said, a single indivisible matter distinct from the control of pollution caused by dumping substances in provincial fresh wasters, as opposed to marine waters. Marine pollution has been, he noted, treated in international conventions and scientific studies as a distinct form of water pollution with its own characteristics and scientific considerations.[56] The fact that fresh waters flow into and mix with marine waters was treated as an indication of "provincial inability"[57]—i.e., that the provincial fresh water and federal ocean water aspects of the matter are inextricably interrelated so that federal legislation offers the only realistic possibility for uniform and effective treatment.

The significance of the decision for federal environmental jurisdiction is clearly shown by the minority judgement of La Forest J. He emphasized the interrelatedness of ecological systems and the difficulty of drawing a clean line between salt and fresh waters in marine areas. He also pointed out that contaminants deposited in fresh water, and even air contaminants produced by activities within provinces contribute significantly to marine pollution. Because effective control of marine pollution may include control of these clearly local and provincial contaminant sources, it is difficult to understand how marine pollution can be regarded as a distinct POGG subject. If it is such a pervasive subject that it includes fresh water pollution and even air pollution, it could, according to La Forest J., "completely swallow up provincial power."[58]

The minority also showed convincingly that under a more "traditional approach" there was ample federal constitutional power to regulate, though narrower, more carefully drafted legislation, pollution affecting fisheries, and pollution originating in provinces and causing harm outside provincial boundaries.[59] A combination of the POGG and criminal law powers could go a long way towards controlling pollution of internal waters as well as territorial marine waters. But the Ocean Dumping Control Act, which covered even dumping that causes no damage, and which could, in the name of marine pollution control, potentially extend to include regulation of local industries and provincial natural resource development, intrudes too much on provincial jurisdiction. It requires, La Forest J. concluded:

> "a quantum leap to find constitutional justification for the provision one, it seems to me, that could create considerable stress on Canadian federalism as it has developed over the years."[60]

The practical importance of the *Crown Zellerbach* decision becomes apparent when one looks at the new federal Canadian Environmental Protection Act (CEPA).[61] This is a prime example of second generation legislation, which includes a consolidation of pre-existing federal environmental statutes, and a core purpose of establishing uniform national standards for the life cycle control and management of toxic substances.

First, the case clarifies the validity of the Ocean Dumping Control Act, which has now become Part VI of CEPA. Second, and more significantly, it strengthens the possibility that Part II of CEPA, which establishes a comprehensive regulatory system for the identification, toxicity assessment, and comprehensive regulation and control of toxic substances, will be upheld under the POGG power.

The problem, prior to *Crown Zellerbach*, was that, while the array of offence provisions and the health protection focus of the Act are consistent with a Criminal Law classification, the toxic substance provisions are essentially regulatory, with offence provisions designed to enforce the regulatory scheme. The authorities suggest that such a regulatory measure is not likely to be characterized as a matter of Criminal Law.[62]

Following the *Crown Zellerbach* reasoning, regulation and control of toxic substances that pose a serious threat to life, health and environmental processes may, like marine pollution, qualify as a POGG subject matter. Such substances are persistent and cross provincial boundaries. Like marine pollution, toxic substance contamination has been treated as a distinct subject matter by reports of international agencies and by international agreements to which Canada is a party.[63] This suggests an extra-provincial aspect appropriate for POGG legislation to establish national standards and control extra-provincial damage. Such toxic substance controls would form a category of environmental regulations distinct from the ordinary array of provincial legislation designed to clean up and impose local controls on less persistent waste.

This extended federal environmental protection jurisdiction is likely to have major federal-provincial relations implications. Provinces resisted CEPA, with the result that equivalency provisions were added in committee following second reading of the Bill.[64] These provide that CEPA regulations do not apply in any province when the provincial and federal ministers agree in writing that provincial environmental laws are equivalent to the particular CEPA regulations. Difficult negotiations on equivalency are now underway. A second major battle is developing over federal jurisdiction to impose environmental impact assessment requirements on developments within provinces.[65]

Provincial officials are concerned that this new federal environmental jurisdiction will provide a handle for federal regulation of the timing and scale of provincial natural resources and energy developments. They worry that the *Crown Zellerbach* approach establishes a back door international treaty power, based on POGG, that could authorize sweeping federal legislation to implement international environmental obligations. The depth of feeling on this issue in provinces such as Alberta and Saskatchewan should not be underestimated. Federal environmental initiatives are seen as a withdrawal from commitments to confirm provincial authority over natural resource development, conservation and management that were enshrined in the Constitution of Canada by the 1982 Resources Amendment.

ADMINISTRATIVE LAW DEVELOPMENTS

Standing to Sue

Perhaps the most important environmental administrative law development is the result of a social welfare case. The Supreme Court of Canada held[66] that a welfare recipient under Manitoba legislation had standing to challenge federal decisions concerning transfer of funds under the Canada Assistance Plan Act to provinces for use in provincial welfare assistance programs. The Court confirmed that discretionary standing could be granted to persons or organizations challenging administrative decisions who lack the traditional special (usually economic) damage, on public interest grounds under the criteria developed in a trilogy of constitutional cases ending with *Borowski* v. *The Queen*.[67] If, (1) there is a serious legal issue to be determined, (2) the plaintiff has a "genuine interest", that may be the record of a non-economic involvement or action and (3) if there is no other reasonable and effective way of bringing the matter before the court, standing may be granted.

Removal of the special damage requirement has opened the door to public interest judicial review actions to challenge governmental decisions that have serious environmental consequences. The door is not wide open. Narrow interpretations of the "genuine interest" and "no other reasonable and effective method of litigating the issue" criteria have resulted in environmental actions being dismissed on standing grounds.[68] But the trend of decisions has been in the other direction so that, for example, where action was taken by a public interest group to challenge the validity of water licences for construction by the Alberta government of a major dam on the Oldman River in Southern Alberta, no serious question was raised about the standing of the group to initiate the action.[69]

Judicial Review of Government Decisions

A second administrative law development is also illustrated by the Oldman River Dam litigation. The grant of the water licences was a Ministerial decision taken under an authorized delegation by the Controller of Water Rights, an official of the Department of the Environment. The applicant and dam proponent was also the Department of the Environment.

Approximately 18 months after the application, the Controller (acting for the Minister) decided that, due to the importance of the project, it was appropriate to waive the Water Resources Act requirements for posting or publishing notice of the application. This decision was taken under s. 19 which provides that:

"The Minister may, if he considers it expedient, fit and proper to do so, waive the requirement for giving public notice of the filing of the application and plans ..."

Chief Justice Moore granted the application by the Friends of the Oldman Society and quashed the water licences. He found that requirements under the Act that specified information to be filed with an application for a water licence are mandatory and had not been followed. These requirements include written permission from municipal authorities having jurisdiction over the site, or if such permission cannot be obtained, written permission of the provincial Public Utilities Board and referral of a copy of the application to the Energy Resources Conservation Board.

The court rejected arguments that the statute gave the minister an unfettered discretionary power to waive the public notice requirements. Chief Justice Moore's approach was that the words "expedient, fit and proper" in section 19 imply some factual basis for the decision. In view of the magnitude of the project and its potential impact on the province, this factual basis must be particularly compelling. His conclusion was that in the circumstances the only purpose behind the Controller's decision must have been to expedite the matter. Waiver of public notice without first obtaining permission of the municipal authorities or the Public Utilities Board and the advice of the ERCB could not be "expedient fit and proper". An argument that Alberta Environment's actions, including staff involvement in the project, provision of information to and solicitation of views of local residents, extensive media coverage of the granting of the licences and establishment of a local project office, provided a sufficient basis for the decision to waive notice, was rejected.

Similarly in *Canadian Wildlife Federation* v. *Canada (Minister of the Environment)*,[70] the Federal Court quashed a licence issued by the federal Minister of the Environment to the Saskatchewan Water Corporation authorizing construction of the Rafferty and Alameda Dams on the Souris River system in Southern Saskatchewan. The court agreed with the Wildlife Federation that the Minister had, before granting the licence to the Water Corporation under the International River Improvements Act,[71] failed to require an environmental impact assessment and review as required by the Federal Environmental Assessment and Review Process Guidelines Order.[72]

The decision came as a surprise to the dam proponents and to Environment Canada officials. Though appeals have not yet been exhausted, it has already had an impact on other environmental controversies. In Alberta, for example, the Friends of the Oldman River Society, in the latest judicial round on the Oldman Dam, has argued, on the authority of the *Canadian Wildlife Federation*

Case, that approvals for the dam under the federal Navigable Waters Protection Act[73] are invalid because no environmental impact assessment was required. The same position is being taken by opponents of pulp mills that are under construction or proposed in Northern Alberta as part of a major provincial pulp and paper industry development policy.[74]

The reason the case evoked surprise is that the Federal Environmental Assessment and Review Process (EARP) has never had a distinct statutory basis.[75] It began as merely a set of guidelines issued under the authority of a cabinet directive. Later it purported to be authorized by a single section of the Department of the Environment Act,[76] which empowers the minister, with cabinet approval, to establish guidelines for use by federal departments and agencies. Since 1984, the process has operated under a Guidelines Order issued as a formal statutory instrument.[77] It had generally been assumed that the result was a set of guidelines that were not formal regulations issued under clear statutory authority and consequently not legally binding.

Cullen J. held that the EARP Guidelines Order is an "enactment" or "regulation" as defined by section 2 of the Federal Interpretation Act[78] because they were issued in the execution of a power—the Department of the Environment Act guidelines power—conferred under the authority of an Act. Consequently, as Cullen J. put it, the Guidelines order is "not a mere description of a policy or program; it may create rights which may be enforceable ..."[79] He decided further that the Guidelines Order specifies that the Guidelines apply to any proposal that may have an environmental effect on an area of federal responsibility and that the issuing of a licence under the International River Improvements Act is such a federal decision making responsibility.

Both the *Canadian Wildlife Federation Case* and the *Friends of the Oldman River Case* involve judicial refusal to defer to broadly expressed discretionary ministerial powers. Government is not permitted to equivocate on environmental decisions, "enforcing" discretionary requirements when it chooses and pleading lack of legal authority and mouthing informal assurances when it chooses otherwise. Both cases are examples of judicial recognition of statutory "sleepers."[80] Neither court was deterred by the fact that these were high level ministerial decisions with a heavy political content.[81] They summarily dismissed any suggestion that the statutory provisions were merely "directory" and not mandatory and that the environmental requirements were satisfied by actions taken by government officials in the spirit of the requirements. The result is a ringing reinforcement of government accountability under environmental laws.

THE CHARTER

The Canadian Charter of Rights and Freedoms has had little direct impact on the development of environmental law.[82] Environmental rights would have to be derived from other Charter protected rights and freedoms, particularly the section 7 right to "life, liberty and security of the person and the right not to be deprived thereof except in accordance with the principles of fundamental justice." It is possible that section 7 rights could be asserted to attack government decisions approving developments that can be shown to be likely to damage health or personal security. There are, however, serious problems of proof, as shown by The Cruise Missile case,[83] and the term "security of the person" has so far received a relatively narrow interpretation. In fact, to date the main impact of the Charter in environmental law has been a negative, dampening one as Charter legal rights have been asserted, with occasional success, by those under investigation or charged with environmental offenses.[84]

In a broader sense, however, it is arguable that the Charter has contributed to courts being relatively more receptive to either constitutional or administrative law challenges to government decisions likely to affect adversely the environment. The reason is that the Charter has forced courts not only to consider seriously direct challenges to government action, but to grapple with difficult conceptions of rights and with competing public values.[85] This increasing judicial comfort with the policy-charged role of measuring government actions against constitutionally protected rights may be seen as one of the factors behind the cases that have held Canadian governments accountable in the administration of their own environmental laws.

LOOKING AHEAD—THIRD GENERATION ENVIRONMENTAL LAWS

A third generation of environmental laws appears likely to follow hard on the heels of the second. These will be the laws that actually implement the concept of sustainable development. Much remains to be done to define further the concept with a view to achieving more than a superficial consensus among interests on its meaning and specific implications. It is clear, however, as Elder and Ross[86] have pointed out, that sustainable development is a normative and not a technical concept. This implies that sustainability determinations must be politically accountable and not merely technical information gathering processes.

The idea of sustainability determinations as part of private and public sector development decisions suggests some kind of structured assessment process. This immediately spotlights existing environmental impact assessment (CEIA) processes as potential models or starting points. Such a sustainability assessment process, however, must extend beyond the scope of existing EIA processes to include a wider range of decisions. More importantly, environmental sustainability criteria must be included in the substantive decision standards on which each proposed action will be judged. Existing EIA processes merely identify environmental impacts so that this information is available to decision-makers.[87] Environmental standards must stand on the same plane as economic standards.

Another area of potential legal changes to foster sustainable development involves enhancement of individual environmental rights. This may be done through statutory environmental "Bills of Rights" or even through constitutional amendment to entrench such rights as part of the Canadian Charter of Rights and Freedoms.

Such enhancement of citizen's environmental rights is a legal technique that appears to be highly compatible with the concept of sustainable development. It increases the legal status of environmental rights relative to existing economic rights and it adds legitimacy to broader citizen participation in environmental decisions. In addition, since such rights would be enforced through citizen actions in the courts, from a government perspective, it is self-implementing.

FEDERAL-PROVINCIAL RELATIONS

The new environmental law has significant implications for federal-provincial relations. In the short term, these legal developments have triggered a flurry of analysis, position development, consultation and negotiation. The longer term prospect is a redefinition of the respective federal and provincial roles in environment protection.

THE CONSTITUTIONAL SHIFT

There are clear indications of a shift in the "political constitution" that has guided federal and provincial legislative action in the environmental field.[88] The idea is that there has been a kind of gloss on the constitutional legalities of federal-provincial relations, based on a range of factors including provincial "sensitivities" and various trade-off considerations. This has resulted in the scope of federal environmental law jurisdiction being perceived by policy-makers and politicians to be somewhat narrower than formal constitutional law would suggest. Thus in the early 1980s a proposed Canada Environment Act aimed at regulation of toxics on a natural scale never emerged from Environment Canada largely because it was perceived that raw provincial nerves, resulting from the aftermath of the 1982 Constitution debate and the federal-provincial energy resources dispute, made such a sweeping federal environmental statute politically unacceptable.

Now, the Canada Environment Act has emerged in the forum of the Canadian Environmental Protection Act. The legal opinions of the early 1980s that suggested that such a statute could be based on the federal peace order and good government power or on a combination of POGG, Criminal Law and Regulation of Trade and Commerce have essentially been dusted off and acted upon. The Supreme Court's decision in the *Crown Zellerbach Case* tends to confirm these opinions and provide the formal constitutional law support for the CEPA initiative. For toxic substances regulation, the political constitution and the legal constitution have now become virtually co-extensive. CEPA's equivalency mechanism under which CEPA regulations do not apply in any province when the federal and provincial ministers agree in writing that provincial environmental laws are equivalent,[89] may be seen as an acknowledgment of this step towards the legal limits of federal constitutional power.

In the case of federal environmental impact assessment requirements the *Canadian Wildlife Federation* ruling has pushed the application of the Environmental Assessment Review Process (EARP) beyond the perceived limits of federal environmental assessment jurisdiction. While the precise question of constitutional power to impose environmental assessment requirements has not yet been resolved, it is likely that a wide range of developments within provinces that produce interjurisdictional effects may be subjected to some type of federal environmental assessment.[90]

PROVINCIAL CONCERNS

Predictably, this apparent constitutional shift has produced concern bordering on paranoia in many of the provincial administrations. There is dismay about the potential for CEPA provisions duplicating basic provincial, environmental legislation. Notwithstanding the potential for negotiating equivalency agreements to render CEPA regulations inapplicable in provinces, there is concern that such negotiations may be protracted so that potential duplication may continue for long periods or that negotiations may be unsuccessful. There is clear potential for duplication of provincial legislation by the CEPA spills and emergency order provisions[91] that are outside the scope of the equivalency agreement powers. Provincial environmental officials are also unhappy about the requirement that provincial equivalent legislation must include citizen application for investigation provisions similar to those in CEPA[92]

Provinces are also under pressure from local industrial interests that have adjusted to provincial environmental regulation and fear the additional burdens, or at least the initial uncertainties, of federal regulations. This industry resistance to new federal environmental requirements and encouragement of provincial officials to resist new federal initiatives was apparent in Environment Canada workshops held as part of the development of its CEPA enforcement policy. In Alberta, for example, there was energy industry concern that the expertise, experience and established environmental regulation patterns of the Energy Resources Conservation Board[93] would be replaced by remote, technical federal regulators not yet familiar with the day-to-day operations of the industry.

In the western provinces these natural resource and energy industry concerns are taken very seriously. Moreover, provincial governments, with memories of the late 1970s—early 1980s energy wars still fresh, are suspicious about possible environmental regulation back doors to federal control of their natural resource industries. Were the energy wars fought and the Resources Amendment to the Constitution guaranteeing provincial jurisdiction over the development, conservation and management of non-renewable and forestry resources won, only to have these powers eroded by federal environmental regulations that can be used to control effectively the scale and timing of provincial natural resource development?[94] The answer, implicit in the *Canadian Wildlife Federation* case and its potential use by opponents of northern Alberta pulp developments to delay or stop the projects, is not comforting for provinces whose economic future is closely tied to expanded natural resource development.

The Supreme Court's approach in *Crown Zellerbach* to definition of subjects as matters of national concern and consequently appropriate for federal POGG jurisdiction is cause for serious provincial uncertainty and apprehension. It had been thought that the specificity requirement for POGG subjects effectively excluded environmental protection, the classic example of an aggregate subject that if brought under POGG had the potential to produce a quantum change in Canadian federalism.[95] Large chunks of the broad "environment" subject now appear to be fair game for federal legislators.

One aspect of this POGG subject characterization was particularly chilling for provincial officials. This was the use by the court of international agreements and studies as evidence to demonstrate the distinctiveness of marine pollution as an appropriate POGG subject.[96] Canadian international activities and obligations may apparently now be pursued to build the "record" necessary to ensure that particular environmental subjects are sufficiently distinguished as distinct or indivisible to bring them under POGG. Notwithstanding the absence of a federal treaty implementation power,[97] this kind of "bootstrapping" may be used to accomplish essentially the same federal purpose under POGG.

Nor is the federal government without its share of pressures and uncertainties about its newly defined environment protection role. There are worries about the cost of CEPA implementation and enforcement and about the provincial feathers that will be ruffled in this process. Will the established federal leadership and research role in environment protection[98] be replaced by a more volatile and decidedly less comfortable role of environmental standard setter, enforcer and frequent adversary of provincial governments and agencies?

There is also pressure on the federal government from another direction. This is the result of Canada putting itself forward as an international environmental protection leader. Canada's leaders have not been short of the latest sustainable development tough enforcement rhetoric whenever international opportunities have arisen.[99] Now the federal government must deal with these self-generated international expectations that Canada has some of the answers to difficult global environmental problems.

CONCLUSION

There is little doubt that environmental law has risen higher in the Canadian legal firmament. It is a reflection of increased Canadian public concern about environment protection and of high profile international environmental law and policy activity. Also relevant are legal developments that include broadened federal constitutional jurisdiction to enact environmental statutes. Relaxed standing to sue requirements, coupled with increased judicial willingness to review ministerial and even cabinet decisions on jurisdictional grounds have improved the prospects for successful legal actions by individuals and public interest groups to enforce environmental law requirements.

Control and regulation of persistent toxics has emerged as the core subject of federal environmental legislation, with the Canadian Environmental Protection Act as the central statute. Human health and environmental dangers presented by toxics have demanded more serious penalties for environmental infractions and tougher, more consistent enforcement. The serious consequences of enforcement actions are causing Canadian industry to reassess its environmental compliance effort.

Because provinces are more directly involved than the government of Canada in promotion of natural resource and manufacturing developments, provincial governments and regulators are now feeling the pressure of the new federal environmental laws. The broadening of federal jurisdiction to enact environmental statutes is likely to increase this pressure. Federal-provincial conflicts concerning CEPA implementation and jurisdiction over environmental impact assessment have already developed.

The real environmental law challenge for both levels of government is now emerging even as the second generation toxics control statutes are implemented. Achieving environmentally sustainable economic development will require legal changes to ensure that the full range of governmental development decisions are assessed under sustainability criteria. There may also be a role for legally defined environmental rights that can be asserted by individuals and groups to maintain environmental sustainability.

Notes

1. The Canadian Environmental Protection Act (CEPA), S.C. 1988, c. 22 (hereinafter "CEPA").
2. E.g., The Environment Act, S.M. 1987, c. 26; The Environmental Statutes Amendment Act, S.O. 1988, c. 54. Recommended for major amendments to provincial environmental statutes were made by the Alberta Review Panel on Environmental Law Enforcement in its report, *An Action Plan for Environmental Law Enforcement in Alberta*. Edmonton: Alberta Environment, January 1988.
3. See R. Franson and A. Lucas, *Canadian Environmental Law* (Toronto: Butterworths—Continuing Service, 1976). The Concept of this service was to limit the field of environmental law covered by focusing on waste control law and legislation.
4. E.g., Department of the Environment Act, R.S.C. 1985, c. E-10.
5. A. Lucas, "Legal Techniques for Pollution Control: The Role of the Public" (1971) 6 U.B.C. L. Rev., 167.
6. See J. Swaigen and G. Bunt, *Sentencing in Environmental Cases* (Ottawa: Law Reform Commission of Canada, 1985).
7. See G. Morley, "Pollution as a Crime: The Federal Response" (1973) 5 Man. L.J., 297; K. Webb, *Pollution Control in Canada: The Regulatory Approach of the 1980s* (Ottawa: Law Reform Commission of Canada Study Paper, 1988) pp. 12-13.
8. A. Lucas, supra, note 5.
9. Criminal Code, R.S.C. 1985, c. C-46, s. 176.
10. See R. Franson and A. Lucas, supra, note 3, vol. 1, ch. 4, "Public Health Provisions" sections.
11. Id., "Natural Resource Management and Use" sections.
12. R.S.O. 1980, c. 141 as amended.
13. R.S.Q. 1977, c. Q-2.
14. R.S.A. 1980, c. C-12.
15. R.S.A. 1980, c. C-13.
16. R.S.A. 1980, c. L-3.

17. R.S.C. 1985, c. C-32. Repealed and partially replaced by the Canadian Environmental Protection Act, supra, note 1, Part V, "International Air Pollution".

18. R.S.C. 1985, c. C-11. Partially repealed by the Canadian Environmental Protection Act, supra note 1. See Part III, "Nutrients".

19. R.S.C. 1985, c. F-14, ss. 34-42; Meat and Poultry Products Plant Liquid Effluent Regulations, C.R.C. 1978, c. 818; Metal Mining Liquid Effluent Regulations, C.R.C. 1978, c. 819; Penalties & Forfeitures Proceeds Regulations, C.R.C. 1978, c. 827; Petroleum Refinery Liquid Effluent Regulations, C.R.C. 1978, c. 828; Potato Processing Plant Liquid Effluent Regulations, C.R.C. 1978, c. 829; Pump and Paper Effluent Regulations, C.R.C. 1978, c. 830; Chlor-Alkali Mercury Liquid Effluent Regulations, C.R.C. 1978, c. 811; Fish Toxicant Regulations, SOR/88-258.

20. E.G., Fisheries Act industry regulations, Ibid. Clean Air Act National Emission Standards Regulations; National Emission Guidelines, and Ambient Air Quality Objectives. See R. Franson and A. Lucas, supra, note 3, vol. 6, Stats. Fed. [2]-[2S].

21. See e.g., *From Cradle to Grave: A Management Approach to Chemicals*, Report of a task force representing industry, governments, labour, environmental groups and consumers (Ottawa: Environment and Supply and Services Canada, 1986).

22. Section 11 of CEPA defines toxic substances to include substances (a) having or that may have an immediate or *long-term harmful effect on the environment*; [or] (b) constituting or that may constitute a *danger to the environment on which human life depends* .... (emphasis added).

23. The preamble of CEPA states in part that: "Whereas toxic substances, once introduced into the environment, cannot always be contained within geographic boundaries . . . And whereas Canada must be able to fulfill its international obligations in respect of the environment."

24. Such an array of enforcement tools is found in Part VII of CEPA.

25. E.g., CEPA, s. 115 provides that:
    Any person who in contravention of the Act intentionally or recklessly causes damage to the environment or a risk of death or harm to persons is guilty of an indictable offence and liable to a fine or to imprisonment for a term of up to five years.
    See *Crimes Against the Environment*, Working Paper no. 44, (Ottawa: Law Reform Commission of Canada, 1985).

26. CEPA, s. 122; The Environmental Protection Act, R.S.O. 1980, c. 141, am. by S.O. 1988, c. 54, s. 49(3); The Environment Act, S.M., 1987, c. 26, s. 35.

27. See R. McLeod, J.A. Langford and J. Swaigen "Environmental Protection Legislation: Personal Liability of Officers and Directors." In Western Canadian Environmental Law and Practice at C-1, proceedings of the Canadian Institute Seminar, Calgary, 31 October—1 November 1988.

28. A recent Gallup Poll showed that Canadians consider the environment to be a more pressing issue than free trade with the U.S. According to an Environics poll, nine out of ten Canadians feel their health has suffered from pollution and 93 per cent fear they are being poisoned by toxins. A majority of respondents in a CROP-Focus poll felt that government does not adequately regulate toxic pollution. See "Public seeks action on the environment" *The Edmonton Journal*, 9 October 1988.

29. Impact Assessment Workgroup I, United States—Canada, *Memorandum of Intent on Transboundary Air Pollution, Final Report* (January 1983); House of Commons Subcommittee on Acid Rain, *Still Waters: The Chilling Reality of Acid Rain* (Ottawa, Supply and Services Canada, 1981).

30. Stephen H. Schneider, "The Greenhouse Effect: Science and Policy" *Science*, 243:771, 10 February 1989; F.K. Hare, "The Global Greenhouse Effect," presentation to the World Conference on the Changing Atmosphere, 27 June 1988 (Environment Canada); J. Janovich, "Is man meddling?" The Globe and Mail, 10 January 1989, at A-7.

31. See B. Morse and D. Nahwegahbow, "The Interaction Between Environmental Law Enforcement and Aboriginal and Treaty Rights in Canada," unpublished paper prepared for the Law Reform Commission of Canada, 1985; "Peigans seek Ottawa's help on dam issue" *The Calgary Herald*, 6 October 1988, at B-8.

32. A Southam News—Angus Reid poll showed that almost one quarter of Canadians feel that environment is the most pressing issue facing the country; only 14 per cent considered jobs and unemployment to be the major issue. See "Environment big issue, poll shows" *The Calgary Herald*, 2 February 1989.

33. W.R.O. Aiken, *The Environment and the Economy* (Kingston: Centre for Resource Studies, C.R.S. Special Paper, June 1988); Ian Smyth, "Industry Perspective on Sustainable Development," presentation to Canadian Institute of Resources Law Conference, "The Legal Challenge of Sustainable Development", Ottawa, 10 May 1989 (Proceedings forthcoming from CIRL); Canadian Petroleum Association, Environmental Code of Practice, undated.

34. Both were members of the National Task Force on The Environment and Economy, whose Report was published by the Canadian Council of Resource and Environment Ministers in September 1987.

35. Report of the U.N. Conference on Human Environment, New York, 1972, U.N. Doc. A/Conf. 48/14 (1972).

36. E.g., Convention on Fishing and the Conservation of the Living Resources of the High Seas, Geneva, 29 April 1958; International Convention for the High Seas Fisheries of the North Pacific Ocean, Tokyo, 9 May 1952.

37. E.g., Agreement Between the Federal Republic of Germany, the French Republic, the Grand Duchy of Luxemborg, The Kingdom of the Netherlands and the Swiss Confederation concerning the International Commission for the Protection of the Rhine Against Pollution, Bern, 29 April 1963; Agreement Between the U.S. and Canada Concerning the Great Lakes Water Quality, Ottawa, 15 April 1972.

38. United Nations Convention on the Law of the Sea, Montego Bay, 10 December 1982 A/Conf. 62/122, (1982).

39. International Maritime Consultative Organization (I.M.C.O.), Intergovernmental Conference on the Convention on the Dumping of Wastes at Sea (London Dumping Convention), London, November 1972.

40. Vienna Convention for the Protection of the Ozone Layer, Vienna, 22 March 1985, (1987) 26 *International Legal Materials* 1516; ratified by Canada, June 1986.

41. R.S.C. 1985, c. A-12. See D. Pharand, *The Law of the Sea of the Arctic with Special Reference to Canada* (Ottawa: University of Ottawa Press, 1973), Part VI; J.A. Beasley (1973) 1 Syracus J. International L. & Comm., 226.

42. Montreal Protocol to Control Ozone-modifying Substances, Montreal, 16 September 1987. (1987) 26 *International Legal Materials*, 1541.

43. E.g., Working Group of the International Law Commission, "International Liability for injurious consequences arising out of acts not prohibited by international law," Year Book of the International Law Commission 1978, Vol. II, Part II.

44. The World Commission on Environment and Development, *Our Common Future* (Oxford: Oxford University Press, 1987).

45. Id., at 8.

46. Id., at 50, 89-90.

47. Id., at 311.

48. Ibid., emphasis added.

49. Id., at 64.

50. Report of the National Task Force on Environment and Economy, supra, note 34.

51. Ibid.; Progress Report of the National Task Force on Environment and Economy, Submitted to the Canadian Council of Resource and Environment Ministers, at p. 3.

52. World Conference on the Changing Atmosphere, Toronto, June 1988. A follow-up meeting of legal experts was held in early 1989.

53. EMR's Commitment to the Environment. Ottawa: Energy, Mines and Resources, Canada, 1988.

54. (1988), 84 N.R. 1 (S.C.C.); A. Lucas, Comment, (1989) 23 U.B.C. L. Rev., 355.

55. S.C. 1974-75-76, c. 55, repealed and substituted by CEPA, Part VI.

56. Supra, note 55, at 41.

57. Id., at 38, 41.

58. Id., at 66.

59. Id., at 67.

60. Id., at 58.

61. Supra, note 2.

62. *Labatt* v. *A-G Canada*, [1980] 1 S.C.R. 914; P. Hogg, *Constitutional Law of Canada* (Toronto: Carswell, 2nd ed., 1985), 414-415.

63. E.g., Organization for Economic Co-operation and Development (OECD), Decision of Council (8 December 1982) Concerning the Minimum Pre-Marketing Set of Data in the Assessment of Chemicals, C (82) 196 (Final), (1983) 22 *International Legal Materials*, 909.

64. *Report of the House of Commons Legislative Committee on Bill C-74*, (23 March 1988), and Committee Proceedings, no. 1 (25 November 1987) at 15ff., and no. 12 (26 January 1988) at 4-16.

65. This is a consequence of the Canadian Wildlife Federation case discussed infra. See "Environmental battle looms" *The Calgary Herald*, 15 June 1989 at A-1.

66. *Finlay* v. *Canada* (Minister of Finance) [1987] 1 W.W.R. 603, 71 N.R. 338 (S.C.C.).

67. [1981] 2 S.C.R. 575.

68. *Sheill* v. *Amok Ltd.* (1988) 58 Sask. R. 141 (Q.B.).

69. *Friends of the Oldman River Society* v. *Alberta Minister of the Environment* (1987-88) 2 C.E.L.R. 234 (Alta. Q.B.). Cf. *Western Canada Wilderness Committee* v. *Strachan* (1987-88) 2 C.E.L.R. 234 (B.C.S.C.).

70. *Canadian Wildlife Federation* v. *Canada (Minister of the Environment)*, Unreported Federal Court Trial Division, Action No. T-80-89, 10 April 1989, Cullen J; affirmed, Federal Court of Appeal, Unreported, 22 June 1989.

71. R.S.C. 1985, c. I-20.

72. S.O.R./84-467.

73. R.S.C. 1985, c. N-22.

74. This has raised the possibility of a constitutional challenge to application of federal environmental assessment law to private sector projects within

provinces. See, "Mills may cause constitutional battle" *The Calgary Herald*, 16 June 1989, at A-1.

75. See D.P. Emond, *Environmental Assessment Law*, (Toronto: Emond-Montgomery, 1978) 227-229; Federal Environmental Assessment Review Office, *National Consultation Workshop on Federal Environmental Assessment Reform, Report of Proceedings* 13 (Ottawa: Supply and Services Canada, 1988).

76. Department of the Environment Act, supra, note 4, s. 6(2).

77. Supra, note 71.

78. R.S.C. 1985, c. I-21.

79. Supra, note 69 at p. 10.

80. See W. Rogers, "The Lesson of the Owl and the Crows: The Rule of Deception in the Evaluation of Environmental Statutes" (1989) 4 J. Land Use and Env't L. 377, 380-81.

81. The cases are consistent with decisions holding that ministerial or even cabinet decisions which purport to override the mandatory duties of administrative tribunals or officials, or to do something for a purpose outside the relevant statutory power, based on irrelevant considerations, or that amounts to failure to exercise the statutory power, may be set aside in judicial review proceedings. See, *Heppner* v. *Alberta Minister of the Environment* (1977) 6 A.R. 154 (Alta. S.C. App. Div.); Re *Public Utilities Review Commission Act* (1986) 26 Admin. L.R. 216 (Sask. C.A.); Re *Doctors Hospital and Minister of Health* (1976) 12 O.R. (2d) 164 (Ont. Div. Ct.); *Padfield* v. *Minister of Agriculture, Fisheries and Food* [1968] A.C. 997 (U.K.H.L.). Even *Monsanto Canada Inc.* v. *Canada (Minister of Agriculture)* (1989) 34 Admin L.R. 277 (F.C.A.), in which the Minister's refusal to accept a recommendation of a Board of review under the Pest Control Products Act, that the cancelled registration of a pesticide be restored, is consistent because the court held that the minister was required to act judicially and to take relevant facts into account, including scientific evidence concerning the relative safety of available alternative products. Ministerial and Cabinet decisions may also be set aside for failure to comply with procedural fairness principles: *Islands Protection Society* v. *The Queen in Right of British Columbia*, [1979] 4 W.W.R. 35 (Alta. S.C. T.D.); *National Anti-Poverty Organization* v. *A-G Canada* (1989) 32 Admin. L.R. 1 (F.C.T.D.).

82. See A. Lucas, "The Impact of the Charter of Rights and Freedoms on Environmental Law" E-1. In Proceedings of the Canadian Institute Seminar on Western Canadian Environmental Law and Practice, Calgary, 31 October—1 November 1988.

83. *Operation Dismantle* v. *The Queen*, [1985] 1 S.C.R. 441.

84. A. Lucas, supra, note 81.
85. In considering the availability of procedural rights in Cabinet appeal proceedings, Muldoon J. stated:
   "Just 8 short years ago in 1980, the jurisprudential world was not quite the same as it is now. Parliament and elected federal and provincial legislators and legislatures have acted decisively and considerably changed the legal and constitutional basis for the lengthy and didactic explanation by Estey J. [in *Inuit Tapirisat of Can.* v. *A-G Canada* [1980] 2 S.C.R. 735, 759-760] as to why the Supreme Court of Canada, in 1980, simply, in black-letter way, followed 'this statutory provision in the context of the pattern of the statute in which it is found'.'
   See *National Anti-Poverty Organization* v. *A-G Canada*, supra, note 80, at 24.
86. P. Elder and W. Ross, "How to Ensure that Development are Environmentally Sustainable," paper presented to Canadian Institute of Resources Law Conference, "The Legal Challenge of Sustainable Development," Ottawa, 10 May 1989 (Proceedings forthcoming from CIRL).
87. Ibid.
88. See A.R. Lucas, "Harmonization of Federal and Provincial Environmental Policies" in J.O. Saunders (ed.) *Managing Natural Resources in a Federal State*, (Calgary: Carswell, 1986) pp. 34-35.
89. Provinces resisted CEPA with the result that the equivalency provisions were added in committee following second reading of the Bill; *Report of the House of Commons Legislative Committee on Bill C-72*, (23 March 1988), and Committee Proceedings, No. 1 (25 November 1987) at 15 ff., and no. 12 (26 January 1988) at 4-16.
90. The *Canadian Wildlife Federation* Case has caused federal officials to reconsider the scope of Federal Environmental Assessment legislation, currently under development, intended to give EARP a clear statutory basis. A federal-provincial dispute appears to be developing. See "Environmental battle looms" *The Calgary Herald*, 15 June 1989, at A-1.
91. Canadian Environmental Protection Act, ss. 35 (emergency orders), 36 (release of toxic substances). All but one province sought exemption from the September 1988 P.C.B. storage order, made under CEPA, which by its own terms provided that provinces can request exemptions if they have legally enforceable requirements with comparable effect. See "All provinces but P.E.I. want P.C.B. rule waiver" *The Globe and Mail*, 14 October 1988 at A1.
92. Under sections 108-110 of CEPA, any two persons resident in Canada who are not less than 18 years of age may apply to the Minister for investigation of an alleged offence under the Act. The minister must then acknowledge,

investigate and within 90 days report to the applicants on the progress of the investigation. If the investigation is discontinued, the minister must report in writing on the information obtained during the investigation and the reasons for its discontinuation.

93. The Board has power to regulate the direct environmental effects of oil and gas, coal and hydro electric projects in the province. See Hunt and Lucas, *Canada Energy Law Service*, vol. 3, Energy Resources Conservation Board Commentary (Toronto: Richard De Boo Ltd.—Continuing Service orig. pub. 1980).

94. A.R. Lucas, Comment on *R. v. Crown Zellerbach Ltd.*, (1989) 23 U.B.C. L. Rev. 355, 370.

95. Mr. Justice Gerald LeDain, who wrote the majority judgement in *Crown Zellerbach*, had himself used this example in his article "Sir Lyman Duff and the Constitution" (1974), 12 Osgoode Hall L.J. 261 at 293.

96. See footnote 64, supra and accompanying text.

97. Though the Supreme Court has suggested that this doctrine may require review: *MacDonald v. Vapor Canada Ltd.* [1977] 2 S.C.R. 134, 171-72 per Laskin C.J.

98. See A.R. Lucas, supra, note 87.

99. See W.E. Rees, "Prosperity, but at what price" *The Globe and Mail*, 9 September 1988 at A7, in which the author quotes from Prime Minister Mulroney's speech to the 1988 Toronto Changing Atmosphere Conference, then points out that less than a month later his government provided over $2 billion in financial aid to a consortium of companies to develop the Hibernia offshore oil field.

NINE

Senate Reform:
Always the Bridesmaid, Never the Bride

Roger Gibbins

Projet maintes fois débattu ces vingt dernières années, la réforme du Sénat est devenue progressivement un quasi-symbole des aspirations politiques des Canadiens de l'Ouest. En réaction contre la présumée prépondérance politique et économique du Québec et de l'Ontario au sein de l'ensemble canadien, les Westerners de toutes tendances se sont ralliés au concept d'un Sénat "triple E" (c-a-d, élu, efficace et à représentation provinciale égale).

Dans ce contexte les radicaux de l'Ouest, résolument hostiles au Québec, voient d'un mauvais oeil la possibilité—même ténue—d'une ratification de l'Accord du lac Meech. Selon eux, un Québec satisfait dans ses revendications constitutionnelles serait aisément enclin à rejeter toute réforme de la Chambre haute qui réduirait, de manière appréciable, sa représentation traditionnelle au Sénat—tel qu'exigé par les provinces de l'Ouest et conformément au principe d'égalité provinciale relatif au "triple E".

De son côté, le gouvernement Getty de l'Alberta tient le pari de la modération; partant, il estime indispensable de souscrire d'abord à l'Accord du lac Meech dans la mesure où la règle de consentement unanime comprise dans l'entente constitutionnelle permettrait éventuellement à l'Alberta de bloquer tout projet de réforme du Sénat qui dérogerait à l'esprit du "triple E".

Enfin le gouvernement albertain a décidé d'aller de l'avant au chapitre du Sénat élu; c'est pourquoi, à l'automne '89, les électeurs de cette province devraient normalement se prononcer à propos d'une liste d'aspirants sénateurs, parmi lesquels le gouvernement fédéral désignerait ultimement le ou les sénateur(s) en titre.

L'auteur conclut son article en souhaitant une réforme du Sénat qui emprunterait, autant que possible, au principe de l'égalité provinciale. A défaut de quoi, Gibbins dit pouvoir s'accommoder simplement d'un Sénat élu. De toute façon, d'ajouter l'auteur, le thème de la réforme du Sénat n'aura de cesse désormais de relancer le débat constitutionnel canadien.

INTRODUCTION

Senate reform has been on Canada's active constitutional agenda from the early 1970s through the current debate over the Meech Lake Accord,[1] and if the Accord is ratified one of its provisions will entrench Senate reform on that agenda for the indefinite future. Yet despite the attention that Senate reform has achieved, despite the number of task forces, legislative committees, organized pressure groups and less-organized scholars who have promoted the principles of Senate reform, reform itself has remained elusive. Indeed, as Franks points out, the Senate has undergone less reform than even the House of Commons, in large part because there has been no agreement on the direction of change.[2] Senate reform has become a staple of Canadian political rhetoric, but not a matter for action. In our long, even prolonged pursuit of constitutional change, Senate reform has been always the bridesmaid but never the bride.

My objective here is *not* to recap the existing models of Senate reform, nor to develop yet another model. I will not extensively review the rationale for Senate reform, a rationale that has remained essentially unchanged over the past decade, nor will I make an impassioned plea for reform.[3] Instead, the present discussion will explore the constitutional and political dynamics of Senate reform, with particular attention being paid to four underlying questions. First, what has been the impact of the Meech Lake Accord on the constitutional and political dynamics of Senate reform? Second, why has Senate reform become such an important issue in western Canada, and particularly in Alberta? Third, what is entailed in the recent initiative by the Alberta government to elect the province's next Senator? And fourth, what impact is the Alberta initiative likely to have on the dynamics of Senate reform as we move into the 1990s? To address these questions, we must begin with the 1984 general election.

THE 1984 ELECTION

If there was any logic to the political world, the 1984 election should have put Senate reform to rest as a political issue. In the first place, the election results dealt a damaging blow, indeed what should have been a crippling blow, to the underlying rationale for Senate reform. Canadians came out of the 1984 election with a national government that was broadly representative of every region of the country. Under Brian Mulroney's leadership, the Progressive Conservatives won 25 of 32 seats in Atlantic Canada, 58 of 75 seats in Quebec, 67 of 95 seats in Ontario, and 61 of 80 seats across the western provinces and northern territories. Gone were the days when entire provinces and almost entire regions were without elected representation on the government side of the House and around the cabinet table. Given, then, that Canadians now had a broadly representative national government, there would seemed to have been little compelling need for institutional reform. Here it is of particular importance to note that western Canadians, who had been all but shut out of the recent national Liberal governments of Pierre Trudeau, and who had become enamoured with Senate reform as a consequence, were at the centre of the new Mulroney government. Alberta, which had not elected a Liberal since 1972, was now represented in the federal cabinet by Harvie Andre, Joe Clark and Dan Mazankowski. In the words of the Toyota commercial, who could ask for anything more?

It should also be noted that the federal Progressive Conservatives had never been very enthusiastic about institutional reform in general, or about Senate reform in particular. In 1978 the Conservatives did release a Senate reform proposal, but this should be seen as an obligatory political response to the nature of the times—it was hard to find Canadians without a Senate reform proposal tucked into their briefcase or purse—rather than as concrete evidence of enthusiasm. Prior to the 1984 election, the Conservatives' message to Canadian voters had been very straightforward; existing parliamentary institutions would work fine if Canadians would only elect the right party—the Progressive Conservative party—and support the right leader. There is no indication that the reform of parliamentary institutions per se caught the imagination of Joe Clark or even the attention of Brian Mulroney. While Mr. Mulroney was certainly alert to the opportunity for, and indeed the necessity of bringing Quebec back into the "constitutional family", he also appeared determined to shift Canadian politics onto a new economic agenda, to move away from the constitutional and institutional politics that had become so characteristic of the Trudeau period. Certainly Quebec's withdrawal from constitutional negotiations following the National Assembly's refusal to endorse the 1982 Constitution Act suggested that, in the short run, there was little political mileage to be gained from wading into the swamp of institutional reform. Nor was there any evidence that Canadians at large would welcome such an excursion. If anything, Canadians appeared to welcome a national government which would give priority to economic management.

For all of these reasons, the 1984 election results should have killed the quest for Senate reform. Yet at another level, the results set up an important test for many of the arguments that had been developed to support institutional reform in general, and Senate reform in particular. In essence, those arguments boiled down to the belief that existing parliamentary institutions were incapable of giving adequate expression to the federal character of Canada, that the combination of an appointed and unequal Senate, a first-past-the-post electoral system, and rigid party discipline in the House of Commons meant that regional interests were denied adequate articulation and defence. Thus the root causes of regional unrest were deemed to be institutional; parties and leaders might well contribute to regional unrest, but Canadians would have to look elsewhere for a cure. However, *what if* Canada had a national government that was truly national, that enjoyed strong support across the country? What if all provinces had powerful, elected spokesmen sitting in the federal cabinet, and Canada had a prime minister committed to national reconciliation? Under these conditions, under the best of conditions rather than under the worst of conditions as Canada had faced during some of the Trudeau governments, would parliamentary institutions be up to the task? In short, could we get by simply by changing parties and leaders, or would more basic institutional reform still be required?[4] The 1984 election set up the conditions under which this question could be addressed.

THE AFTERMATH OF THE 1984 ELECTION

In retrospect, it is surprising how things turned out. Western alienation proved to be much more resilient than one would have expected given the strength of the West within the Mulroney government, and given a generally favourable policy response by that government to western Canadian concerns.[5] Admittedly, the government's decision to award the CF-18 maintenance contract to Canadair in Montreal rather than to Bristol Aerospace in Winnipeg,[6] and Bill C-72's extension of official bilingualism were unpopular. Still, there was every reason to expect that any losses suffered on those fronts would be more than offset by the Western Energy Accord, by generous financial relief for prairie grain farmers, by Ottawa's free trade initiative, and by the 1987 establishment of the Department of Western Economic Diversification, with headquarters in Edmonton and a five-year budget of $1.2 billion. Although the Conservatives' track record in the West was not unblemished, it met *reasonable* expectations for a national government facing the reality of regional trade-offs.

As it turned out, however, the combination of positive policy and strong representation in the governing caucus and cabinet was not enough to contain a resurgence of western alienation. In the unduly harsh but nevertheless widely shared assessment of McCormick and Elton, "it does not seem to have made any difference whether western MPs sat noisily but impotently on the opposition benches or quietly and impotently on the government benches."[7] Nothing, it appeared, or at least nothing the Conservative government was able to deliver, would satisfy large numbers of western Canadians. Thus as Mr. Mulroney neared the end of his first term, the Conservatives were experiencing unexpected difficulties in the West: regional alienation had recovered from the blow dealt by the 1984 election results and a radical new regional party, the Reform Party of Canada, had appeared on the scene, a party which danced to the traditional music of regional discontent and placed Senate reform at the top of its dance card.

Western Canadians appeared to have answered the question posed above in the affirmative; institutional reform was still required despite the efforts of Mazankowski and the Conservative government. Ironically, and somewhat inexplicably, the acquisition of real and effective influence in Ottawa's corridors of power[8] was coupled with a resurgence of western alienation. Thus the latter part of Mr. Mulroney's first term witnessed the re-emergence of institutional critiques as the Reform Party, the Triple E Senate Committee, the Canada West Foundation and provincial parties sounded the clarion call for Senate reform.

The developments in the West were not the only surprise. With the defeat of the Parti Québécois government in 1985, movement was suddenly possible on the constitutional front. Under specified conditions Premier Robert Bourassa's Liberal government was prepared to bring Quebec back to the constitutional table, and thus events were set in motion that were to culminate in the Meech Lake Constitutional Accord, signed by the 11 first ministers in the spring of 1987. Suddenly Mr. Mulroney and his Progressive Conservative government were thoroughly entangled in the politics of constitutional reform, as Mr. Trudeau and his Liberal governments had been before.

MEECH LAKE AND SENATE REFORM

This is not the place to present a general review or assessment of the Meech Lake Accord.[9] Rather, the focus here is on the provisions of the Accord which deal with Senate reform, and on the more general impact of the Accord on the dynamics of Senate reform. Although Senate reform is by no means central to the Meech Lake Accord, the Accord touches upon the issue in a number of ways.

First, the Accord alters, or would alter, the amending formula by bringing the powers of the Senate, the method of selecting Senators, the number of Senators by which a province is entitled to be represented, and the residency qualifications of Senators under Section 41 of the Constitution Act, 1982. If the Meech Lake Accord is ratified, any subsequent changes to the above would require the unanimous consent of Parliament and the ten provincial legislative assemblies. This provision of the Accord has been roundly condemned by proponents of Senate reform who argue, understandably, that the need for unanimous consent will make Senate reform even more difficult to achieve. In practice, however, it is not clear that this change will have any great effect. The 1980 Supreme Court decision on the Bill C-60 reference case strongly implies the need for something close to unanimous provincial consent, and Quebec has argued that Section 38 (3) of the 1982 Constitution Act already provides means by which that province could block Senate reform. Even putting this defence aside, it is unlikely that any federal government would proceed in Parliament with Senate reform until a virtual consensus had been reached on the principles of reform and, more specifically, until *both* Ontario and Quebec were on board.[10] As supporters of Meech Lake also point out, the Accord itself along with prior agreements in 1940, 1951 and 1964 on unemployment insurance and pensions[11] demonstrate that unanimous consent is attainable across a fairly broad constitutional front. So, while this provision of the Accord will not facilitate Senate reform, it may not be the deathblow to reform which many western Canadian opponents of the Accord have claimed.[12]

Second, the Meech Lake Accord amends the 1982 Constitution Act to state that a First Ministers' Constitutional Conference will be held annually, and that such conferences shall include on their agenda "Senate reform, including the role and function of the Senate, its powers, the method of selecting Senators and representation in the Senate." This provision has been widely acknowledged as a concession to Alberta's Premier Don Getty; if the Accord was not going to address Senate reform directly, then the price of Mr. Getty's support was the commitment to discuss Senate reform in future constitutional conferences, and to keep on discussing it year after year until some resolution was found. Of course, the agreement to discuss Senate reform falls well short of reform itself, and it does not dictate the direction that any such reform might take. There is no commitment that future reforms to the Senate will follow the trajectory mapped out by the supporters of the Triple E concept, and no commitment that a reformed Senate will be elected, equal and effective. Nonetheless, the provision for ongoing constitutional negotiations should not be dismissed too lightly as it does ensure that Senate reform remains on the nation's constitutional and hence political agenda, assuming of course that the Meech Lake Accord is ratified. Mr. Getty may not have achieved much, but he did achieve something.

Third, and perhaps most important, the preamble to the Accord states that "until the proposed amendment relating to appointments to the Senate comes into force, any person summoned to fill a vacancy in the Senate shall be chosen from among persons whose names have been submitted by the government of the province to which the vacancy relates and must be acceptable to the Queen's Privy Council for Canada." Taken by itself, this is a substantive albeit interim reform as one of the major criticisms leveled in the past has been that Senators are not only appointed, but are appointed by the federal government without even the need to consult with provincial governments. This procedure, it has been argued, effectively emasculates Senators as regional representatives. Now, with the Meech Lake Accord, the federal government has brought the provinces into the appointment process. While the federal government still makes the appointments, it *shall* make appointments from lists submitted by provincial governments. The Prime Minister can veto but cannot initiate Senate appointments.[13]

There is a certain irony here in that provincial appointment has been steadily losing ground as a reform option. Although many of the "House of Provinces" reform models which appeared in the late 1970s and early 1980s featured provincial appointment, the more recent trend has been towards models featuring the direct popular election of Senators.[14] In the case of Alberta, for example, a 1982 government discussion paper calling for a provincially-appointed Senate has been superseded by the 1985 Report of the Select Special Committee on Upper House Reform, a report calling for a Triple-E Senate.[15] To the extent that the Senate reform issue has been probed by public opinion surveys, virtually no support for provincial appointment has been unearthed. When Canadians are asked, or are forced, to speculate about Senate reform, their preferences in descending order are: an elected Senate, the abolition of the Senate, and the status quo; the reform embedded in the Meech Lake Accord attracts no enthusiasm or support. Somewhat paradoxically, however, and as will be discussed in more detail below, the Accord's appointment provision has been cleverly exploited by the Alberta government as a means by which Senators can be elected even if no further Senate reform is achieved. It is this provision, then, that is likely to keep Senate reform in play as a political and constitutional issue both inside and outside Alberta.

Apart from these three specific provisions, the Meech Lake Accord alters the dynamics of Senate reform in a number of other, albeit somewhat contradictory ways. Ratification of the Accord will bring Quebec back into the constitutional fold and, in so doing, permit ongoing constitutional negotiations. As Jim Horsman, Alberta's Minister of Intergovernmental Affairs, has argued, "the Accord will end the constitutional isolation of Quebec and make no mistake, there will be no senate or any other constitutional reform without Quebec at the table as a full partner in Confederation."[16] In this very important respect, the ratification of the Accord is a necessary precondition for Senate reform to take place. It can be argued, however, that ratification will also reduce if not extinguish Quebec's interest in constitutional change *including Senate Reform*. Bluntly put, it may be very difficult, once Quebec's constitutional aspirations have been met, to convince the Quebec government that Senate reform should proceed. (Given the changes in the amending formula, Quebec's agreement will be essential.) While the Accord's provision calling for an annual constitutional conference was designed to ensure that the Quebec government would not leave the table once the Accord had been ratified,[17] staying at the table does not ensure a sympathetic stance towards Senate reform.

Here it should be noted that the Triple E model of Senate reform emerging from western Canada is inherently inimical to Quebec's interests. After all, the entire rationale of Senate reform is based on the assumption that such reform would entail some real shift in power from the two central Canadian provinces to the eastern and western peripheries. Based on the principle of provincial equality, the Triple E model would require that Quebec's representation in the Senate be reduced from 23 per cent at present to 10 per cent, and indeed even less once representation is provided for the northern territories. However, it is difficult to square the Accord's recognition of Quebec as a distinct society with the principle of equal provincial representation, and it is unlikely that Quebec, after achieving recognition as a distinct society in the Accord, would consent to a reform of parliamentary institutions in which Quebec's status and power would be identical to smaller and less-distinct Canadian provinces. Although Quebec might be content with some form of double senatorial majority whereby "no legislative action could be taken derogating from the province's linguistic, cultural, or other rights without the assent of a majority of Quebec Senators ...,"[18] such a provision would not be an easy sell in the West. Nor, for that matter, would it be an easy sell in Quebec's National Assembly, which would be asked to entrust the defence of Quebec's interests to elected Senators beyond the Assembly's control. A more likely prognosis is that a truly effective Senate in which Quebec's power would equal that of Prince Edward Island or Manitoba is not in the Meech Lake cards.

The dynamics of Senate reform have also been altered in that the federal government has adopted the same procedural approach to Senate reform as was used to achieve the Meech Lake Accord. In the latter case, Ottawa let the Quebec government act as the pointman; Quebec produced its five conditions, and then proceeded to sell the five in a series of bilateral meetings with other provincial governments, and in the multilateral forum provided by the 1986 Premiers' Conference in Edmonton. In a like manner, Ottawa has passed the Senate reform ball back to the Alberta government and its quarterback, Premier Don Getty. The Alberta government in turn has established a Senate Reform Task Force[19] which has gone on the road selling Senate reform to other governments and, where possible, to the media and public. Presumably, if the Alberta government is able to cobble together an intergovernmental consensus, then and only then will the federal government come on board. This abdication of federal leadership, however, does not augur well for the success of any Senate reform initiative. Certainly it places a very heavy load on Mr. Getty's shoulders. It is passing strange, and indeed alarming, to have the federal government adopt a bystander's roll with respect to the reform of the country's central institutions.

MEECH LAKE, SENATE REFORM AND THE CANADIAN WEST

The western Canadian debate over the merits and demerits of the Meech Lake Accord was slow to get underway. The Accord, with little legislative debate and virtually no public debate was quickly ratified by Alberta, British Columbia and Saskatchewan. Then the free trade debate in the 1988 federal election campaign effectively pushed Meech Lake off the political agenda. This debate, incidentally, was especially problematic for the Reform party which opposed the Accord and strongly advocated Senate reform, but which also supported free trade. The party became trapped by a one-issue federal campaign focused on free trade; a party committed to fundamental political and institutional reform found itself agreeing with the government of the day on the most important issue of the day. Furthermore, the free trade issue so dominated the campaign that the Reform party was unable to provoke much debate on its own agenda, including Senate reform and opposition to the Accord. However, after the free trade issue had been laid to rest, the Reform party was able to bring its own agenda items to the fore. Not coincidentally, both Meech Lake and Senate reform climbed back up the western Canadian political agenda, locked arm in arm. When the Meech Lake ratification process ground to a halt in Manitoba, the stage was set for a wide-ranging regional debate.

Two sides to this debate can be readily identified. The first side argues that Meech Lake will kill the chance for Senate reform, that both the need for unanimous consent and Quebec's indifference to further constitutional reform once its aspirations have been met will raise insurmountable barriers to Senate reform. Therefore, the argument goes, Meech Lake must be blocked if Senate reform is to be saved. Unfortunately, simply killing Meech Lake would also kill any immediate prospects for Senate reform, and thus the more pragmatic argument is that western Canadians should insist upon a parallel accord that would bring about Senate reform in conjunction with the ratification of Meech Lake. (At the time of writing, the proposal for a parallel Accord has not evoked any support from the federal or Quebec governments.) Here it should be noted, of course, that the Meech Lake Accord is also opposed on other grounds in the West, and indeed is supported on other grounds quite removed from the issue of Senate reform. Yet the point to be stressed is that the supporters of Senate reform see such reform as being tightly linked to the fate of the Accord; they argue either that passage of the Accord will kill reform, or that Senate reform can only be achieved if it can be presented as a precondition for the Accord's ratification. More rarely one encounters the argument that Quebec's stake in Meech Lake finally gives the West the leverage it needs to achieve Senate reform. In the words of Link Byfield, Publisher of *Alberta Report*, "if Ottawa and Quebec are so fearfully anxious to get Meech Lake approved, they can be forced to reform the Senate first."[20]

Conversely, the point is made that if the Accord is ratified without prior or at least concurrent agreement on Senate reform, then western Canadians will have no cards left to play in future rounds of constitutional negotiations. As Peter McCormick and David Elton argue:

> if the West meekly acquiesces now, on the grounds that it is selfish and unCanadian to insist on some linkage of issues, it will have nothing to bargain with, nothing to trade off, when discussions on the western agenda finally begin. (The record also suggests that it will be a long time indeed before the issues will be addressed; the meek may inherit the earth, but they won't accomplish much in the way of amendments to the Canadian Constitution.) Only an eccentric labour union negotiator would advise the union to agree to everything management suggested and just hope they felt generous afterward, but this is precisely the behaviour that seems to be expected of western Canadians.[21]

The other side of the debate is most clearly associated with the Alberta government. Here the argument is that the Accord has been good for the West not only because it makes Senate reform possible, by bringing Quebec back to the table, but also because it facilitates Senate reform by entrenching the issue on the nation's constitutional agenda. Put somewhat differently, the Alberta government defends its support of Meech Lake, in the face of growing and increasingly vociferous opposition,[22] by arguing that the Accord promotes Senate reform. (Given that Alberta has already ratified the Accord, the provincial government cannot now adopt the strategy of demanding reform per se as a precondition for supporting the Accord.) In a somewhat different argument, the Alberta government also makes the point that the unanimous consent provisions of the Accord will enable Alberta to block Senate reform which is not to its liking, reform that departs too radically from the Triple E model. As Horsman puts it:

> It is wrong to impose Senate reform on any partner of confederation without their consent. And Alberta, for one, will not accept a senate with slight adjustments or mere tinkering in the guise of reform! We cannot—and will not—have undesirable or cosmetic changes rammed down our throats.[23]

Given that the Alberta government is spearheading the drive for Senate reform, and given that the federal government has abandoned the field, it is not clear that any other government has an alternative model that they would try to ram down anyone's throat, including Alberta's.

The problem, however, is that a commitment to talk is not a commitment to reform, and thus the Alberta government is having some difficulty convincing Albertans that merely having Senate reform on the constitutional agenda justifies support for Meech Lake. Something more is needed, and something more has been found in the Accord's provision stating that future appointments to the Senate shall be made from lists submitted by the provinces. It is this provision which enables the Alberta government to proceed unilaterally with Senate reform. The Alberta government has proposed that it will turn to the people of Alberta in drawing up its list, that Albertans will vote not to elect their next Senator, but to decide upon the composition of the list that the Alberta government will then submit to Ottawa.

Initially, the federal government reacted with considerable reservation to the Alberta initiative, stating that it would have the final choice regardless and that Alberta would have to submit a list of five names, and not simply the name of the one individual topping the polls. As the Prime Minister observed, a list with only one name would be "incomplete and therefore unacceptable."[24] Ottawa's opposition, however, merely strengthened the popularity of the initiative in Alberta; if the federal government was opposed to the idea, then even confirmed sceptics were forced to admit that the Alberta initiative must have some merit. More importantly, Ottawa's opposition cannot be sustained. There is nothing in the Accord which states that a list must have five names, or any set number. Moreover, even if the Alberta government was required to submit five names, it could simply pass along the front page of the *Calgary Herald* or the *Edmonton Journal*, listing the election results. It would take a great deal of courage on the part of the federal government to appoint an individual who had finished second, third, fourth or fifth, and individuals who had not even been candidates could not be appointed for the Accord states that the Senators *shall* be appointed from provincial government lists. Here it should also be noted that this is not a hypothetical exercise; there is an Alberta opening in the Senate now, and the "election" is likely to be held by November 1989. A second Alberta Senator is due to retire in less than two years.

The details of the Alberta initiative first appeared in the draft of Alberta's *Senatorial Selection Act, 1989*, tabled shortly before Albertans went to the polls in March. Although Bill 1 died when the legislature was prorogued for the election, it was re-introduced when the legislature reconvened, and was passed in August. The Act is a carefully crafted document that tries to avoid any constitutional challenge, even to the extent of referring to the democratic *selection* rather than to the *election* of Senators. The Act states that "persons declared elected under this Act shall have their names submitted by the Government of Alberta to the Queen's Privy Council as persons who may be summoned to the Senate of Canada for the purpose of filling vacancies relating to Alberta." It also contains the following provisions:

- although senatorial elections will generally be held in conjunction with provincial elections, they may also be held at the same time as municipal elections or provincial by-elections, or they may be held on their own;

- elections will be held on a province-wide basis;
- voters will have one vote per senatorial vacancy; candidates will be elected on a first-past-the-post, plurality system, and only the name/s of the winning candidate will be submitted to the federal cabinet;
- candidates cannot be members of the House of Commons or the Alberta Legislative Assembly;
- party labels will appear on the ballot, although candidates can also run as independents; in either case, 1500 electors must sign the candidate's nomination papers and a $4,000 deposit must be posted;
- campaign contributions from federal parties will not permitted.

It should be noted that the Alberta legislation is constrained by the fact that the actual appointment to the Senate is made by the federal government. Therefore Alberta candidates must conform to the constitutional provisions that Senators be Canadian citizens, be at least 30 years old, hold $4,000 in real property, and be a resident in the province for which they are appointed. Senators chosen under the Senatorial Selection Act would also have the right to serve until reaching the mandatory retirement age of 75, although considerable moral suasion would be exercised to encourage Senators to seek re-election or, more properly, re-selection.

Alberta's initiative, which owes its genesis to the prior spadework of the Canada West Foundation and the Canadian Committee for a Triple E Senate, draws upon a good deal of regional support for Senate reform. The four western premiers endorsed the Triple E concept at a 1986 meeting in Parksville, British Columbia, and in Manitoba, where the Meech Lake debate is the most intense, all of the contending parties have made Senate reform a necessary albeit not sufficient condition for support of the Accord. Senate reform has also picked up considerable support through the Meech Lake debate outside the West; both New Brunswick Premier Frank McKenna and Newfoundland Premier Clyde Wells have stated that the Accord should not be ratified until Senate reform can be assured.

It is in the West, however, and particularly in Alberta, that the quest for Senate reform finds its greatest political resonance. Senate reform has come to rival the role played by the Crow rate in the more distant past, and by the National Energy Program in the more recent past; it is the new regional issue *and symbol* which anchors political discourse and shapes the partisan contours of political life. Apart from the common assertion that the NEP would never have happened had a Triple E Senate been in place, discussions about Senate reform are not usually linked to specific policy objectives.[25] There has been, for example, very little discussion of how the Conservatives' free trade initiative might have fared in a Triple E Senate, or how such a Senate might promote stronger export markets or economic diversification. Rather, a reformed Senate is seen as an essential symbolic step in recognizing the West's contributions to and aspirations within Confederation. More specifically, if the intent of the Meech Lake Accord is to make Canada whole again by bringing in Quebec, then the argument is made that Senate reform should be pursued for the same reason with respect to the West, and with the same vigour and enthusiasm. In this sense the federal government's passive involvement in Senate reform, its decision to let Alberta carry the ball alone, is a cause of some distress.

It is also in the West that the Senate reform issue is likely to have the greatest impact on the next federal election campaign. The Reform party has nailed its colours to the mast of Senate reform, and has successfully integrated the Senate reform issue into both a broader critique of Canadian political life and a more focused critique of the Meech Lake Accord. Note, for example, the maiden House of Commons speech by Deborah Gray, MP for Beaver River and the first elected member of the Reform party:

> Our people are not unsympathetic to constitutional amendments to make Quebec more at home in confederation, but they want concurrent constitutional amendments; namely, meaningful Senate reform to make the West feel at home in confederation. In the past generation, Mr. Speaker, it is the West that has experienced the National Energy Program and the CF-18 decision, not Quebec. It is the West's grievances which the government should be addressing with at least as much fervour as it brings to Quebec's demands.[26]

The challenge for the traditional parties will be to respond to the Reform party's stance on Senate reform without alienating potential support in Ontario or Quebec, a strategic dilemma that does not confront the regionally-based Reform party. For all three parties, Senate reform promises to be a troublesome issue. Both Brian Mulroney and Joe Clark have positioned the Progressive Conservatives in opposition to Alberta's Reform initiative; and if the Meech Lake Accord has not been ratified by the next federal election, the influential Quebec wing of the party will make it next to impossible for Conservatives to swing behind Senate reform. For the NDP, Senate reform has always posed a problem; on traditional and ideological grounds New Democrats favour abolition rather than reform, but western Canadian New Democrats have recently been much more supportive of the reform option. It is the Liberals, however, who will first confront the Senate reform issue when they hold their June 1990 leadership convention in Calgary. At that time Senate reform, the climax of the Meech Lake debate, the potential for a Liberal resurgence in the West, and the need for the party to recapture lost ground in Quebec should create a fascinating political brew.

IMPACT OF THE ALBERTA INITIATIVE

The Alberta government hopes to accomplish two objectives with the Senatorial Selection Act. First, the Act should provide important political support for the provincial government's continued endorsement of the Meech Lake Accord; the Act demonstrates that Alberta, and by extension the West, achieved something of tangible value from the Accord. Second and undoubtedly more importantly, the Act enables the Alberta government to move Senate reform forward even if further constitutional change is not forthcoming in the near future. The Act will, in effect, keep Senate reform in play. However, the impact of the Act will depend on the extent to which the Alberta initiative is followed by other provinces, for Alberta's action alone will not yield a reformed Senate. In addressing the impact of Alberta's initiative on the other provinces, it is useful to look at each of the Triple Es in turn.

There is no question that the Alberta initiative constitutes a bold and significant step towards an elected Senate. The question to be asked, however, is whether the Alberta Act will create such an important democratic precedent that the other provinces will be forced, willy-nilly, to follow suit. Within the Alberta Senate reform movement, there is considerable optimism that this snowball effect will occur. Repeated reference is made to the American experience where, after Oregon introduced Senate elections in 1904, the other American states quickly followed suit and supported the passage of the Seventeenth Amendment in 1913. (It should be noted that Americans already had a Double-E Senate— equal and effective—and thus had only to reach agreement on the third and least contentious E.) Yet, while Alberta's *Senatorial Selection Act* creates an important precedent that other provincial governments will be forced to grapple with, there are a number of reasons to expect that they will exercise considerable caution in leaping aboard the Alberta bandwagon.

First, much will depend on the results of the upcoming Alberta Senate election. If the Progressive Conservative candidate loses that election, if Mr. Getty's government finds itself having to cope with an elected Reform or Liberal Senator claiming to speak for the province at large, then there is little doubt that other provincial governments will question the wisdom of electing Senators. Certainly Premiers Vander Zalm and Devine would be leery about providing a senatorial stage for the New Democrats, just as Premier Filmon would be justifiably uneasy about an elected Liberal Senator from Manitoba. It should be stressed, moreover, that such an elected Conservative Senator could challenge Mr. Getty's role as Alberta's spokesman in national affairs. This simply underscores the more general threat that Senate reform poses for provincial premiers, and indeed for MPs. Power shared is power diminished.

Here it should also be noted that Mr. Getty's influence as the national pointman for Senate reform has been damaged by recent electoral setbacks, both personal and partisan. A Conservative loss in the upcoming Senate election would further damage Mr. Getty's credibility, and thus the cause of Senate reform. Second, the interim appointment provision of the Accord gives provincial governments virtual control over the most lucrative patronage plums that Canada has to offer, and there is no reason to expect that provincial governments will be eager to relinquish this control to a fickle electorate, although admittedly Mr. Mulroney relinquished his control to equally fickle premiers. Third, there are important principled grounds for resisting the Alberta initiative. It is unlikely, for example, that either the Quebec government or National Assembly would welcome another tier of elected federal politicians claiming to speak for Quebec, politicians who could well undercut the ability of the Quebec government to speak for Quebec in national affairs. For the same reasons that the Alberta Government opposed an elected Senate in the past,[27] Quebec may well be expected to oppose an elected Senate in the future. More generally, provincial premiers have little to gain in surrendering their high-profile role as regional spokesmen to elected Senators. While all of these reasons do not mean that the other provinces will vigorously resist the Alberta bandwagon, greater democracy being difficult to resist at the best of times, they do suggest that rapid endorsement of the Alberta initiative is unlikely.

The Alberta initiative does not and cannot address the powers of the Senate, and thus the extent to which the Senate will be an "effective" chamber of regional representation. It should be noted, however, that the current "ineffective" Senate has virtually unrestricted formal powers, albeit powers that appointed Senators have found difficult to deploy with any legitimacy. Apart from the Senate's inability to initiate money bills or to block constitutional amendments for more than 180 days, and apart from the fact that only the House is a confidence chamber, the Senate's formal powers are equivalent to those of the House. Potentially, the Alberta initiative might begin to unleash those formal powers by strengthening the democratic legitimacy of the Senate. Here it should also be noted that the unanimous consent provision of the Accord would enable Alberta to block any reduction in the Senate's powers. Alberta, then, may be able to trade support for a modest reduction in those powers, a reduction that the federal government would certainly support, for constitutional movement on an elected and equal Senate.

Finally there is the question of the impact of Alberta's initiative on the quest for a Senate based on equal provincial representation. Here the point to stress is that the Alberta initiative per se creates no movement with respect to equal provincial representation; an equal Senate can only be attained with the unanimous support of all ten provinces and the federal Parliament. While the unanimity provision of the Meech Lake Accord may recognize the principle of provincial equality with respect to changes to federal institutions, and while this recognition *might* be extended in discussions of Senate reform,[28] the Alberta initiative provides no additional momentum. This in turn raises the question as to whether Alberta and the West would be better off if Canada moved towards an elected Senate with the current distribution of Senate seats. Would Alberta be well served, for example, by six elected Senators facing 24 elected Senators from Ontario? Here it should be noted that at the present time both Alberta and the western Canadian region have fewer Senators than they would be entitled to on population grounds alone. This reality simply underscores the centrality of provincial equality, or at least some rough approximation of that principle, for western Canadian models of Senate reform. An elected Senate alone would be a mixed blessing at best for the West.

Thus the Alberta initiative takes us a step closer to only one of the three Triple Es. As a consequence, it might promote a mishmash of Senate reform—significant movement towards an elected Senate coupled with deadlock on the equality principle and disagreement on the powers of the Senate. At the same time, however, the Alberta initiative does keep Senate reform in play. If the Meech Lake Accord is ratified, its appointment provision, coupled with the Alberta Senatorial Selection Act, will keep the door to Senate reform open. Even if the Accord is not ratified, it seems unlikely that Ottawa will be able to revert to a system of exclusive federal appointment. Alberta, then, has put a small wedge in the door that cannot be easily removed. While the door is not open enough to admit the entire Tripe E model of Senate reform, it is open enough to encourage ongoing public and constitutional debate. Senate reform is no closer to being the bride, but its stranglehold on the role of bridesmaid seems secure.

Notes

1. For some of the earlier reform proposals, see the *Report of the Special Joint Committee of the Senate and the House of Commons on the Constitution of Canada*, Ottawa, 1972; "Reform of the Canadian Senate", British Columbia's Constitutional Proposals, 1978; *A Future Together: Observations and Recommendations*, The Task Force on National Unity, Ottawa, 1979; *Regional Representation: The Canadian Partnership*, A Task Force Report Prepared by Peter McCormick, Ernest C. Manning and Gordon Gibson, Canada West Foundation, Calgary, 1981; and *Senate Reform*, Report of the Special Joint Committee of the Senate and of the House of Commons, Ottawa, January 1984.

2. C.E.S. Franks, "The Canadian Senate in an Age of Reform", *Queen's Quarterly*, vol. 95, no. 3, Autumn 1988, p. 672.

3. For an article that neatly accomplishes both tasks, see Howard McConnell, "The Case for a "Triple E" Senate" *Queen's Quarterly*, vol. 95, no. 3, Autumn 1988, pp. 683-698.

4. For a useful discussion of "Good Man/Bad Man" explanations of western discontent, see Peter McCormick and David Elton, "The Western Economy and Canadian Unity," *Western Perspectives* (Calgary: The Canada West Foundation, March 1987) p. 6.

5. For empirical evidence, see McCormick and Elton, "The Western Economy."

6. McConnell, "The Case for a "Triple E" Senate," p. 690.

7. McCormick and Elton, "The Western Economy," p. 13.

8. Charlotte Gray, "How the West Won" *Saturday Night*, June 1989, pp. 15-17.

9. For general discussions of the Accord, see: Roger Gibbins, (ed.), *Meech Lake and Canada: Perspectives from the West* (Edmonton: Academic Printing and Publishing, 1988); Donald Johnston, (ed.), *With a Bang, Not a Whimper: Pierre Trudeau Speaks Out* (Toronto: Stoddart, 1988); K. E. Swinton and C. J. Rogerson, (eds.), *Competing Constitutional Visions: The Meech Lake Accord* (Toronto: Carswell, 1988). See also a special edition of *Canadian Public Policy* on the Meech Lake Accord, published in September 1988.

10. J. Peter Meekison, "Meech Lake and the Future of Senate Reform", in K. E. Swinton and C. J. Rogerson, *Competing Constitutional Visions: The Meech Lake Accord* (Toronto: Carswell, 1988), p. 117.

11. Ibid.

12. For more optimistic assessments, see David Elton, "The Enigma of Meech Lake for Senate Reform," and Peter McCormick, "Senate Reform: Forward Step or Dead End?", in Gibbins, *Meech Lake and Canada*, pp. 23-32 and 33-36.

13. Peter Dobell, "The Senate: New-Found Levers of Power?" *Parliamentary Government*, vol. 8, no. 2, p. 16.

14. Franks, "The Canadian Senate", pp. 677-8.

15. See *A Provincially-Appointed Senate: A New Federalism for Canada* (Edmonton: Government of Alberta, 1982); *Strengthening Canada: Reform of Canada's Senate*, Report of the Alberta Select Special Committee on Senate Reform (Edmonton: Plains Publishing, 1985).

16. Hon. Jim Horsman, "Senate Reform and Meech Lake" *Canadian Parliamentary Review*, vol. 12, no. 1, Spring 1989, p. 7.

17. Meekison, "Meech Lake and the Future of Senate Reform", p. 116.

18. McConnell, "The Case for a "Triple E" Senate," p. 695.

19. The Task Force is headed by Jim Horsman, Minister of Intergovernmental Affairs, and includes MLA Stan Schumacher, Bert Brown, chairman of the Canadian Committee for a Triple E Senate, an alternating MLA, and Peter Meekison, Academic Vice-President of the University of Alberta.

20. *Alberta Report*, 23 January 1989, p. 4.

21. McCormick and Elton, "The Western Economy", pp. 5-6.

22. An Environics poll conducted between 12 March and 25 March 1989, showed that there was less support for the Meech Lake Accord in the West than elsewhere in the country. Nationally, 29 per cent of the respondents favoured the Accord while 34 per cent opposed it (36 per cent were undecided). The proportion supporting the Accord ranged from 43 per cent in Quebec to 30 per cent in Atlantic Canada, 24 per cent in Ontario, and only 22 per cent in the West, *Globe and Mail*, 1 April 1989, p. A3.

23. Horsman, "Senate Reform", p. 9.

24. *Alberta Report*, 20 February 1989, p. 10.

25. For an exception, see McCormick and Elton, "The Western Economy."

26. Cited in the *Alberta Report*, 1 May 1989, p. 12.

27. See *A Provincially-Appointed Senate: A New Federalism for Canada*, Government of Alberta, August 1982.

28. Horsman, "Senate Reform and Meech Lake", p. 7.

TEN

Canadian Federalism and Trade Policy: The Uruguay Round Agenda

Douglas M. Brown

Jusqu'à quel point les négociations commerciales et multilatérales du GATT se refléteront-elles sur la dynamique interne du Canada, aux plans politique et économique, à l'issue de l'actuel Uruguay Round? Partant de cette réflexion maîtresse, l'auteur examine d'abord un à un les dossiers, prioritaires pour le Canada, du commerce international traités dans le cadre de l'organisme. Il s'agit en l'occurrence de l'accès aux marchés publics, des textiles et des vêtements, de l'agriculture, des subventions et, nouveaux sujets à l'étude, des services et de l'investissement.

Les questions commerciales et multilatérales discutées au GATT ne suscitent pas, et de loin, un engouement auprès de l'opinion publique canadienne, encore moins donnent-elles lieu à une effervescence idéologique comme ce fut le cas précédemment lors des négociations canado-américaines sur le libre-échange.

Par ricochet, cette situation laisse plus ou moins dans l'ombre certains problèmes régionaux canadiens tel, notamment, le contentieux agricole entre les provinces de l'Ouest et celles de l'Est, conditionné en bonne partie par la conjoncture internationale. De fait l'Ouest réclame à cor et à cri la libéralisation commerciale des grains tandis qu'à l'opposé, les provinces de l'Est récusent toutes réformes éventuelles qui porteraient atteinte à l'intégrité des offices de commercialisation des produits de la ferme.

Dans un troisième temps, Brown soulève l'épineux problème des chevauchements juridictionnels au Canada entre le fédéral et les provinces au regard du commerce international. Déjà, il est manifeste que les juridictions provinciales en matière d'agriculture, subventions et services—entre autres domaines—permettront de plus en plus aux provinces d'avoir prise sur des secteurs stratégiques touchant leur économie régionale. Cependant le problème relatif aux responsabilités commerciales et internationales des provinces, à l'intérieur des limites de leurs juridictions, reste toujours entier mais il importe qu'il soit abordé incessamment.

En conclusion, l'auteur estime que le rôle accru des provinces au sein de l'économie internationale s'incrit à contre-courant de la tendance mondiale actuelle conviant plutôt à une plus grande discipline collective dans l'intervention gouvernementale.

INTRODUCTION

With the great free trade debate of 1988 behind us, the intense public attention on trade policy has abated. However, trade issues may gather attention again as the "Uruguay Round" of multilateral trade negotiations is now, finally down to a hard bargaining stage. By September 1989, three years will have elapsed since the sweeping declaration at Punta Del Este in Uruguay launched a new round of negotiations under the auspices of the General Agreement on Tariffs and Trade (GATT). The final push to the end of the Round scheduled for late 1990 has now begun. The success or failure of the Uruguay Round will have profound effects for the international trading system in which Canada has a vital stake.

As the globalization of the Canadian economy increases, the trade regime takes on greater importance for our domestic economy. Canada's trade policy must, however, reflect the domestic considerations of a federal constitution and political culture, and a strongly regionalized economy with a long tradition of competing trade interests. Regional conflict and federal-provincial politics may not generate the same degree of public interest and heat in the Uruguay Round as they did in the bilateral negotiations with the United States. Nonetheless, the outcome of the Round will be important to Canada, and there are a number of sensitive trade policy issues which Canada must face.

This paper reviews the negotiating agenda of the Uruguay Round from the perspective of the unique domestic politics imposed by Canada's federal system. The intent is first, to summarize the trade negotiation agenda in terms of its overall impact on Canada's general interests and on the total dynamics of the success or failure of the world trading system and second, to review these issues from the perspective of Canada's internal regional political economy. Third, the intent is to review federal-provincial relations in light of the jurisdictional responsibility for Uruguay Round agenda items. The focus there will be on consultation with provinces on Canada's negotiating position and on the still unresolved problems of reaching agreement on trade policy matters where the provinces are involved.

THE URUGUAY ROUND AGENDA

The Uruguay Round is now widely perceived as the last chance for the ailing GATT. The forty-year old system has fallen into disrepute in many circles as incapable of handling the many stresses upon it, in particular the proliferation of trading agreements and arrangements which have grown outside its disciplines. The grain subsidy war, the growing use of voluntary export restraint agreements and the increased recourse to contingency protection through safeguards, countervail and anti-dumping measures, have all served to reduce dramatically the effect of the trade liberalization achieved in previous rounds of multilateral trade negotiations. Countries which led in the creation of the multilateral system in the 1940s are now viewed as leading the trend to a new era of protectionism. Nowhere is this more true than in the United States where trade legislation in the past decade has provided the means for the world's largest economy to dictate unilateral terms for solving its trade problems.

This is not the place to review the complex developments that led to the significant trade imbalances of the late 1970s and the 1980s, fueling the new protectionism.[1] Suffice it to say that the most active parties of the GATT have been attempting since 1982 to re-start the trade liberalization momentum by launching a new round of multilateral trade negotiations. Partly because progress in addressing the growing number of trade problems at the multilateral level was slow if not altogether stalled in the mid-1980s, Canada sought out bilateral trade liberalization with the United States. Canada's interests in these negotiations were mainly to get inside the raging U.S. protectionism. For its part, the United States sought to pursue through the bilateral route what it could not yet achieve through the multilateral route, that is, a kick-start to renewed liberalization to forestall the need for even worse protectionism at home and abroad.[2]

Finally, however, a new multilateral attempt to restore the international trading system began in September, 1986.[3] The Ministerial Declaration on the Uruguay Round breaks new ground in a number of areas. As a whole, it reflects the fact that the negotiations involve a much broader club than the earlier Rounds, with a much more varied set of actors, especially from among the developing countries. Issues which set apart the traditional protagonists of the United States, EC, and Japan can be matched with equally important issues which separate the developed countries with developing countries. The role of the developing countries in the "pre-negotiation" of the Punta del Este meetings demonstrates the increasing role and importance attached by them to the international trading system and an increased determination that the system act not only in the interests of the most developed economies.[4]

The ambitious scope of the negotiations is unprecedented. The negotiations encompass the more traditional issues of market access for the trade of goods, including a major attempt to discipline trade distortions in agriculture. They also address for the first time trade in services and trade-related matters involving intellectual property and investment. Equally ambitious are the attempts to improve on trade laws or contingency protection measures including safeguards, subsidies and countervailing measures. The negotiations are also a significant attempt to give more life and clout to the institutions of the GATT to deal with trade disputes, to monitor trade relations, and to generally improve the linkages between the international trading regime and other international economic organizations.

Finally, the agenda demonstrates that the interdependent world economy has gone well beyond trade in goods.[5] Merchandise trade is increasingly tied to trade in services and to investment. The globalization of financial markets and the development of a global information society makes possible, if not inevitable, conditions whereby labour, technology, market size, and public policy environment are continuously compared in the race for competitive advantage. The Uruguay Round is an attempt to ensure that this competitive process reaps its potential for increased international welfare.

A failure of the Round would be critical to all the players in the trading world, although arguably more so for those smaller trading partners which do not have the ability to manage trade through unilateral measures. As Canada's Minister for International Trade, John Crosbie is fond of saying , "The law of the jungle is all right if you're the King of the Beasts, but if you're not King of the Beasts you don't want the law of the jungle." Despite our more secure relationship with the United States through the FTA, our position as a small open economy makes it in our interests to have a successful outcome to the Uruguay Round. This is true not only for our non-North American trade, but also within our bilateral trading relationship, where many unresolved issues are on the multilateral agenda.

The Uruguay Round, as launched at Punta del Este in September 1986 and as further defined by the establishment of trade negotiations modalities agreed upon in January 1987, comprises 16 separate issues and negotiating fora. In addition to an initial "standstill and rollback" agreement on the imposition of new protectionist measures, the parties to the GATT agreed on a set of negotiations as shown in Figure 10.1.

In practically all of these negotiating issues there is an element of domestic politics which affect the Canadian position, and in many of them there is a strong element of regional politics and provincial jurisdiction. The intent here is not to explore in detail the Uruguay Round agenda.[6] Rather, in this and succeeding sections of this paper, certain issues have been highlighted which are most likely to indicate the federal-provincial and regional dimensions of Canadian trade policy. These issues are: (1) market access, (2) textiles and clothing, (3) agriculture, (4) subsidies, and (5) the new issues of services and investment.[7] Before exploring at length the regional political economy of these issues and federal-provincial relations over trade policy, it is important to review briefly these five issues in terms of their overall significance to the Round and to Canada's general interests.

Figure 10.1
Uruguay Round of Multilateral Trade Negotiations

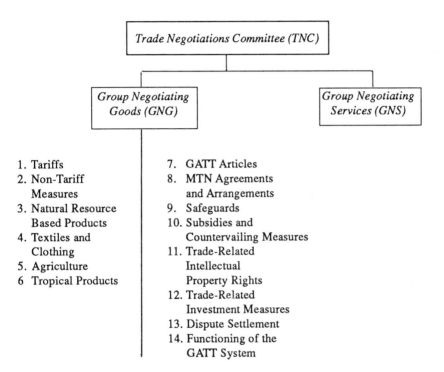

MARKET ACCESS

There are five different negotiating groups that fall under the general category of market access in goods: tariffs, non-tariff measures, natural resource-based products, textiles and clothing, and tropical products. (For our purposes we divide the issues into market access for Canadian exports and treat separately the issue of textiles and clothing, given its overwhelming import sensitivities.)

The *tariff* negotiations will be less prominent in this Round than in previous negotiations, largely because they are not really a priority for the big three industrialized parties, the United States, Japan and the European Community. Nonetheless they are important to a number of countries, including Canada, who have banded together in the "de la Paix" group to push for substantial tariff reductions. The group has succeeded, at least so far, in having this objective recognized in the negotiating instructions for the remainder of the Round, but there is as yet no commitment to a "formula" approach that would favour smaller parties. The elimination of tariff barriers, especially tariff escalation for finished products as compared with their semi-processed inputs, is a major priority for Canadian resource-based manufacturing.

Non-tariff measures cover a broad range of quantitative restrictions, import restrictions such as licensing and other government measures including procurement and technical standards. While the negotiating instructions are rather vague, this is another area where progress is important to Canada and where lack of progress could stymie substantial movement on tariffs. It is worth noting that one objective is to have non-tariff measures transformed to tariffs in cases where the elimination of such measures is not possible.

The group negotiating market access in *natural resource-based products* is looking primarily at extending the general liberalization of this and previous rounds to forest and fishery products and non-ferrous metals. At least this is the Canadian objective. In some areas, such as fish, Canada may find itself isolated in seeking significant liberalization. Canada's objectives will be met in part by the extent to which the negotiations proceed as if there were no distinctions made between resource and other goods in trade.

TEXTILES AND CLOTHING

Textiles and clothing is one of the "make or break" issues for the developing countries. Their chief objective is to bring the managed trade of the Multi-Fibre Agreement (MFA) and its system of voluntary export restraint arrangements into the discipline of the GATT. At the December 1988 GATT Ministerial meeting in Montreal, the developing countries held back from general agreement on the overall negotiating instructions pending agreement on this item. While the developing countries did not succeed in getting a freeze on measures under the MFA, they did get a commitment to negotiate the terms of its replacement with a new set of rules under a strengthened GATT when the MFA expires in 1991. Canada, as one of the import-sensitive parties to the MFA, may seek to continue to shelter its textiles and clothing industries, in particular the garment sector. However, the developing countries could block the success of the entire Round if substantial liberalization is not achieved in this area. Some of the debate on this issue may arise in the review of GATT rules governing safeguard measures, but the heart of the matter is the attempt to "tame" the MFA. Canada will not be alone among industrialized countries in having acute import sensitivities in this area.

AGRICULTURE

Reform of agricultural trade rules is perhaps the single most difficult issue for the vast majority of participants in the Uruguay Round. Canada is not an exception. A subsidy war in grain and other agricultural commodities led by the United States and the EC has completely disrupted export markets. In the past three years, the Government of Canada has had to increase its fiscal deficit to finance a set of special deficiency payments, mainly to grain farmers, to cover the losses sustained in the dropping prices for export commodities.[8] This grain subsidy war is a symptom of a larger problem of pervasive agricultural protectionism, where food surpluses created by government support programs have completely distorted world trade in practically all commodities.[9]

Canada's interests in these negotiations have been effectively served to date by its active involvement in the "Cairns" group of agricultural exporters, which has been aggressively pursuing a multilateral commitment to a more liberalized trade. The group has been particularly effective in getting the European Community and the United States to the bargaining table. This objective appeared to be beyond their grasp in December 1988, when the EC continued to balk at the firm U.S. position of the total elimination of all trade distorting agricultural subsidies. By April 1989, however, the GATT Trade Negotiations Committee was able to report that the parties would begin negotiations aimed at "substantial progressive reductions" of trade restrictive practices including measures that control imports, subsidies, and export assistance. They further agreed to begin negotiations towards a new set of GATT rules covering agriculture applicable to all parties, to freeze agricultural support at current levels, and to undertake a roll-back of support by 1991.

As important as the liberalization of agriculture is for Canada, the Round will not be without its costs. There are significant import sensitive agricultural sectors that will seek to limit the impact of the negotiations on their activities. Canada's system of supply management for commodities such as dairy, eggs, and poultry is maintained by import quotas which have long been labelled as protectionist by our trading partners. The Government of Canada has thus far been careful to distinguish between what it terms as trade-distorting and non-trade distorting support programs, defending Canada's marketing boards as belonging in the latter category. This is unlikely to be entirely convincing as a negotiating position.[10] The Canadian government will be forced in the market access part of the agriculture negotiations to make concessions in terms of import access to Canada if it is to make any gains for export access elsewhere. Similarly, in the general rule-making negotiations, any derogation by Canada from the multilateral norms will exact a heavy price. This is complicated by the large measure of provincial jurisdiction exercised in agricultural support programs. There will be a lively domestic debate on these issues (see below).

SUBSIDIES

The negotiating group on *subsidies and countervail* has a special interest for Canada in this Round in light of the failure to reach immediate agreement on these issues in the FTA. Chapter 19 of the FTA calls for the negotiation of a substitute set of laws affecting subsidies within the next five to seven years. This time frame was chosen at least in part to give the Uruguay Round a chance to work out some of the solutions which eluded Canadian and American negotiators. For the United States agreement on subsidy practice and countervail laws within the broader context of the multilateral trading system would make any change to its own stringent countervail regime more acceptable to Congress. Thus the multilateral negotiations could get to the heart of some of the thornier issues in the bilateral discussions: the definition of a trade distorting subsidy, the concept of when a subsidy is injurious to domestic industry, and the settlement of disputes about the use of trade remedy laws. The December 1988 statement of the GATT indicated that negotiations will attempt to define subsidy practice in terms of three general categories: prohibited practices, practices that are not prohibited but are "actionable" through countervailing measures, and non-actionable subsidies (i.e., not significantly trade distorting). It is of course too early to judge, but progress here could significantly alter the environment for industrial and regional development policy in Canada.[11] Other major trading partners, such as the European Community, also have sensitivities in this area for regional development.

THE NEW ISSUES

Three new issues take the Uruguay Round beyond the traditional focus of the GATT system on goods. These are negotiating groups on trade-related intellectual property, trade-related investment measures, and services. While not to denigrate the importance of the debate on intellectual property, the latter two issues are likely to generate more debate in regional/federal terms in Canada.

Canada has already reached agreement with the United States on the issue of *trade related investment measures* through the FTA. Any agreement in the Uruguay Round is not likely to be more extensive. However, any discipline on performance requirements for foreign investment in the GATT will meet with competing interests in Canada, as did the provisions of Chapter 16 of the FTA. Large Canadian-based firms will welcome curbs on such practices, while some provinces, labour and other interests may not wish to see any further restrictions on the use of a developmental tool of some perceived value.

As with the investment issues, in the negotiations on trade in services, Canada has the benefit of having defined and consolidated its interests through the bilateral process. However, progress in the FTA, as limited as it was, was more easily achieved given the relative similarity of business practice and culture in North America when compared with the many parties to the GATT. Nonetheless, the December 1988 statements of the GATT Ministerial meeting did outline an ambitious framework for negotiation, including the following elements: transparency of regulatory measures, progressive liberalization of restrictive practices, the principle of national treatment, some form of non-discrimination principle, some recourse to safeguard actions, and rules regarding what services would be covered. There is still a very wide gap between the interests of the developed and developing countries in this area. In any case, success in the Uruguay Round may well be marked by bringing services into the trade-rules system by preventing further protectionism and by laying the ground work for future liberalization on a sectoral basis. Canada's interests, especially our potential export interests, are likely to be met by such achievement notwithstanding concern expressed in some quarters about the services chapter of the FTA. Should the services negotiations go beyond the "grand-fathering" of all existing measures that occurred in the FTA, more immediate problems of provincial jurisdiction will have to be faced.

Each of the above issues is ambitious, to say the least, and each has its own negotiating complexities and dynamics. However, apart from making work for international bureaucrats, this massive attempt to revitalize the international trading system does have significant domestic consequences not always easily discerned. These negotiations are an attempt to tame the many domestic political responses to a world economy which is surging well ahead of attempts to contain it.

As the GATT regime moves beyond border measures and into integral domestic policies, the traditional divisions between trade policy and domestic economic policy break down. This has consequences for both the Canadian regional political economy and for Canadian federalism, to which we now turn. In this discussion it will become clear that our domestic policy environment is being transformed by international regimes at least as much as our domestic politics is determining our international response.

CONSIDERATIONS OF REGIONAL POLITICAL ECONOMY

The regionalized political economy has dominated domestic consideration of Canada's trade policy throughout most of our history. Canada, as an economic unit, was created in 1867 partly in response to the abrogation of the Reciprocity Treaty with the United States. Free trade or protection was a constant political theme throughout the nineteenth century. With the inauguration of a more comprehensive national tariff structure in 1879 (the National Policy as it would later be called), the stage was set for the integration of an East-West economy behind relatively high tariff walls. The putative effects of the National Policy in determining the regional division of labour within Canada were not necessarily evident in the nineteenth century. Manufacturing only slowly declined in the Maritimes. The West was too busy coping with the settlement boom to notice, especially after 1896. Only in the 1920s and onward has the national tariff become an essentially regional issue. (It had always been a sectoral issue, as the farming community across Canada was in favour of free trade at least until the end of the World War II.)[12]

With the eventual concentration of manufacturing in Ontario and Quebec, especially after 1921, the primary economic activity in the Western and Atlantic provinces has been in the export-oriented resource sectors. The regional alienation fueled by growing disparities in wealth, population, economic growth and diversity, has often focused on the perceived disproportionate benefits and costs of Canada's essentially protectionist trade policy. The policy has been blamed for raising consumer and industrial costs in the resource-producing regions, keeping the Canadian dollar higher than it should be to the detriment of exporters and preventing the diversification of Western and Atlantic industry based on export markets. Such political perceptions are buttressed by economic analyses that support the traditional view of the outlying regions that the National Policy had negative effects on their economies as well as on the country as a whole.[13]

The progressive liberalization of Canada's tariff structure through successive GATT Rounds since 1947 has considerably lessened the overall impact of protection in Canada, but not the political desire in certain regions for more liberalization. Canada as a whole has become more, not less, trade dependent. This has been especially so in the resource-producing provinces. With the rise through the 1970s and 1980s of neo-protectionism in Canada's trading partners, so too has intensified the continuing regional debate about Canada's use of these same neo-protectionist measures and the constraints imposed by them on the export interests of the resource-producing provinces.

The current reality does not only reflect a simplistic dichotomy of resource versus manufacturing regions in Canada. The negotiations and implementation of the FTA have significantly altered both the dynamics and the relative importance of regional trade issues. The Report of the Macdonald Royal Commission in September 1985 confidently predicted that its proposed freer trade with the United States would not generate the same regional divisions as had traditionally surrounded the National Policy. This was because, in their view, the proposed freer trade would benefit all regions and would indeed "make a major contribution to Canada's regional development and to national competitiveness and overall confidence."[14]

The ensuing debate over the free trade agreement illuminated a number of features of a changed Canadian domestic environment for trade policy. First, every province, including Ontario and Quebec, had become dependent on U.S. export markets for employment and economic activity. Indeed the Ontario economy had become overwhelmingly dependent on U.S. exports, largely through the automobile sector. During the Tokyo Round the Quebec government had taken its rather traditional position of seeking protection for its "soft sectors." However, by 1985 it came out firmly in favour of liberalized trade with the United States. Quebec's changed perspective illustrated a new confidence in international business within the province, a growing regional dependence on the U.S. market, and the fact that the United States was not perceived to be the primary threat to its soft sectors.[15]

Third, and perhaps most important, the regional debate over free trade was simply not as important as the ideological debate. For much of the period up to and just after the conclusion of the FTA, public controversy had become focused on the premiers as regional spokesman culminating in December 1987, when each provincial government declared itself on the agreement. A clear regional cleavage emerged between the three western-most provinces, Quebec and three of the Atlantic provinces in favour of the agreement and Ontario, Manitoba and Prince Edward Island opposed. The campaign and results of the federal general election of 21 November 1988, however, demonstrated that the ideological debate over free trade was significantly more determining of the issue. Polls showed that support and opposition to the agreement cut across all regional lines.[16] This is not to downplay the regional element, but to make the point that the national party system through the election campaign served to channel the debate into terms that were much less regional than had historically been the case. While the ideological debate was divisive, paradoxically it dampened the potential damage to national unity that a totally regionalized debate would have wrought.

What of the Uruguay Round, will the regional dimension be equally muted as it was in the last stages of the FTA debate, and will the same regional coalitions remain intact? Almost certainly the dynamics will be different. The stakes are different in the Uruguay Round, the issues are more diverse and the role of multilateral trade in the various regional economies differs from their trade with the United States alone. To the extent to which the Uruguay Round focuses Canada's attentions on trade with countries other than the United States, the MTNs could be said to be of importance to a more select group of provinces. As Table 10.1 shows, only British Columbia, Newfoundland, Saskatchewan, Manitoba, and Prince Edward Island send more than 40 per cent of their exports to countries other than the United States. B.C. and Saskatchewan are the most "multilateral", the former's trade concentrated in the Pacific Rim and the latter with grain exports around the world. And while practically every province felt keenly the threat or actual impact of U.S. protectionist measures in the lead-up to the FTA, only the western grain-producing provinces have the same sense of urgency about the Uruguay Round.

The Uruguay Round will also involve many issues of significance to Canada-U.S. bilateral trade. There is the unfinished business of the FTA, which was put off to the Uruguay Round or after, such as agreement on a substitute set of laws affecting subsidy countervail and anti-dumping and further agreement on agricultural subsidies, services, and intellectual property. Second, many of the general rules and dispute settlement procedures of the GATT integrally affect the operation of the FTA and could, if changed, alter the bilateral relationship accordingly. Finally, concessions to third parties for market access in the Uruguay Round could impair the benefits to either Canada or the U.S. from the FTA. So in all of these ways it is important to bear in mind that while the Uruguay Round is a multilateral negotiation, it also affects trade with the United States and therefore an emphasis only on non-North American trade can be misleading. All of Canada's provinces will be affected by these negotiations, regardless of their dependence on U.S. or non-U.S. trade.

The positions of Ontario and Quebec will be particularly important to the overall Canadian position. Quebec, as a strong supporter of the FTA, played a critical role in its successful negotiation. This time, however, Quebec's import sensitive sectors in agriculture and textiles and clothing may force it to take a more protectionist position than in the bilateral negotiations. Ontario, moreover, is the least dependent of all Canadian provinces on non-North American trade, with only 10 per cent of its exports going to offshore markets in 1986 (although that 10 per cent constituted $6.3 billion in 1986, or 23 per cent of total Canadian exports to offshore markets). In the debate over the FTA, the Ontario government trumpeted multilateral liberalization over bilateral free trade as the more effective Canadian strategy. Will this rhetoric hold and will the perceived gains from multilateral liberalization for Ontario's more advanced manufacturing and service economy outweigh the perceived costs in terms of its import sensitive sectors?

Table 10.1
International Commodity Trade (Exports) by Province—1986

1. Thousands of current Canadian $

	United States	Other Countries	Total
British Columbia	6,299,138	7,207,116	13,506,254
Alberta	7,788,233	2,914,044	10,702,277
Saskatchewan	1,797,406	2,523,348	4,320,754
Manitoba	1,429,709	1,119,126	2,548,835
Ontario	56,248,550	6,344,544	62,593,094
Quebec	15,795,225	4,999,500	20,794,725
New Brunswick	1,723,680	905,431	2,629,111
Nova Scotia	1,453,889	666,644	2,120,532
Prince Edward Island	87,794	58,806	146,600
Newfoundland	549,461	468,978	1,018,439
Yukon and NWT	9,170	105,075	114,246
Canada*	93,182,255	27,312,612	120,494,867

2. Percentage

	United States	Other Countries	Total
British Columbia	46.6	53.4	100.0
Alberta	72.8	27.2	100.0
Saskatchewan	41.6	58.4	100.0
Manitoba	56.1	43.9	100.0
Ontario	89.9	10.1	100.0
Quebec	76.0	24.0	100.0
New Brunswick	65.6	34.4	100.0
Nova Scotia	68.6	31.4	100.0
Prince Edward Island	59.9	40.1	100.0
Newfoundland	54.0	46.0	100.0
Yukon and NWT	8.0	92.0	100.0
Canada	77.3	22.7	100.0

* total figures may not be exact due to rounding
Source: External Affairs, "Canada's Trade Statistics", 2nd edition (Ottawa: Supply and Services, 1987).

To answer these questions in even a tentative way one must return to the individual negotiating issues of the Uruguay Round. The overall dynamics of the Round are of course important, but Canada is hardly in a make or break position with respect to the Round's overall success or failure. This contrasts with the negotiations over the FTA. Also unlike the FTA, the Uruguay Round will not top the nation's political agenda. Therefore, it may be argued that individual provinces, sectors and other interests could militate against various aspects of multilateral liberalization without incurring the wrath of a federal government for whom other issues will be more vital. This is not to say, however, that such positions would not be antithetical to Canada's overall interests in the Round, as will be shown.

From the agenda items reviewed above, there are five main issues which can be examined from a regional political economy perspective: market access, textiles and clothing, agriculture, subsidies, and the new issues of trade related investment and services.

As already noted, Canada has taken a strong stand on the importance of *market access* issues by virtue of our overall status as a smaller trading partner with a greater than average dependence on export trade. The Canadian position is also led by the particular demands of the resource and resource-related manufacturing sectors, which are important to every province. Tariff and non-tariff barriers for Canadian exports are significant, especially in terms of further processed resource products. The Western provinces and the Atlantic provinces are particularly concerned that the Uruguay Round will neglect the resource sectors, as they contend has occurred in past rounds.

There is not much controversy in the Canadian position on market access as such: everybody wants the same thing, i.e., expanded export markets. What controversy there is will arise in the real and perceived difficulty in achieving the market access objectives when they must be paid for by concessions from our domestic trade barriers. Here the group negotiating *textiles and clothing* will be a good test of Canada's will for liberalization. The concentration of this sector in Quebec will pose problems given the perceived influence of that province in Ottawa, although the garment sector is also important in British Columbia, Manitoba, and Ontario. This regional effect will influence the Canadian position and may make hollow Canada's more pious objectives with respect to the developing world. On the other hand, the issue is sufficiently central to the overall success of the Round that the federal government may find the will to take on these uncompetitive sectors.

The *agriculture* issues are vital to Saskatchewan and the other grain produc-ing provinces. The Government of Saskatchewan has taken a lead role in calling for liberalization and has followed closely the basic Cairns group line. The general Canadian position is of course constrained by the issue of the marketing boards. According to some sources, the federal government is prepared to consider replacing the import quotas, which support the marketing board system, with tariffs.[17] In any case, Canada will have to face up to the view held widely among the GATT parties that the system is a protectionist device. How and whether the marketing board ox is gored depends in part on the way in which support programs across all agricultural commodities are calculated and how they are reduced. Almost certainly sector specific support programs will be affected and it seems doubtful that the supply management system as we know it will survive intact.

The agricultural community across Canada is understandably nervous about this issue, but again there are significant concentrations of interest. Farm production in Ontario, Quebec, British Columbia, and the Atlantic provinces is much more subject to the marketing board system, especially the big three of dairy, eggs, and poultry, than are the prairie provinces.[18] Faced with the prospects for progress in market access and subsidy discipline in the export oriented sectors, the Uruguay Round is bound to expose the sharply competing regional interests within Canadian agriculture. Provincial governments such as Saskatchewan will be anxious that Canada do what is necessary to ensure that a freer market prevails in grain.

Under the rubric of trade rules, any tightening of *the subsidies and counter-vail code* will affect the policies and programs of both the federal and provincial governments in the area of regional and industrial development. Here the urgency of U.S. protectionism has worn off and the political acceptance of disciplining government intervention may also be waning. However, any progress in the Uruguay Round may be the best that can be achieved in terms of our bilateral relations with the United States.

The public debate over these issues is unlikely to be as intense as it was over the FTA, but there is certainly room for anxiety at the regional level. Canada has submitted a proposal to better define trade-distorting subsidies. This proposal would seek to prohibit certain practices, better define the conditions for countervail for other practices, and provide rules on a third category of practices that would be permitted as non-trade distorting.[19] There is considerable public confusion as to what constitutes a trade-distorting industrial or regional development practice, thanks in large measure to the rhetorical debate over the FTA. The new rules may be less constraining of federal and provincial regional and industrial policy than is commonly assumed. Nonetheless, there are bound to be particular sets of regional and sectoral interests affected by the transformation of offending government programs into programs which are consistent with any new GATT obligations.

Finally the new issues of *services and trade related investment* do not as yet seem to have generated the same sort of potential regional controversy as have the more traditional issues related to trade in goods. This may simply be because the issues are new and extensive adjustment is not expected within Canada this time around. The business community and most of the provinces would appear, however, to recognize the importance to Canada's overall competitiveness of bringing these areas into the trading system.

These issues do involve matters of provincial jurisdiction (see below) and sensitive issues of national sovereignty. At the moment they may be too esoteric and diffuse to generate significant regional debate. Depending on the degree of progress in the Uruguay Round, however, concessions for market access or the discipline of new rules could go well beyond the easy "grandfathering" of existing Canadian measures in the FTA. In such a case, messy jurisdictional problems will arise for Canada, complicating an already complex set of negotiations. So too, the value of existing service and investment measures to specific regions will be tested and could generate debate. For example, access to basic telecommunications markets, access to transportation markets, preferential purchasing, and other performance requirements on investment, access to technology, the subsidization of services and the mobility of labour in the service sector, are all sensitive regional issues.

From this discussion of the regional political economy of Canada's trade-policy environment, it is now appropriate to turn to the federalism dimension. The processes of Canadian federalism pose some specific challenges for Canadian trade policy, not only in terms of how policy is made, but also in terms of sharpening some of the substantive issues which arise from the regional political economy.

FEDERAL-PROVINCIAL RELATIONS

Provinces are involved in Canadian trade policy in two ways. First, they have, by virtue of constitutional jurisdiction, ultimate authority in many matters that arise in international trade including a number of items on the Uruguay Round agenda. Second, through the processes of executive federalism, provincial governments represent the regional interests of their province in numerous intergovernmental interactions with the federal government. These two facts of Canadian political life become intertwined when the jurisdictional support of provinces required to reach international agreements affords the provinces an influential advocacy role in overall policy affecting their regional economies.

The intent of this paper is not to get into the detail of constitutional law respecting international trade[20] It is important, however, to review some important long-standing points and some recent developments. Throughout much of the debate over the FTA, the issue of provincial jurisdiction was thoroughly discussed.[21] The role of provinces in the law of international treaties, as basically determined by the *Labour Conventions* case in 1937, has not changed. The Government of Canada cannot legislate to implement an international treaty if that legislation intrudes on provincial jurisdiction. Debate during and since the FTA has revolved not around this point, but rather on whether the federal trade and commerce power has sufficient clout to encompass the totality of the FTA, or indeed the Uruguay Round agenda. This proposition has not yet come to a legal test although legal scholars contend that in the light of recent case law there is sufficient evidence to indicate that a new, more centralist definition of the trade and commerce power may be made by the courts.[22] The certainty of this position was, nonetheless, in sufficient doubt during the last phase of the Canada-U.S. free trade talks that the federal government did its best to limit the impact of the agreement on provincial jurisdiction. This was to avoid a court challenge from Ontario and possibly the other provinces opposed to the FTA. This did not stop the Ontario government from obtaining legal advice that several areas of provincial jurisdiction were touched by the FTA, beyond the obvious area of alcoholic beverages.[23]

To what extent the Uruguay Round results will touch on provincial jurisdiction is, of course, too soon to tell both in terms of substantive provisions and evolving constitutional law. However, an examination of the agenda reviewed above reveals quite a number of provincial measures which could be affected. These include: resource pricing, resource taxation designed to favour local processing, resource export controls, liquor board regulations, government procurement, agricultural support programs, agricultural marketing board legislation, agricultural standards, industrial and regional subsidy practices, investment performance requirements such as local content rules, preferential purchases on mega-projects, local equity requirements and product mandating, and finally, a diverse range of service-sector regulation affecting among other things, establishment, investment, and the mobility of labour.

These provincial measures are well known to our trading partners and many of them will be targeted for removal or modification according to new rules or specific Canadian concessions sought in the Uruguay Round. However, thanks to the recent liquor board case, the parties to the GATT will also be asking for assurances of provincial compliance to the Round agreements. The dismal history of the liquor board dispute has unfortunately demonstrated to the EC and others that not only are the Canadian provinces adept at weaseling out of commitments, but that the federal government is more or less powerless to prevent them from doing so.

The evidence and arguments presented before the GATT panel on this case were especially instructive.[24] Article XXIV.12 of the GATT requires each party to "take such reasonable measures as are available to it" to ensure compliance by "regional and local governments." This is the so-called federal state clause.

Canada essentially argued before the panel that "reasonable measures" as required in the GATT did not extend to constitutional *force majeure*, even if such action could be guaranteed of success before the courts. The EC argued that the provinces violated GATT commitments and that the federal government had the power to force the provinces to keep those commitments. Upon hearing both sides, the GATT panel concluded that Canada (plural) did not meet its obligations, but wisely gave Canada a few more months to get its act together, without stipulating how it should do so.

Canada's admission of federal impotence in the face of provincial measures that were inconsistent with the GATT might raise a few questions about the adequacy of the federal state clause of the GATT. To the author's knowledge this issue has not come up in the negotiations to date. Canada's trading partners will probably leave it as a matter for Canadians to sort out in the certain knowledge that we will pay the price if concessions are not delivered or if Canadian national objectives are not met due to provincial blockage.

Thus, the issue of how the provincial governments agree to international trade obligations is a thorny one. It leads to the other aspect of provincial involvement: as trade-policy advocates for their regions. The federal government realizes that the provinces have exercised jurisdiction over a range of non-tariff measures which have become key issues in trade negotiations, at least since the beginning of the Tokyo Round in 1974. Since then Canadian politics has also been marked by the rise of executive federalism.[25] These two phenomena combined have led to a significant increase in the scope, depth, and significance of federal-provincial relations over trade policy.

The federal government agreed to an elaborate but workable mechanism for consulting the provinces on the progress of the bilateral trade negotiations with the United States.[26] The results of that process have been described by the author elsewhere, but a few important points are of relevance to federal-provincial relations on the Uruguay Round. First, the involvement of the provinces in the FTA has sensitized them to trade policy in all its nuances and complexity. The multilateral negotiations will not have the same profile in the provincial capitals as did the bilateral, but in even the smallest governments there exists an expertise and interest in trade matters, at least in terms of the direct impact on the provincial economies. This means that even if the federal government were not to consult the provinces, the provinces have enough competence to make their views known and to stir up public debate.

Second, however, the politics of the final phase of the FTA negotiations has left more than a few wary players who may be less certain of the intentions of the other side. The federal government in particular may be seeking to limit as much as possible the role of the provinces, given the conflict which arose in late 1987 when federal-provincial consensus on the negotiations broke down.

However much federal trade negotiators may wish not to have provincial colleagues second-guessing their negotiating strategy, federal-provincial dialogue on the Round continues. John Crosbie has met with his provincial counterparts on at least three occasions in the eight months since the general election and a committee of senior federal and provincial officials meets about once every two months to review the negotiating agenda, discuss the Canadian position and exchange data and analysis. Provincial Ministers and officials have been welcomed in Geneva and have been assisted by the Canadian Delegation in making the rounds to other delegations. Provincial representatives were observers at the Montreal Ministerial meeting in December 1988 and at other international trade fora, such as Cairns group meetings.

Apart from this consultative process, the provinces are active in general advocacy: speeches, position papers, missions and briefings, consultations with the private sector, and direct representation to other GATT parties. The impact of this advocacy is difficult to judge, but if all such interventions are of the general quality of the recent Western Premiers Conference Report, *Western Trade Objectives*,[27] provincial positions will be influential.

Notwithstanding this advocacy, executive federalism, as it relates to trade policy, is not a decision-making process. The federal-provincial meetings do not have formal procedures, there are no votes and even a unanimous provincial consensus does not preclude federal decisions to the contrary. On the basis of current arrangements, provincial representatives are not members of the Canadian delegation, are not privy to the negotiations and will not be there to take the final Canadian decision. Some of the provinces have been proposing a more elaborate and more formal structure to ensure federal-provincial collaboration in the Uruguay Round. Thus far the federal government has not relented. Difficult issues involving provincial jurisdiction may arise and if Canada is to be a party to agreement which involves provincial jurisdiction more than was the case in the FTA, some means of closing the gap in ways which are final and certain must be found.

This issue has been reviewed by a number of commentators including the Macdonald Commission Report. In a commentary for the C.D. Howe Institute in 1986, Murray Smith outlined four options: (1) the federal government goes it alone; (2) a federal-provincial consensus approach; (3) a "Canadian Fast-Track Process" that would involve constitutional amendment to empower the federal government to impose international economic agreements on all provinces when it has the support of a majority of the provinces; and (4) a series of federal-provincial agreements to implement commitments.[28] In the negotiations for the FTA the federal government tried the second option and when that did not work, took the first. The Macdonald Commission Report recommended what is essentially the third option, a constitutional amendment to have international obligations imposed on provinces across Canada only after the measures are approved by the legislatures of two-thirds of the provinces, having half of the population (i.e., the general amending formula of the Constitution Act of 1982).[29] In the prevailing climate over the Meech Lake Accord, it seems unlikely that a constitutional amendment to settle such matters can possibly be passed in time for the conclusion of the Uruguay Round in late 1990.

As noted above, the degree of provincial jurisdiction involved in Uruguay Round commitments is unclear at the moment. Nonetheless, it must be demonstrated to other GATT parties that provincial commitments will meet a better fate than the 1979 Statement of Intent on provincial liquor boards. Whether or not this is demanded by our GATT partners, the federal government itself may seek to have some sort of commitment, even if it is only a political agreement morally binding on the provinces.

If provinces are to be expected to sign, for example, memoranda of agreements on the implementation of Uruguay Round results, then the onus will be on the federal government to ensure that provincial representatives are fully involved and informed of the Geneva negotiations. This will require a more elaborate form of relations than has to this point been implemented. This would include, among others, a way of ensuring provincial cabinet approval. This sort of federal-provincial "concertation" could proceed under the rubric of a new constitutional era inaugurated by the Meech Lake Accord as some prefer.[30] Or it could build on the conventional growth of executive federalism in Canada; which will not matter in the short term. However, in the longer term, federal-provincial collaboration must proceed in such a way that at the end of the day, binding decisions can be taken which apply to all jurisdictions. Short of constitutional amendment or jurisprudence to change the current rules, federal and provincial governments might consider some sort of political accord on a process for taking decisions regarding international economic obligations where unanimous consensus is not the only operative rule.

CONCLUSIONS

Canadians may be forgiven if they have not taken much notice of the Uruguay Round of multilateral trade negotiations until now. Just to say the words is to launch into an arcane world of legal and economic jargon largely unintelligible to the average citizen. The general public responded to the complexities of the free trade debate of 1988 largely through a symbolic and emotional campaign. The public may never get the chance to come fully to grips with the Uruguay Round where the issues seem so diffuse and technical. This may present problems if the domestic politics of the Uruguay Round are fought only in terms of special interests and if appeals are not made to the broader national and consumer interests. There are, nonetheless, some important issues involving regional perspectives and which affect the process of Canadian federalism. These issues may not attract top media billing, but they will significantly affect Canada's overall interests.

The interests of Canada in the Uruguay Round are manifested every day in our domestic economies. No sector of the Canadian economy is untouched by the competitive international environment. The pervasiveness of this economic challenge and its threat to established communities, distributions of income and indeed the entire post-war welfare state, translate into pressure on political institutions. This pressure is not discriminating. It applies with equal force to provincial governments as to the federal government in Canada.

Thus the domestic politics in Canada and its uniquely regional characteristics, as filtered through a decentralized federalism, cannot help but be involved in the broader politics of international trade relations. Provincial governments are taking an increased interest and involvement in the international economy. At the same time, the efforts of the Uruguay Round and other international forces will continue to constrain the ability of all governments to intervene in their local economies. It is, nonetheless, clearly in Canada's interests that the Uruguay Round succeeds because Canada's prospects will steadily shrink in the more protectionist, regionalized world of big power bullies that will displace the GATT system if it fails. This is a conclusion that may not be as widely shared in Canada as one would hope and begs for a broader public debate of the issues.

The Canadian regional issues in the Uruguay Round will be different than in the debate over the FTA. The main indicators of regional and federal-provincial debate in this Round will be in five issues: market access especially for resource products, textile and clothing, agriculture, subsidies and the new issues of services and trade-related investment measures. Debate over these issues may be a throw-back to the older East/West cleavages of previous trade policy debates. Agriculture in particular will expose some sharp regional differences, but so too will the issues of subsidies and textiles and clothing. In a set of negotiations where the overall political stakes may not seem to be as high as in the FTA debate, and where the ideological lines may not be as firmly drawn, the old regional chestnuts could be the most difficult domestic political issues of the Round.

Finally, added to the regional issues, and indeed the chief forum for their expression, is the problem of federal-provincial relations. The role of the provinces, especially their role in implementing Canadian international commitments which fall within provincial jurisdiction, is still not resolved. It presented difficulties in the negotiation of the FTA and it will come back to haunt Canada in the conclusion of the Uruguay Round. It is an issue that should be resolved sooner rather than later on the Canadian intergovernmental agenda.

Notes

1. For general background to the rise of protectionism and trade imbalances in recent years from a macroeconomic perspective see Lester Thurow "Adjusting the U.S. Trade Imbalance: A Black Hole in the World Economy," *Berkeley Roundtable on the International Economy*, Working Paper No. 24, March 1987; for a more "micro" view, see Stephen S. Cohen and John Zysman, *Manufacturing Matters: The Myth of the Post-Industrial Economy* (New York: Basic Books, 1987). Two recent overviews of the Canadian perspective may be found in Sylvia Ostry, "Global Trends: Global Solutions," paper delivered at Queen's University School of Policy Studies, 13-14 April 1989; and Murray Smith, *Canada's Stake in the Uruguay Round and the GATT System* Discussion Paper 8801 (Ottawa: Institute for Research on Public Policy, October 1988). From a U.S. perspective, see G.C. Hufbauer and Jeffrey J. Schott, *Trading For Growth: The Next Round of Trade Negotiations* (Washington: Institute for International Economics, 1985).

2. The Government of Canada pursues what it has called a "two-track" trade policy of bilateral and multilateral trade liberalization. During the debate over the FTA and since there has been a continuing discussion about the impact of bilateral liberalization on the multilateral system. See, for example, Jeffrey J. Schott, "Implications for the Uruguay Round" in Jeffrey J. Schott and Murray Smith (eds.), *The Canada-United States Free Trade Agreement: The Global Impact* (Washington: Institute for International Economics, 1988). For a good summary of the official view, see Germain Denis in "The FTA and the GATT: The Link," paper delivered at the Inaugural Conference of the Canadian Centre for Trade Policy and Law, Ottawa, 5 May 1989.

3. Ministerial Declaration, Punta del Este, October 1986; and Trade Negotiations Committee: Texts adopted on 28 January 1988, GATT Secretariat, *Basic Instruments and Selected Documents*, published in Kenneth R. Simmonds and Brian H.W. Hill (eds.), *Law and Practice Under the GATT* (New York: Oceana Publications, 1988).

4. See Gilbert Winham, "The prenegotiation phase of the Uruguay Round", *International Journal*, XLIV: 2, Spring, 1989, pp. 285-86.

5. For a good overview of the concept of interdependence see Sylvia Ostry, *Interdependence: Vulnerability and Opportunity* (Washington, D.C.: The Per Jacobsson Foundation, 1987).

6. For a basic introduction to the Uruguay Round issues, see J. Michael Finger and Andrzej Olechowski (eds.), *The Uruguay Round: a Handbook on the Multilateral Trade Negotiations* (Washington D.C.: The World Bank, 1987).

7. Information on the negotiating mandate and agreement reached at the December 1988 Ministerial Meeting and the April 1989 Trade Negotiations Committee meetings has been obtained from the following documents: GATT Secretariat, Multilateral Trade Negotiations, Uruguay Round, Document #MTN.TNC/7 (MIN) 9 December 1988 "Trade Negotiations Committee Meeting at Ministerial level" Montreal, December 1988; Government of Canada, Department of External Affairs, (Multilateral Trade Negotiations Office) "Situation Report" of January 1989 and April 1989; Canada, Minister of International Trade News release and annex, 8 April 1989: "Canada Welcomes Agreement in Geneva Trade Talks". See also *Globe and Mail* for 6, 8, and 10 April, 1989.

8. While it is not always easy to separate out the cause of low grain prices as attributable solely to subsidy escalation by Canada's trade partners, the effect is nonetheless very tangible. The Special Canadian Grains Program of 1986-87 and 1987-88 cost a total of $1.0 billion and $1.1 billion respectively. Other major programs which compensated grain farmers for low prices are payments under the Agricultural Stabilization Act and the Western Grain Stabilization Act. Total net direct payments for producers of wheat barley and oats combined were $1,162 million for 1986-87 and $997 million for 1987-88. (See Minister for International Trade, Canada, News Release and Backgrounder No. 130, 6 June 1989 "Support Levels Agreed to Under Canada-U.S. Free Trade Agreement").

9. Harry Johnson called this problem "agriculturalism": "the protection of domestic agricultural production by a host of direct and indirect interferences with freedom of trade in agricultural products far transcending in complexities the protectionist measures applied to industrial trade." See Harry G. Johnson, "Mercantilism: Past Present and Future" in Harry G. Johnson (ed.), *The New Mercantilism* (Oxford: Basil Blackwell, 1974) pp. 7 and 15.

10. Canada's insistence in this area may already have produced difficulties within the Cairns group. Canada had to exclude itself from parts of the July 1988 Cairns proposal to the GATT that specified changes to Article XI of the GATT affecting marketing boards. See *Globe and Mail* 6 April 1989.

11. Canada submitted a "comprehensive" proposal on subsidy-countervail rules in June 1989. See Minister for International Trade, News Release no. 158, 28 June 1989.

12. On the legacy of the National Policy see G. Stevenson, *Unfulfilled Union: Canadian Federalism and National Unity*, (3rd ed.) (Toronto: Gage, 1989) pp. 75-81; see also articles by Paul Phillips, David E. Smith and T.W. Acheson in D.J. Bercuson (ed.), *Canada and the Burden of Unity* (Toronto: Macmillan, 1977); see also P.M. Leslie, *Federal State, National Economy* (Toronto: University of Toronto Press, 1987) pp. 4-7; and *Report of the Royal Commission on the Economic Union and Development Prospects for Canada*, vol. 1, (Ottawa: Minister of Supply and Services, Canada, 1985) pp. 213-224.
13. See Economic Council of Canada, *Looking Outward: A New Trade Strategy for Canada* (Ottawa: Information Canada, 1974) esp. chap. 4, pp. 39-46; a good summary of the economic literature and an effective presentation of the evidence may be found in Ronald A. Shearer, "Regionalism and International Trade Policy", in J. Whalley (ed.), *Canada-United States Free Trade* vol. 11 of the Research Studies commissioned for the Royal Commission on the Economic Union and Development Prospects for Canada (Toronto: University of Toronto Press, 1985) pp. 325-366.
14. *Report*, vol. 1, p. 331.
15. For an assessment of the Quebec government's hands off role in industrial adjustment in the textile and clothing sector see Denis Robert, *L'ajustement structurel et le fédéralisme canadien: le cas de l'industrie du textile et du vêtement*, Notes de recherche (Kingston: Institute of Intergovernmental Relations, 1989).
16. See the article in this volume by Darrel Reid on the federal general election campaign of 1988.
17. See *Globe and Mail* of 23 March 1989.
18. The Economic Council of Canada calculated the share of total farm receipts influenced by supply management boards in each province in 1978 as follows: British Columbia 41.7(%); Alberta 8.3; Saskatchewan 2.9; Manitoba 13.1; Ontario 37.7; Quebec 58.1; New Brunswick 38.1; Nova Scotia 53.8; Prince Edward Island 20.8; Newfoundland not available. See Economic Council of Canada, *Reforming Regulation* (Ottawa: Minister of Supply and Services Canada, 1981) p. 57.
19. Supra, note 11.
20. For useful summaries, see Ivan Bernier and André Binette, *Les provinces canadiennes et le commerce international: dynamique économique et ajustment juridique* (Québec: Centre québécois de relations internationales, 1988) pp. 115-204; I. Bernier, *International Legal Aspects of Federalism* (London: Longman, 1973); and G.Z. Szablowski, "Treaty-Making Power in the Context of Canadian Politics: An Explanatory and Innovative Approach," in C. Beckton and W. MacKay (eds.), *Recurring Issues in*

Canadian Federalism, Macdonald Commission Research Studies, vol. 57 (Toronto: University of Toronto Press, 1985).

21. See "Anonymous," "The Canada-United States Free Trade Agreement: Issues of Constitutional Jurisdiction," in P.M. Leslie and R.L. Watts (eds.), *Canada: The State of the Federation 1987-88* (Kingston: Institute of Intergovernmental Relations, 1988); and contributions by M. Pilkington, I. Vernier, H. Scott Fairley and D. Bigson in Chap. 4 of M. Gold and D. Leyton-Brown (eds.) *Trade-Offs on Free Trade* (Toronto: Carswell, 1988), pp. 89-129.

22. See J. Whyte, "Federal Powers over the Economy: Finding New Jurisdictional Room," *Canadian Business Law Journal,* vol. 13, (1987) p. 257.

23. Attorney General for Ontario, *The Impact of the Canada-U.S. Trade Agreement: A Legal Analysis,* May 1988.

24. GATT Secretariat, Panel on Import, Distribution and Sale of Alcoholic Drinks by Canadian Provincial Marketing Agencies, *Report of the Panel,* 12 October 1987.

25. For an explanation of the concept of executive federalism, see D.V. Smiley *The Federal Condition in Canada* (Toronto: McGraw-Hill Ryerson, 1987) Chap. 4.

26. See the author's "The Canada-United States Free Trade Agreement: The Federal-Provincial Consultation Process," in Leslie and Watts, *Canada: The State of the Federation 1987-88,* pp. 77-93.

27. *Western Trade Objectives: Report of the Western Ministers Responsible for Multilateral Trade Negotiations to the Western Premiers Conference* (Camrose: Alberta, 27-28 June 1989).

28. M. Smith, "Closing a Trade Deal: The Provinces' Role", C.D. Howe Institute, *Commentary,* no. 11, August 1986.

29. See *Report,* vol. 1, pp. 368-72; 383-84. See also Sablowski, "Treaty-Making Power in the Context of Canadian Politics".

30. See Bernier and Binette, *Les provinces canadiennes et le commerce internationale.*

IV

Chronology

ELEVEN

Chronology of Events January 1988–June 1989

Darrel R. Reid and Dwight Herperger

An index of these events begins on page 285

2 January 1988
Free Trade

Prime Minister Brian Mulroney signs the Canada-U.S. Free Trade Agreement, promising to introduce enabling legislation for the agreement into the House of Commons as soon as possible. From his Ottawa office Mr. Mulroney calls the signing ceremony a "note of hope" and confidence for 1988. In a parallel signing ceremony U.S. President Ronald Reagan terms the deal a "win-win situation for both countries" which would create jobs and lower consumer prices.

6 January 1988
Hydroelectricity—
Exports—Quebec

Governor Mario Cuomo of New York and Quebec Premier Robert Bourassa sign a memorandum of understanding between Hydro-Québec and the State of New York for the sale, over 21 years, of 1,000 megawatts of hydroelectricity worth $17 billion beginning in 1995. This is the largest hydroelectricity contract signed in Hydro Québec's 25-year history.

7 January 1988
Regulation—
Securities

Securities Commissions from Ontario, Quebec, and British Columbia sign a memorandum of understanding with the U.S. Securities and Exchange Commission calling for closer cooperation between the commissions in the investigation of possible securities violations. The agreement, which still requires enabling legislation to take effect, is to give regulators the authority to pursue information and witnesses in their own country on behalf of the other country, even though no violation of domestic law has occurred. The agreement also obliges regulators to share information from their own jurisdiction which is required by officials from the other jurisdictions.

18 January 1988
Regional Development—Prince Edward Island

Following nearly two months of intense debate, Prince Edward Island voters approve of the building of a 14-kilometre fixed link between the Island and the mainland, by a margin of nearly 60 per cent. Premier Joe Ghiz had called the plebiscite following the federal government's announcement that it was asking seven Canadian firms to submit detailed designs for a bridge or tunnel across the Northumberland Straight. Of the result, Mr. Ghiz notes that "It is a clear mandate to negotiate with the federal government while respecting the concerns of the many Islanders who voted against it."

19 January 1988
Environment—Nuclear Power

The Commons Environment Committee issues a unanimous report on the nuclear power industry in Canada entitled The Eleventh Hour, which proposes that the federal government declare a moratorium on the construction of nuclear power plants until an acceptable solution is found to the waste disposal issue. The committee also recommends that the provinces that produce nuclear waste—Ontario, Quebec, and New Brunswick—should bear primary responsibility for storing it.

26 January 1988
Senate Appointments; Meech Lake Accord

The first Senator to be appointed under the new Meech Lake constitutional formula is sworn in. Gerry Ottenheimer, a former Newfoundland cabinet minister, was chosen by Prime Minister Mulroney from a list provided by Newfoundland's Conservative government. Even though the Accord has yet to be ratified by most provinces, the federal government is honoring the agreement to appoint senators from lists provided by provinces with Senate vacancies.

28 January 1988
Supreme Court—Abortion

Citing Section 7 of the Canadian Charter of Rights and Freedoms that guarantees "security of the person," the Supreme Court of Canada rules 5-2 that a British Columbia law restricting access to abortion is unconstitutional, holding the law to be so "manifestly unfair" that it could not be allowed to remain on the books. As a result, the little-used Criminal Code law, which provided sentences of up to two years for those seeking abortions, is no longer enforceable. Dr. Henry Morgentaler, who had been charged under the law, terms the decision a "vindication of a lifetime of struggle." In Ottawa, federal Justice Minister Ray Hnatyshyn announces that the decision must be studied by the federal government and discussed with the provinces. Provincial responses to the decision differ: both Manitoba Attorney General Vic Shroeder and Ontario Attorney General Ian Scott announce that their provinces would drop all abortion-related charges against Dr. Morgentaler; British Columbia announces that, despite the ruling, public money would not be spent to finance abortion on demand.

28 January 1988
Meech Lake Accord
—Northwest
Territories

An attempt by former N.W.T. government leader Nick Sibbeston to launch a legal attack on the Meech Lake Accord is turned down by the Northwest Territories Court of Appeals, agreeing with a federal government request to dismiss the suit. In seeking a full hearing for his client's case, Sibbeston's lawyer had argued that sections of the Accord violate the Charter of Rights and Freedoms, and that Ottawa had ignored the rights of the Yukon and Northwest Territories in concluding its agreement with the ten provinces. The three judges reject these arguments, holding, among other things, that the Charter of Rights cannot be used to challenge other parts of the Constitution, and that the federal government was not required to make the Territories part of the negotiations leading to the Meech Lake Accord.

4 February 1988
Regional Develop-
ment—ERDA—
British Columbia

British Columbia Finance Minister Mel Couvelier announces the unilateral withdrawal of his province from a $1 billion federal-provincial Economic and Regional Development Agreement (ERDA), stating his government's concern that the ERDAs offer unfair competition to existing companies and an artificial stimulus to the economy. Though more than 100 ERDA grants worth $5.2 million had been announced in mid-January, Couvelier said the government had simply "grandfathered" those already in the system, giving them consideration under former terms and conditions. According to Couvelier, there are to be no further grants pending the outcome of talks with Ottawa. The suspension of provincial participation in the ERDA comes one year in advance of the agreement's 1989 expiry and is part of a review of all federal-provincial agreements by the Government of British Columbia.

10 February 1988
Budgets—Federal

Federal Finance Minister Michael Wilson delivers his fourth budget in the House of Commons. In what is widely interpreted as an election budget, Mr. Wilson dwells largely upon the Conservative government's achievements since it came to office in 1984. The budget is aimed primarily at continuing the government's deficit-cutting policies, with no new spending initiatives announced.

12 February 1988
Canadian Radio-Television and Telecommunications Commission (CRTC)

A federal cabinet decision allows Call-Net Telecommunications Ltd. to continue its long-distance service to its customers for at least six months despite a Canadian Radio-Television and Telecommunications (CRTC) ruling that its service violates federal policy. The Toronto-based firm sells call time to customers over long-distance lines it leases from Bell Canada and CNCP Telecommunications. Manitoba Telephones Minister Gary Doer announces that he plans to organize a multiprovince protest of the decision, citing his fears that this service—if allowed to continue—amounts to competition in long-distance service, something the provinces fear will lead to large rate increases in local service for provincial telephone utilities similar to those that occurred in the United States when AT&T's monopoly was dismantled.

15 February 1988
Regional Development—ACOA

Senator Lowell Murray, the minister responsible for the Atlantic Canada Opportunities Agency, announces cabinet approval authorizing that agency to spend $1 billion of development money over the next five years, despite the fact that legislation confirming the mandate of ACOA is still before Parliament.

25 February 1988
Supreme Court—
Language—
Saskatchewan

In a 6-2 ruling, the Supreme Court of Canada holds that Saskatchewan's English-only laws are invalid and that the Saskatchewan government must either translate all laws into French within a reasonable time, or invalidate, as soon as possible, the right to French-language laws. In the ruling the court states that Section 110 of the Northwest Territories Act contains French-language guarantees which are still valid in Saskatchewan and must be either respected or repealed by the province's legislature. In response, Saskatchewan officials request more time to study the ruling. The decision also has implications for Alberta, where the same law was applied when the province was formed 1 September 1905. Francophone spokesmen hail the ruling as a victory and asked for help from the federal government and Quebec in defending French rights in Saskatchewan and Alberta.

29 February 1988
Council of
Maritime
Premiers;
Regional Develop-
ment—ACOA

Following a meeting of the Council of Maritime Premiers, the three Maritime premiers and Newfoundland's premier Brian Peckford request a meeting with Prime Minister Brian Mulroney to obtain details on how Ottawa is going to operate the new Atlantic Canada Opportunities Agency. Premier John Buchanan notes that the premiers are not asking for a say in governing the agency but want to harmonize its operations with that of their provinces.

1 March 1988
Hydroelectricity—
Quebec

Quebec Premier Bourassa announces that his government will go ahead with construction of a second James Bay hydroelectric development. According to Mr. Bourassa, James Bay II is to cost $7.5 billion over ten years, and will involve the construction of three dams and a transmission line to the U.S. border. The project is to create 40,000 new jobs.

8 March 1988
Elections—
Manitoba; New
Democratic Party—
Manitoba

The New Democratic government of Manitoba Premier Howard Pawley falls after an unexpected defeat on a motion of non-confidence following its annual budget. In addition to the combined opposition Conservatives and Liberal leader Sharon Carstairs, NDP backbencher Jim Walding voted for the motion. After announcing a provincial election, to be held 26 April, Mr. Howard

Pawley, Manitoba premier since 1981, stuns observers by announcing his resignation as leader of the Manitoba New Democrats. At dissolution, the party standings are: NDP 29, Conservatives 27 and Liberals 1.

8 March 1988
French Language Education— Prince Edward Island

The Supreme Court of Prince Edward Island rules that the province's School Act and certain of its regulations are inconsistent with the Canadian Charter of Rights and Freedoms, in that the Act does not recognize the right of the French language minority to participate in French language program development and its delivery in the province. Among its findings, the court rules that section 5.32(1) of the School Act, which reserves the sole discretion in the regional school board to determine if a sufficient number of students can be assembled for providing French language education, to be inconsistent with the Charter and, therefore, ultra vires.

15 March 1988
Regulation— Securities Industry

Federal Minister of State for Finance Thomas Hockin announces an agreement between Ottawa and Quebec on supervision of the securities industry, a major sore point since financial deregulation last year cleared the way for mergers between federally- and provincially-regulated companies. According to Mr. Hockin, the deal protects Quebec's traditional jurisdiction over the securities industry, even when stock brokerages are taken over by federally-regulated institutions. In return, Quebec will guarantee federal regulators access to information concerning, among other things, the capital adequacy of securities operations owned by banks and federally-regulated financial institutions. A similar agreement has been struck with Ontario. Both provinces agree to notify Ottawa six months ahead of any changes in the rules governing the securities industry.

17 March 1988
Meech Lake Accord; Interprovincial Energy Relations

Quebec Premier Bourassa and New Brunswick Premier McKenna sign an energy agreement. The six-year, $650 million agreement will see New Brunswick receive access to cheaper hydroelectricity in return for the province dropping its opposition to a major Hydro-Québec sale of electricity to the New England states.

During discussions the New Brunswick premier also outlines six major changes to the Meech Lake Constitutional Accord before his province can ratify it. These conditions are:

• parliament should be required in the Constitution to "promote" as well as to simply "preserve" bilingualism across the country. The Accord provides that only Quebec would be committed to "preserve and promote" its identity;

• the removal of the stipulation in the Accord that jurisdiction over fisheries be discussed at constitutional conferences every year;

• the Accord must be rewritten to remove any doubt that womens' rights might be affected;

• the section on appointment of Supreme Court appointments should be amended to allow federal-provincial bar committees to make nominations to the Supreme Court;

• the issue of Senate reform must be settled before the Accord is ratified; and

• New Brunswick wants clearer language to ensure that limitations placed by the Accord on federal-provincial shared cost programs will not deprive have-not provinces of badly needed federal assistance.

21 March 1988
International Trade—GATT

Federal Trade Minister Pat Carney announces in the House of Commons that Canada will accept two GATT rulings that call for the elimination of protectionist measures involving alcoholic beverages and Pacific salmon and herring, but that Ottawa will decide how to make the necessary changes. The European Community had launched its GATT case protesting that pricing practices by provincial liquor control boards favoured domestic beverages over foreign ones. Ms. Carney announces she will continue to consult with the provinces on what actions will be taken by the federal government. Canada has until the end of the year to inform GATT how it plans to comply with the rulings.

30 March 1988
Meech Lake
Accord

Former Prime Minister Pierre Trudeau addresses a Senate Committee of the Whole on the Meech Lake Accord. In his presentation he urges the Senate to block the Accord by amending it, and outlines other possible ways to turn back the agreement: a Supreme Court reference and a federal election. In his address, he portrays Prime Minister Brian Mulroney as a weak leader who bought peace with the provinces at any price: "Mr. Mulroney's government of national reconciliation was able to bring temporary peace to federal-provincial relations by negotiating a sweetheart constitutional deal whereby enormous amounts of power were transferred to the provincial governments and particularly to the premiers." He portrays the Accord as a "Rubicon—once you've crossed it you can't go back."

1 April 1988
Health Policy—
Federal-Provincial
Agreements

A new federal-provincial agreement on the interprovincial portability of health benefits comes into effect today. Under the agreement, patients from any province or territory—except Quebec, which is not party to the agreement—will be insured for all benefits offered by the province or territory in which they are treated. The agreement on portability of health care insurance gives effect to a principle enshrined in the federal government's Canada Health Act. It makes billing arrangements easier, eliminating any extra costs or the need for special insurance to cover benefits not insured in the province of residence.

4 April 1988
Language Policy—
Saskatchewan

Saskatchewan Justice Minister Bob Andrew tables Bill 2 in the legislature, to repeal Section 110 of the Northwest Territories Act, 1877. The bill is the government's response to the Supreme Court decision of 25 February that ruled the province's English-only laws to be invalid unless either translated into French or declared to be valid in English alone. Among the bill's provisions are the following:

• Section 110 of the 1885 Northwest Territories Act—which guaranteed the right to French trials, the right to French versions of all laws and the right to speak French in the legislature—will be repealed and replaced;

• validation of past and existing statues, even if they were passed only in English; and

• validations of future statues and regulations, even if passed in English only.

In addition, the bill states that bills may still be passed in English only and does not set out a time limit or put onus on the government to translate old laws into French. Response to the bill by federal politicians and minority language groups alike is swift and negative. The bill is passed by the Legislature and becomes law on 25 April.

7 April 1988
Environment—
Provincial-Inter-
national Relations

The province of Ontario joins with nine U.S. states in a court action to force the United States Environmental Protection Agency to order reductions in emissions that cause acid rain. The province and the states file a petition asking the agency to release two 1981 decisions that determined acid rain was a threat to the environment. Under U.S. procedures, the decisions had to be made public before the agency could order states to reduce emissions of acid-rain producing pollutants.

13 April 1988
Tax Reform

Finance Minister Michael Wilson releases 360 pages of draft legislation on the reform of personal and corporate income taxes; this legislation is meant to give force to the first stage of the government's two-stage tax reform plan.

13 April 1988
Language Policy—
Saskatchewan

In a visit with his Saskatchewan counterpart, Quebec Premier Robert Bourassa voices his support for the controversial Saskatchewan language legislation, Bill 2. Characterizing the bill as a step forward, Mr. Bourassa notes that "I understand the Saskatchewan position. When Premier Devine says this is a delicate and emotional question and we have to apply the law with prudence, I think he's talking common sense." Mr. Bourassa's support for the government of Saskatchewan is criticized by francophone groups living outside Quebec as a betrayal of their minority language rights.

18 April 1988
Environment—
Atlantic Ocean

Citing its concern for the environmental safety of the region's rich fishing grounds, the federal government declares a 12-year moratorium on oil and gas exploration for the Canadian portion of Georges Bank, off Canada's east coast. The decision is fully supported by Nova Scotia Premier John Buchanan.

19 April 1988
Provincial-Inter-
national Relations—
Ontario

Ontario Premier David Peterson and Michigan Governor James Blanchard sign agreements aimed at ensuring the "mutual benefit" of the jurisdictions and establishing new "plateaus of friendship." The agreements include a declaration of partnership which calls for regular meetings between cabinet ministers and senior officials on matters of joint concern; and memoranda of understanding on cooperation in fighting forest fires, the regulation of maritime commerce and communication on accidental pollution discharges.

21 April 1988
Meech Lake
Accord—Senate

The Senate passes an amended version of the Meech Lake Accord, sending it back to the Commons for further debate followed by another vote. The Senators propose nine changes to the resolution—in essence the same changes as proposed by the Liberals during the earlier Commons debate. The key amendment would ensure that the clause in the agreement which acknowledges Quebec to be a "distinct society" is subordinate to the Canadian Charter of Rights and Freedoms. Other amendments would expand protection for official-language minorities, toughen provisions allowing provinces to opt out of new national programs, make it easier for the Yukon and Northwest Territories to become provinces, and provide for the election of senators. Senator Lowell Murray, Minister of State for Federal-Provincial Relations, calls the changes "killer amendments" aimed at destroying the Accord.

26 April 1988
Elections—
Manitoba

Manitoba voters elect a Progressive Conservative minority government. The Conservatives, led by Gary Filmon, win 26 seats—down from 27 in the last house. The big winners are the provincial Liberals, under Ms. Sharon Carstairs, who become the official opposition, going from one seat in the previous house to 20 in this one. The New Democrats elect 12 members, down from 29 in the previous legislature.

26 April 1988
*Provincial-International Relations—
Environment*

The Governments of Quebec and New York State sign a five-year extension of an acid rain control treaty originally concluded in 1982. The treaty requires the sharing of acid rain research, educational material and strategies to lobby for tougher environmental laws. For the first time, the treaty specifies that Quebec and New York will lobby other states to support tougher environmental protection laws.

5 May 1988
Environment

The House of Commons unanimously adopts the government's new Canadian Environmental Protection Act, which the government describes as being the strongest environmental legislation in the western world. The bill consolidates federal environmental laws and creates a new system for regulating the development, production, use and disposal of toxic chemicals. It also creates stiff sanctions for polluters, including unlimited fines and jail terms for the worst offenders. The bill includes provisions for agreements with provinces to allow provincial laws and regulations to stand for federal regulations where such measures are equivalent.

13 May 1988
*Meech Lake Accord
—P.E.I.*

With a single dissenter, the legislature of Prince Edward Island ratifies the Meech Lake Accord, becoming the fourth province to do so.

18-21 May 1988
*Western Premiers'
Conferences*

The Western premiers hold their annual meeting at Parksville, B.C. All four premiers affirm their support for free trade, and criticize Ontario premier David Peterson for his government's opposition to the agreement. On Senate reform, they are unanimous in supporting Premier Getty's call for a "Triple-E" Senate (Effective, Equal and Elected). The premiers call for a meeting of federal and provincial agriculture ministers on how to deal with conditions in the drought-stricken West.

24 May 1988
*Supreme Court—
Appointments*

Prime Minister Brian Mulroney names John Sopinka, a practicing lawyer, to the Supreme Court of Canada, filling the vacancy created by the resignation of J.W. Estey.

24 May 1988
Free Trade;
Federal-Provincial
Relations

International Trade Minister John Crosbie introduces his government's free trade legislation to the House of Commons. The bill amends 27 existing statutes to end, among other things, all cross-border tariffs over a ten year period. It will also ensure the compliance of such diverse legislation as the Bank Act, the Meat Import Act, the Income Tax Act and the Canadian Wheat Board Act with the terms of the Free Trade Agreement signed on 2 January 1988. While the legislation promises to trigger a bitter parliamentary debate, much of the attention is focused upon how Ottawa will guarantee to the United States that the provinces will comply with the agreement. Contained in the act are two clauses designed to bring about this effect. The first is Section 6, which states "For greater certainty, nothing in this act, by specific mention or omission, limits in any manner the right of Parliament to enact legislation to implement any provision of the agreement or fulfil any of the obligations of the government of Canada under the Agreement." Under second Section 9, Ottawa reserves the right the bring in further legislation after the deal is in effect to override new provincial legislation that would violate the agreement. Although the premiers of Alberta, Quebec and Nova Scotia indicate their concerns about these provisions, none of them withdraw their support for the agreement.

25 May 1988
Meech Lake Accord

Nova Scotia becomes the fifth province to ratify the Meech Lake Accord; the motion in support of the agreement passes by an overwhelming majority.

26 May 1988
Regional Develop-
ment—Western Di-
versification Office

Deputy Prime Minister Donald Mazankowski announces that $27 million will be allocated from the Western Diversification Fund to help Ontario Hydro afford Western Canadian coal. A 1987 task force report concluded that the Ontario utility could reduce acid rain emissions and create up to 26,000 permanent jobs in Western Canada by switching to western coal. The money will go towards subsidizing the transportation of the coal to Ontario.

2 June 1988
Health Policy—
Ontario

The Ontario government introduces its Independent Health Facilities Act into the Ontario legislature; the legislation could be a direct challenge to the Canada-U.S. Free Trade Agreement. The new law sets rules for the licensing and funding of clinics that provide health services covered by medicare, and appears to contravene the FTA with its assertion that "despite any international treaty or obligation to which Canada is a party or any law implementing such a treaty or obligation," preference will be given to proposals for clinics that are to be owned and operated by Canadians. In Ottawa the next day Trade Minister John Crosbie dismisses the Ontario legislation as a "propaganda ploy."

2 June 1988
Supreme Court—
Meech Lake Accord

The Supreme Court of Canada rejects an attempt by the Yukon and Northwest Territories to challenge the constitutionality of the Meech Lake Accord. Without giving reasons, Chief Justice Brian Dickson dismisses a request from these governments for permission to appeal lower court rulings that Ottawa had no obligation to consult them before signing the Accord.

6 June 1988
Regulation—
Financial Institutions

Federal Finance Minister Michael Wilson announces a joint federal-provincial moratorium on the sale and leaseback of libraries and other assets by universities and hospitals. In "sale and leaseback" arrangements, a tax-exempt institution, which cannot benefit from depreciation allowances, sells its assets to a private company that can benefit from tax write-offs. The tax-exempt institution receives some of those benefits in the form of fees or preferential leasing rates. Such arrangements hurt both federal and provincial treasuries, which lose tax revenue from the private company. Ontario had imposed a unilateral moratorium on sale and leasebacks imposed in that province 7 May.

6 June 1988
Health Policy

Federal Health Minister Jake Epp announces a $40 million joint federal-provincial program to battle the prevalence of family violence. Of this money, $22.2 million is to go to the federal housing agency to build or acquire the units expected to provide temporary housing for 25,000 abused women a year. According to Mr. Epp, the provinces are to be responsible for operating expenses for the program, but will be able to draw funds from the Canada Assistance Plan. The federal contribution—paid 50-50 on a matching basis—is expected to be $3 million annually.

9 June 1988
Supreme Court—
Hydroelectricity;
Interprovincial
Energy Relations

In a decision Newfoundland premier Brian Peckford calls "extremely disappointing," the Supreme Court of Canada rejects Newfoundland's battle for a greater share of the hydroelectricity generated by the giant Churchill Falls hydro project. The government of Newfoundland had wanted to renegotiate a 65-year contract between the government of Joseph Smallwood and Hydro-Québec under which Quebec buys Labrador power at low prices and then resells it, as part of its surplus, to the United States at ten times the price. In an unanimous judgement, the Supreme Court judges concur with two previous rulings by senior courts in Quebec and Newfoundland upholding the sanctity of the contract. The decision is the second time in four years that the Court has ruled unanimously against attempts by Newfoundland to alter the Churchill Falls agreement. Later, at a meeting in Newport, R.I., Premiers Peckford and Bourassa announce their willingness to investigate the possibility of further joint hydroelectric developments in Labrador.

9 June 1988
Regional Develop-
ment—Quebec

Prime Minister Mulroney announces the conclusion of a 5-year regional development agreement between Ottawa and Quebec. Under the agreement, the two governments will spend $970 million to help underdeveloped areas revitalize existing industries and attract new ones, to boost tourism and to improve transportation systems. The program is to be jointly managed by both governments.

13 June 1988
Environment—
Interprovincial
Relations

Meeting in Montreal, Premiers Bourassa of Quebec and Peterson of Ontario sign an agreement committing their respective provinces to share information with each other both on hazardous shipments passing from one territory to the other and on emerging environmental problems of interest to both provinces.

14-15 June 1988
Eastern Canadian Premiers and New England Governors

The Eastern Canadian Premiers and New England Governors meet in Newport, R.I. for their annual conference. Atop the agenda for the two-day meeting is the Canada-U.S. Free Trade Agreement, with the participants being briefed by U.S. free trade negotiator Peter Murphy and Canadian Ambassador to the U.S. Alan Gotlieb. A particular point of contention for premiers McKenna, Peckford and Buchanan is the attendance of anti-free trade Ontario premier David Peterson as a guest; according to Premier Peckford "There's no place for Ontario at this conference, geographically or any other way." Also discussed are energy matters and environmental issues—particularly acid rain and the environmental threat posed by oil exploration on the American portion of George's Bank.

15 June 1988
Language Policy— Saskatchewan

Federal Secretary of State Lucien Bouchard and Saskatchewan Education Minister Lorne Hepworth announce that their respective governments have reached an agreement on French-language eduction in Saskatchewan. Ottawa will pay up to $56 million over as many as ten years to support francophone school boards, improve French-language education and immersion programs, rebuild the province's only French-language high school which recently burned, and create a language training centre at the University of Regina. Another $6 million is to be provided for the translation of some of the province's laws into French, establishing a French language coordination and translation office, and increasing the use of French in the provincial legislature.

20 June 1988
Transportation— Newfoundland

The federal and Newfoundland governments announce a 15 year, $800 million federal-provincial agreement that would close the Newfoundland railway, making Newfoundland the only Canadian province without rail service. Ottawa is to provide a package of highway improvements and benefits for displaced workers. Municipalities hit by the layoffs and loss of related revenue from the railway will also receive compensation in the form of development grants.

22 June 1988
Language Policy—
Alberta

Alberta introduces its new language legislation in response to the Supreme Court ruling of 25 February that significant French rights are guaranteed in Saskatchewan and, by implication, in Alberta. Bill 60 will permit Alberta MLAs to speak French in the legislature, and courts will operate in either English or French. It validates all existing provincial laws, even though they exist in English only. The law also invalidates Section 110 of the 1886 Northwest Territories Act which would have meant all laws had to be in both languages. Like the language legislation introduced in Saskatchewan 4 April, the Alberta bill meets with strong criticism from federal politicians and French-language groups.

22 June 1988
Meech Lake Accord

The House of Commons endorses the Meech Lake Constitutional Accord with a 200-7 vote. The Accord, which had been passed by the House in October 1987, required a second vote to override the Senate approved amendments to the Accord. Opposition votes are cast by four Liberals, one Conservative, one New Democrat and one independent.

23 June 1988
Regional Develop-
ment—Prince
Edward Island

Representatives of the federal Government and the Government of Prince Edward Island sign a new five-year forestry development agreement worth $24.1 million.

24 June 1988
Aboriginal Self-
Government—
British Columbia

The Sechelt Indian Band of British Columbia officially becomes a self-governing municipality. The Sechelt Indian Government District is the first of its kind in Canada.

27 June 1988
Council of
Maritime Premiers

The Council of Maritime Premiers meet for the seventieth session of the Council of Maritime Premiers in Charlottetown. Leaving broader issues such as free trade and Meech Lake—over which there is disagreement within the Council—off the agenda, the premiers discuss the proposed fixed link to Prince Edward Island and the future energy needs of the maritime provinces.

27 June 1988
Jurisdiction,
Provincial—
Ontario

The Government of Ontario introduces changes to two pieces of legislation—the Power Corporation Act and Wine Content Act—which appear to go against provisions of the Canada-U.S. Trade Agreement. Changes to the first would require Ontario Hydro, "notwithstanding anything to the contrary in the trade agreement," to sell energy only if it is surplus to Canadian needs and to charge higher prices for exported energy. Changes to the Wine Content Act set up a timetable for the elimination of markups over 12 years, as opposed to the seven-year schedule under the agreement.

28 June 1988
Jurisdiction,
Provincial—Water—
Ontario

The Government of Ontario tables its Water Transfer Control Act, asserting provincial control over any future sales of water from the Great Lakes. The government argues that because water exports are not expressly excluded under the Canada-U.S. Free Trade Agreement, domestic supply would be jeopardized by large-scale water diversion schemes.

29 June 1988
Meech Lake Accord
—Ontario

The Ontario Legislature votes 112-8 to ratify the Meech Lake Constitutional Accord. The vote—which makes Ontario the sixth province to endorse Meech Lake—was opposed by three New Democrats and five Conservatives.

29 June 1988
Meech Lake Accord
—British Columbia

The British Columbia Legislature becomes the seventh province to ratify the Meech Lake agreement, voting 42-5 in favour of the agreement.

5 July 1988
Regulation—
Energy—National
Energy Board

The National Energy Board grants Pan-Alberta Gas Ltd. a 24-year license to sell natural gas it may not yet have to Southern California, while rejecting Ontario concerns that the deal will erode valuable Canadian reserves. The decision marks the first application of the NEB's new policy to eliminate the surplus test, which for decades has required Alberta to stockpile enough gas for up to 30 years future use in Canada before exports were allowed. During the NEB hearings, however, Ontario and its regional fuel buyers were virtually alone in demanding some sort of retention of the surplus test. Quebec, the other major consuming province, had joined forces with Alberta before the NEB hearings on the sale earlier this spring.

7 July 1988
Environment—
Nova Scotia

The federal and Nova Scotia governments conclude the Canada-Nova Scotia Sub-accord on Sustainable Development for Central Nova Scotia, which aims at ensuring that any economic development in the central part of the province protects the environment. As part of the agreement, a study is launched to identify existing or potential conflicts between economic development in the area and the environment.

7 July 1988
Language Policy

The Commons passes Bill C-72, its proposed bilingualism legislation over the protests of nine Conservative dissidents. The bill, which updates the 19 year-old Official Languages Act allows more public servants to work in the official language of their choice and guarantees the right to trial in either French or English. The bill now moves on to the Senate, where it is passed on July 27.

8 July 1988
*Meech Lake Accord
—Newfoundland*

Newfoundland becomes the eighth province to ratify the Meech Lake Accord. Twenty-eight voted in favour of the accord, with ten Liberals dissenting.

12 July 1988
*National Parks—
British Columbia*

The federal and British Columbia governments sign a $31 million agreement—of which the federal government will provide $24 million—to establish the South Moresby national park reserve in the Queen Charlotte Islands. Issues left unresolved are compensation for resource companies working in the region and the as yet unresolved land claims of the Haida Indian band.

13 July 1988
Day Care

Health Minister Jake Epp announces in the Commons that the federal government will contribute an additional $1 billion for day care, raising the cost of its already announced, federal-provincial day-care program to $6.4 billion over seven years. Although the extra funds will not create any more than the 200,000 new day-care spaces promised under the program announced last December, they will be used largely to cover a shortfall in the original estimated price—$5.4 billion—of the program.

18 July 1988
*Megaprojects—
Newfoundland*

The federal and Newfoundland governments, together with a Mobil Oil-led consortium sign a long-awaited agreement to begin construction next year on an $8.5 billion development of the Hibernia oil field. According to the agreement, Ottawa is to contribute $2.6 billion towards the project, $1 billion grant towards pre-production costs and $1.6 billion in loan guarantees. Newfoundland is to receive the major share of the construction contract for the massive drilling platform that will be built in Come by Chance. The project is to provide 1,000 permanent jobs over its 20 year production life, as well as about 1,400 jobs during six years of construction.

20 July 1988
Free Trade—
Liberal Party

Opposition Leader John Turner announces that he has instructed the Liberal-dominated Senate not to pass legislation to implement the free trade agreement until Prime Minister Brian Mulroney calls a federal election on the issue. "This issue is so fundamental that the people of Canada deserve and must have the right to judge," Mr. Turner says at a news conference. "I think the issue becomes democracy. Let the people decide." Senate leader Alan MacEachen announces that the Liberal majority in the Senate will accede to Mr. Turner's wishes. During Question Period in the Commons Prime Minister Mulroney attacks Mr. Turner's announcement. "In an act of desperation, the leader of the Opposition no longer wants the House of Commons to consider this important matter. He wants to resign his leadership in favour of the Senate, and I say that's not good enough for the people of Canada."

30 July 1988
Elections—
Nova Scotia

Announcing that this election "is about leadership—strong leadership for new ideas," Nova Scotia Conservative Premier John Buchanan calls a provincial election for his province, to be held 6 September. At dissolution, the Conservatives hold 40 seats, the Liberals six and the NDP three.

4 August 1988
Energy Policy

The federal government releases *Energy Options*, a report suggesting possible federal energy policies for the future. Among its significant departures from previous policy would be equal weight given to environmental considerations and to have a non-discriminatory fiscal and expenditure policy.

9 August 1988
Free Trade

The United States House of Representatives gives overwhelming approval to legislation covering the Canada-U.S. Free Trade Agreement, voting 366-40 to implement the trade pact. The agreement still requires the approval of the U.S. Senate and the Canadian Parliament before it can be implemented.

18 August 1988
Regional Development—ACOA

Parliament passes Bill C-103—the legislation establishing the Atlantic Canada Opportunities Agency—after third and final reading in the Senate.

19 August 1988
Annual Premiers' Conference

Canada's ten premiers meet in Saskatoon for their annual premiers' conference. On the agenda for the meeting is monetary policy, Senate reform and the Meech Lake Accord. Regarding monetary policy, the ten premiers agree unanimously to demand an immediate reduction in interest rates by the Bank of Canada. Saskatchewan Premier Grant Devine is delegated to go to Ottawa to meet Bank of Canada Governor John Crow to make the demand on behalf of the ten premiers. Although Alberta Premier Don Getty pushed for a First Ministers' Conference on Senate reform to be staged before the end of the year, the premiers agree that an Alberta task force, headed by Alberta Intergovernmental Affairs Minister Jim Horsman, will tour the country in the fall to conduct bilateral discussions aimed at developing a plan for Senate reform with Ottawa and the other provinces. Premiers Peterson of Ontario and Bourassa of Quebec make it clear, however, that reform of the Senate cannot be negotiated until the Meech Lake Accord has been ratified by all ten provinces.

25 August 1988
Hydroelectricity— Prince Edward Island

Prince Edward Island signs a six-year agreement with New Brunswick and Quebec to buy as much as $175 million worth of electricity. Whereas P.E.I. buys 90 per cent of its power from New Brunswick, the deal allows the province to buy power from Quebec to offset interruptions in the New Brunswick supply. Under the agreement, P.E.I. will be allowed to determine how much power it wants to buy from New Brunswick and how much it wants from Quebec to cushion the impact of sharp increases in the price of oil. New Brunswick will then buy the electricity from Quebec and send it on to P.E.I.

25 August 1988
Free Trade—Water
Exports

Reacting to concerns that the Canada-U.S. Free Trade Agreement does not protect the country from large-scale diversions of water to the U.S., Environment Minister Tom McMillan introduces a bill in the Commons that would ban outright large-scale projects to divert water across the border and provide million-dollar fines and jail sentences for anyone breaking the law.

31 August 1988
Free Trade

After months of heated exchanges, the government's free trade legislation is passed by the House of Commons by a vote of 177-64. The bill now passes on to the Senate, where the Liberal majority in the upper chamber has said it will delay the legislation until a federal election is held on the issue as demanded by Opposition Leader John Turner.

2 September 1988
Megaprojects—
Saskatchewan

The federal government and the governments of Alberta and Saskatchewan announce the construction of a $1.3 billion Husky oil upgrader plant in Lloydminster, Saskatchewan. The three governments will put up almost 75 per cent of the cash for the project, with Husky Oil Ltd. providing the rest. The federal government will pay $399 million for 31.67 per cent equity, Alberta about $300 million for 24.17 per cent equity, and Saskatchewan $222 million for 17.5 per cent equity. According to Deputy Prime Minister Don Mazankowski, the deal will provide a means of strengthening Canada's energy security while conventional reserves of crude oil continue to dwindle.

5 September 1988
Aboriginal Land
Claims—
Northwest
Territories

Prime Minister Brian Mulroney signs an agreement-in-principle that would make the Dene and Métis the largest non-government landowners in North America. It will give the 15,000 natives in the Northwest Territories $500 million in cash and ownership, including subsurface rights, to about 10,000 square kilometres of land. The deal splits royalties received from the land between the natives groups and the federal government. The groups also are to receive special rights and interests in a total of 180,000 square kilometres, including a voice in land, wildlife and water management decisions. Left out of the agreement are such contentious issues as aboriginal title and self-government, which are to be negotiated later.

6 September 1988
Hydroelectricity—
Exports—Regula-
tion

Federal Energy Minister Marcel Masse announces a new policy easing the restrictions on large, long-term exports of Canadian electricity. Under the policy, the National Energy Board will be able to approve electricity exports without a public hearing. Consuming provinces will have to convince the board and federal cabinet that a hearing is necessary to protect the national interest, and will have to demonstrate that they want to purchase the electricity, in order to block exports. For their part, the exporters must show that the power was made available to Canadians first at a price no higher than the export price. "My objective," according to Mr. Masse, "is to streamline the regulation of electricity exports so as to make it easier for exports. At the same time, the powers of the National Energy Board will be retained to guarantee the protection of the Canadian public interest."

6 September 1988
Elections—
Nova Scotia

Nova Scotia Premier John Buchanan leads his Conservative Party to victory in the Nova Scotia election, although with a much-reduced majority. The Conservatives win 28 seats, losing 14 from their pre-election total; the Liberals win 21 seats, up from six; and the New Democrats win two, down from the three they held before the election. One Independent is re-elected.

7 September 1988
Federal-Territorial
Relations—Energy

Prime Minister Brian Mulroney and Northwest Territories Government leader Dennis Patterson sign a tentative northern accord on energy, hailing it as a huge step towards achieving the territory's ambition of provincehood. The agreement-in-principle gives the territory "province-like" legislative and management responsibilities for on-shore oil and gas revenues and a share of all royalties. The management of off-shore royalties is to be negotiated later. Although the deal does not include ownership of the resources, revenues from them are to be shared between the two governments. According to Mr. Patterson, with the energy pact now entering the final negotiation phase only certain federal powers relating to inland fisheries, labour relations and the attorney general's department prevent the territory from having the same powers as provinces.

15 September 1988
Free Trade

In a 19-0 vote marked by the absence of Liberal Senators, the Canada-U.S. Free Trade Agreement is given approval-in-principle by the Senate, and moves on to the Foreign Affairs Committee, where it is expected to languish until a federal election is called.

19 September 1988
Procurement—Inter-provincial Relations

Meeting in Saint John, N.B., federal and provincial trade ministers from the ten provinces conclude a deal on procurement that participants hail as a first step towards the dismantling of interprovincial trade barriers. The agreement—concluded after ten months of negotiation—would disallow provincial tendering policies that give preference to goods from companies based within the province. Services and public works contracts are not affected by the agreement. Pending final approval from premiers, provinces will adopt non-discriminatory national tendering for contracts to supply goods worth more than $25,000 by 1 April 1992. The deal also applies to federal government contracts, although Ottawa may continue to use procurement selectively to promote regional development.

19 September 1988
Environment—Federal-Provincial Relations

Invoking special interim powers provided for in the Canadian Environmental Protection Act and in the wake of a toxic chemical fire in Saint-Basile-le-Grand, Quebec, Environment Minister Tom McMillan announces that all depots for PCBs must meet federal or equivalent provincial standards for fire and security measures within 30 days, or the operators will face stiff fines. The special interim order changes existing federal suggestions for safe storage of PCBs into binding requirements. Provinces that fail to show they have standards or permit systems comparable to the federal system will be subject to federal inspection of sites.

22 September 1988
Federal-Territorial Relations—Energy

The federal and Yukon governments sign an agreement-in-principle that gives the territory a role in oil and gas development. According to Yukon Government Leader Tony Penikett, the agreement finally recognizes the territorial government's stake in energy development. The two governments agree to share the regulation and management of oil and gas in the Beaufort Sea, subject to negotiations with the Northwest Territories. The agreement mirrors Ottawa's deal with the Northwest Territories signed on 6 September.

22 September 1988
Federal-Provincial
Relations—Energy

The federal and British Columbia governments announce the construction of a $485 million natural gas pipeline to connect Vancouver Island with the mainland. The two governments are to fund 50 per cent of the project, with Ottawa providing a $100 million grant and a $50 million interest-free loan and British Columbia matching the federal contribution with a $25 million interest-free loan, $55 million to help consumers convert from oil to natural gas and $70 million to cover cost overruns. The project is to begin as early as 1989.

24 September 1988
Megaprojects—
Alberta

The federal and Alberta governments announce that they have reached an agreement that will allow a proposed $4 billion Alberta oil sands project to go ahead. A group of six companies known as the OSLO consortium worked out the $2 billion package with the two governments, paving the way for a final study of the project. Under the deal, the federal and provincial governments would give the consortium $850 million in loan guarantees. If the price of oil falls below $19 U.S. a barrel, the consortium is to receive $160 million—70 per cent to be paid by Alberta and 30 per cent by Ottawa. If, in turn, oil prices are higher, the two governments will share 16 per cent of operating revenues.

26 September 1988
Senate—
Appointments

Prime Minister Mulroney announces the appointment of four new Senators from Quebec. The four named to the upper house are: Solange Chaput-Rolland, a former member of the Pepin-Robarts Task Force and past-member of the Quebec National Assembly; constitutional expert Gerald Beaudoin; Roch Bolduc; and Jean-Marie Poitras. The appointments were made from a nominations list provided by Quebec Premier Bourassa, as stipulated by the Meech Lake Constitutional Accord, which requires that all new senators be named from lists supplied by the provinces.

28 September 1988
Free Trade—United States

Hailing the agreement as a "landmark," and an "idea whose time has come, " United States President Ronald Reagan signs into law the U.S. legislation to enact the Canada-U.S. Free Trade Agreement, ending the American process for approving the agreement.

28 September 1988
Health; Regional Development— Manitoba

Federal Health Minister Jake Epp announces the federal government's decision to locate a new virology laboratory in Winnipeg on a site near Manitoba's largest hospital. Construction is scheduled to start in 1990 at a cost of about $93 million.

1 October 1988
Elections—Federal

Inviting "the people to judge us," Prime Minister Mulroney dissolves Parliament and calls a federal election to be held on 21 November. At dissolution the Progressive Conservatives hold 211 seats, the Liberals 40, the New Democrats 30, and one Independent. The key issue is expected to be the Canada-U.S. Free Trade Agreement, which has received approval in the U.S. and passed through the Commons, but which has been stalled in the Liberal-dominated Senate since Liberal leader John Turner requested Liberal Senators to delay the bill until after an election on the issue. Among those bills which die on the order paper are the free trade legislation, the government's day-care legislation, the new Broadcasting Act, amendments to the Criminal code defining pornography, conflict of interest legislation and a bill banning large-scale exports of water to the U.S.

17 October 1988
Interprovincial Relations—Energy

In an agreement that may bring an end to the acrimonious battle between the Alberta gas producers and Ontario consumers, Alberta's largest natural gas marketer, Western Gas Marketing Ltd., signs a package of 15-year supply contracts with six central Canadian distributors. The new contracts with gas distributors in Manitoba, Ontario and Quebec are said to be worth roughly $20 billion over the next 20 years, and may avoid the need for "spot-market" shopping by consumer firms. The deals give "essential service" customers—those who can least tolerate a disruption of service—15 years of firm gas supply, with prices to be renegotiated annually after 1990.

24, 25 October 1988
Elections—Federal

The leaders of the Conservative, Liberal and New Democratic Parties contest two three-hour debates, the first in French and the second in English, broadcast nation-wide. The debates were marked by several angry exchanges between Prime Minister Mulroney and Liberal leader John Turner over the issue of free trade.

27 October 1988
Regulation—Financial Institutions

Consumer and corporate affairs ministers from the four western provinces sign an agreement in Winnipeg to share information on the economic health of financial institutions to protect consumers and strengthen the industry. The information is to alert provincial governments to potential problems within banks, trust companies and other credit firms so as to avoid problems such as the June 1987 collapse of Principal Group Ltd.

2 November 1988
Sports

At their annual meeting in Winnipeg, provincial sports ministers from across the country agree to work together to fight the use of drugs in amateur athletics. According to Manitoba Sports Minister Jim Ernst, the ministers "unanimously agreed that our priority must be the development ... of educational programs relating to the use of prohibited substances in sport."

8 November 1988
Interprovincial Relations—Law Enforcement

The governments of Quebec and Ontario sign an accord in Montreal to share traffic offence information, ensuring that tickets issued to motorists visiting from either province would not be left behind at the border.

8 November 1988
Elections—Federal

New Democratic Party leader Ed Broadbent rejects a statement made 4 November by a group of Quebec NDP candidates who asserted that only Quebec should have the power to override the Charter of Rights—and only to protect the French language and culture. The position of the Quebec candidates, he asserted "is not the position of the party as a whole." Rather, the notwithstanding clause, insomuch as it exists in law, should continue to be available to all governments.

8 November 1988
Monetary Policy

Saskatchewan Premier Grant Devine meets in Ottawa with Finance Minister Michael Wilson and Bank of

Canada governor John Crow in an attempt to convince them to lower the bank's interest rates. Mr. Devine had been delegated by the provincial premiers to carry their concerns about the high interest rate policy to this years' Annual Premiers' Conference. Emerging from the meeting, the Saskatchewan premier tells reporters that he is now more confident that Mr. Crow was looking at a wide range of policy options rather than just resorting to interest rates as the only tool to manage the economy.

8 November 1988
Aboriginal Land
Claims—Yukon

An agreement-in-principle is concluded between the federal government and the Yukon Council of Indians that is to give the Council's 6,500 members $230 million and about nine per cent of Yukon Territory. The deal involves the transfer of about 41,000 square kilometres of land to the territory's 13 Indian bands. In negotiations, the main issue in dispute had been the size of the federal financial compensation package. The Yukon Indians sought $234 million while Ottawa was offering $214 million. The two sides reached agreement of $230 million after the Indians agreed to make some tax concessions. Most of the cash will be used to finance native development corporations.

10 November 1988
Jurisdiction,
Provincial—Water—
Ontario

The Ontario government introduces legislation into its legislature banning the transfer of large amounts of water from the province to the United States or any other country. The amendment to the Water Transfer Control Act states that, despite the proposed free trade deal with the United States or any Canadian legislation implementing that agreement, the Ontario government "shall refuse to give approval to a transfer of water out of a provincial drainage basin to a place outside Canada."

21 November 1988
Elections—Federal

The Progressive Conservative Party under Brian Mulroney wins its second consecutive majority government—the first federal government in 35 years and the only Conservative government this century to do so. The Conservatives win 170 seats in the new Parliament, down from 211 in the previous one; the Liberals win 83, up from 40 in 1984; and the New Democrats win 43, up from 30 previously. Throughout, the election campaign was dominated by the free trade debate, and featured bitter accusations and counter-accusations from those on both sides of the issue. Six cabinet ministers went down to defeat, including Communications Minister Flora MacDonald, Solicitor General James Kelleher, Justice Minister Ray Hnatyshyn, Environment Minister Tom McMillan, Public Works Minister Stewart McInnis and junior transport minister Gerry St. Germain. Given that the election was fought around the free trade issue, the Conservative victory ensures the passage of that agreement.

26 November 1988
Parti Québécois

In a convention in St. Hyacinthe, Quebec, the Parti Québécois adopts a policy to start negotiations to make Quebec independent if the PQ ever forms a government in Quebec. According to party leader Jacques Parizeau, in the next provincial election "a vote for the PQ is a vote for the sovereigntist party."

28 November 1988
*Council of
Maritime Premiers*

The Council of Maritime Premiers meets in Saint John to discuss their concerns over the free trade agreement, and agree to form a united front to press the federal government to help industries that could be weakened by free trade with the United States. According to Premier Frank McKenna, "We have pledged to work together in providing a common voice to Ottawa urging adjustment programs where necessary." All three premiers identified the food processing industry as being in particular need of assistance, with Nova Scotia Premier John Buchanan adding textiles to the list and P.E.I. Premier Joe Ghiz calling for support for family farms and manufacturers of farm implements. They agree, as well, that training, marketing information, access to new technology and exporting skills are all required to help businesses in their region compete. The premiers plan to appoint deputy ministers to a committee which will formulate the region's approach to Ottawa.

6 December 1988
*Education, French
Language—Alberta*

The Conservative government of Alberta Premier Don Getty announces a new policy that recognizes French language rights in education. While the policy emphasizes proficiency in English as a major key to success in Alberta, it also commits school boards to guarantee and finance French language education as provided "where numbers warrant" in the Charter of Rights and Freedoms and the new Alberta School Act.

7 December 1988
Fisheries

Federal Fisheries Minister Tom Siddon rejects a request by a Quebec-New Brunswick consortium known as Nova Nord to gain a share of northern cod stocks. Asserting that there had been a rise in cod stocks, Nova Nord had asked Ottawa for 548,000 tonnes of fish over ten years. Mr. Siddon states that he will continue to be guided by the principles of adjacency and historic sharing, after which—if there is a demonstrated increase in the stock—his main objective is to rebuild the inshore fishery on Newfoundland's northeast coast.

9 December 1988
Regulation—Financial Institutions

Provincial ministers responsible for financial institutions agree to work toward harmonizing their laws and regulations governing trust and other financial companies under provincial authority. The protocol affirms that each province has jurisdiction over all financial institutions operating within its borders and has primary responsibility for the companies incorporated under its laws. It calls for the home province of a financial institution to provide information on request to other provinces where it operates and states that provinces will keep one another posted on investigations to avoid duplication of efforts. In addition, the ministers agree to form a committee, chaired by British Columbia Finance Minister Mel Couvelier, to begin exploring areas where they might harmonize laws and regulations governing their financial companies.

15 December 1988
Supreme Court—Language—Quebec

In an unanimous judgement, the Supreme Court of Canada strikes down the French-only sign provisions of Quebec's language law, Bill 101, as an unreasonable violation of freedom of expression, as prohibited by the Quebec Charter of Rights and the Canadian Charter of Rights and Freedoms. Although the five judges recognize the survival of the French language as a "pressing and substantial concern" and strongly endorse Quebec's right to require the use of French, they hold that Quebec has not proven the need to ban the use of English or other languages. In its ruling, the court indicates that it would accept a law requiring the "markedly predominant" display of the French language as a valid way of promoting the French identity of Quebec. But the court recognizes non-francophones' right to freely express themselves in the language of their choice. "Language is so intimately related to the form and content of expression that there cannot be true expression by means of language if one is prohibited from using the language of one's choice." The ruling carefully examines Quebec's use of the federal "notwithstanding clause" to grant blanket exemption to its statutes in 1982, calling it a valid exercise of the province's power.

18 December 1988
Language Policy—
Quebec

Quebec Premier Bourassa announces that his government will invoke the "notwithstanding" clauses of the Canadian and Quebec Charters of Rights to ensure that French alone will be used on commercial signs outside stores in the province. According to Mr. Bourassa, this is a compromise meant to preserve the French face of Quebec while guaranteeing individual rights to freedom of expression. Noting that his government was following the Supreme Court's suggestion in invoking the notwithstanding clause, he acknowledges that he knows this decision is asking anglophones "to make an enormous concession." Premier Bourassa suggests, as well, that invoking the notwithstanding clause was necessary because the Meech Lake Accord, which gives Quebec extra powers to protect its French language and culture, has not yet been ratified.

19 December 1988
Meech Lake Accord
—Manitoba

Manitoba Premier Gary Filmon, citing his grave concerns over Quebec Premier Bourassa's response to the Supreme Court language ruling, withdraws his government's Meech Lake Accord resolution from its legislative agenda. Only Manitoba and New Brunswick have yet to ratify the Accord. Response to Mr. Filmon's action is swift. Quebec Justice Minister Gil Remillard noted that ten provinces are needed to complete the Accord and that "those responsible for the failure of Meech Lake must bear the consequences." Mr. Bourassa's response is that "the first loser if Meech Lake is not ratified will be the country, not Quebec."

20 December 1988
Language Policy—
Quebec

Three of Premier Bourassa's four anglophone ministers quit his cabinet saying they cannot support the government's language policies. Environment Minister Clifford Lincoln, Public Security Minister Herbert Marx and Communications Minister Richard French, who represented mainly English ridings, state that they intend to remain in the Liberal caucus and sit as backbenchers in the National Assembly. A fourth anglophone cabinet minister, Energy Minister John Ciaccia, remains in the cabinet, stating that "someone must make the first move to end the language wars. By staying I can do more than by leaving."

23 December 1988
Language Policy

The Department of the Secretary of State announces that the federal government is to contribute $1.2 billion over the next five years to minority and second-language education across the country. According to a press release, the money is to be used to help develop educational programs for minority languages and for English and French second languages. Priority is to be placed upon improving access to minority-language education, expansion of French in post-secondary schools, expansion of programs for teachers and more opportunities for second-language learning.

30 December 1988
Free Trade

With the Liberal majority abstaining from the vote, the government's free trade legislation passes the Senate and is given royal assent by Supreme Court Justice Antonio Lamer on behalf of Governor General Jeanne Sauvé. The legislation amends 27 Canadian laws to conform with the obligations of the trade agreement. On 31 December Canadian and U.S. representatives exchange diplomatic notes stating that each country is ready to put the treaty into effect. The treaty is to come into effect 1 January.

4 January 1989
Provincial-Inter-
national Relations

British Columbia Premier Bill Vander Zalm and Washington State Governor Booth Gardner sign two cooperation agreements pledging their respective jurisdictions to knocking down trade barriers and launching joint tourism and business promotions.

10 January 1989
Senate—Reform

Senator Lowell Murray, the minister for federal-provincial relations, begins talks on the next stage of Senate reform with the provinces. Senate reform is scheduled as the first item of a constitutional conference of first ministers to be held after the Meech Lake Accord is ratified by all ten provinces.

16 January 1989
Provincial-International Relations

The Alberta government agrees for the first time to participate in a meeting of the Organization of Petroleum Exporting Countries (OPEC). Neil Webber, provincial Energy Minister, says that Alberta has not agreed to cooperate with production quotas set by OPEC to prop up world oil prices at the London meetings on 25 and 26 January, but will lend "moral support" to the organization's most recent agreement to limit oil production. The federal government was not invited to attend.

17 January 1989
Elections—Yukon

Yukon Government Leader Tony Penikett calls a general election for 20 February. Penikett, leader of the country's only New Democratic Party government, says that the election will be fought on his government's record of creating 3000 new jobs since it was elected in May 1985. At dissolution, the party standings are: NDP—seven; Conservatives—six; Liberals—one; and, one seat is vacant.

21 January 1989
Progressive Conservative Party —Newfoundland

Newfoundland Premier Brian Peckford announces that he will step down from office at the end of January. The fiery orator took office in June 1979 and fought almost continuous battles with the federal government, particularly Prime Minister Pierre Trudeau, over offshore oil and fisheries jurisdictions. At a press conference Peckford says he no longer has the "ruthlessness" to perform the job required as premier and that he is worn down by his partial failure to achieve his dream of making Newfoundland an equal partner in Confederation.

23 January 1989
Supreme Court— Appointments

Prime Minister Brian Mulroney names two appointments to the Supreme Court of Canada. Mr. Justice Charles Joseph Gonthier, a judge of the Quebec Court of Appeal, and Mr. Justice Peter de Carteret Cory of the

Ontario Court of Appeal were named to replace Jean Beetz and Gerald Le Dain, both of whom resigned in November 1988 because of illness. The appointments, effective 1 February, bring the court back to full compliment and were welcomed by Chief Justice Brian Dickson, who earlier had delayed four constitutional cases until a full court could hear them. This brings to five the number of appointments that Brian Mulroney has made to the Supreme Court since becoming Prime Minister in 1984.

26 January 1989
Federal-Provincial Agreements

The Federal Court makes public a ruling that has ordered Ottawa to freeze $168 million in transfer payments to the province of Manitoba because that provincial government has been deducting 5 per cent of monthly welfare cheques to make up for past overpayment. Mr. Justice Max Teitelbaum says the practice is a violation of a federal-provincial agreement, and until violations stop, Ottawa must halt its transfer payments to Manitoba. The payments amount to $14 million each month (see entry for 23 February 1989)

7 February 1989
Senate—Reform

Prime Minister Brian Mulroney rejects one-name Senate lists. Speaking to reporters Mulroney says that provinces have the right to nominate whomever they want as potential senators, but a list from any one province with only one name on it will not be accepted. This appears to call to a halt suggestions by Alberta Premier Don Getty that his province will provide only one nominee to the Senate following an election. As part of the Meech Lake Accord it was agreed that provinces with a vacancy in the Senate could submit a list of names to the federal cabinet with Ottawa choosing from the list.

20 February 1989
Elections—Alberta

Alberta Premier Don Getty calls a general provincial election for 20 March. The election call comes two years and 45 weeks after the previous election produced a majority Conservative government. "The people I'll be dealing with—on Senate reform, a Senate election, low interest rates and a fight against the national sales tax—they understand strength" says Getty in justifying the election call.

20 February 1989
Elections—Yukon

Yukon Government leader Tony Penikett and his New Democratic Party are returned to power in a general territorial election, keeping in power the only NDP government in Canada. Of the 17 seats, the NDP took nine and the Conservatives, seven.

23 February 1989
Environment

Environment ministers from three western provinces agree to improve recycling programs. Paper recycling will be studied in Saskatchewan; oil recycling, in British Columbia; pesticide container recycling in Manitoba; and Alberta is expected to study the recycling of used tires. The ministers also promise to support a ten-year federal program to ban chemicals that harm the ozone layer.

23 February 1989
Federal-Provincial Agreements

The federal government appeals a Federal Court ruling that says that Manitoba must change its welfare system or lose millions of dollars a month in federal payments under the Canada Assistance Plan (CAP). Most other provinces have similar agreements and would be affected by the Manitoba ruling. The federal government is also talking with the provinces on a political solution to what has become a national problem (see entry for 26 January 1989).

27 February 1989
Meech Lake Accord —First Ministers' Meeting

At a meeting of the Prime Minister and nine of ten provincial premiers (Premier Bill Vander Zalm of British Columbia was ill), no consensus is reached on the constitutional impasse over the Meech Lake Accord. "There are realities ongoing in the province of Quebec and elsewhere that would be ignored only at very considerable risk and peril," Mulroney warned the two premiers, McKenna and Filmon, whose provincial legislatures have yet to ratify the Accord. All the premiers admit that they had made no progress in appeals to Ottawa to do something about rising interest rates.

28 February 1989
International Trade, GATT

The Canadian Government and the European Community (EC) sign an agreement to open Canadian markets to beer, wine and spirits. Signed in Brussels, the agreement commits Canada to phase out provincial liquor board regulations that discriminate against EC alcoholic beverages—the liquor board regulations had earlier been ruled an unfair trading practice by the parties of the General Agreement on Tariffs and Trade (GATT). As well, the provinces must stop putting higher prices on EC wines than on Canadian wines within seven years—the same deal Canada gave the United States under the free trade agreement. Ontario continues to oppose the deal, wanting to extend protection for its wine and grape industry for 12 years.

1 March 1989
Industrial Development

Regional Industrial Expansion Minister Harvie André announces that the new national space agency will be located in Montreal. The agency will coordinate the work of several federal departments and private industry working in the space program. The decision ends three years of lobbying efforts for Quebec Premier Robert Bourassa and Ontario Premier David Peterson who wanted the agency located in Montreal and Ottawa, respectively.

3 March 1989
Meech Lake Accord —Manitoba

Manitoba Premier Gary Filmon announces plans for an all-party committee to hold public hearings across the province on the Meech Lake Accord. Liberals and New Democrats are seeking amendments to the Accord, while Filmon says he might be satisfied with a set of written assurances. The committee will include three MLAs from the governing Conservatives, two Liberals, one New Democrat and a neutral chairman, political scientist Waldron Fox-Decent of the University of Manitoba. Filmon says that his minority Conservative government will not submit an official position on Meech Lake to the committee for the public to comment on. The hearings begin 6 April.

4 March 1989
New Democratic Party—Canada

Federal New Democratic Party leader Ed Broadbent resigns after 14 years and four election campaigns as leader. As leader since 1974, he managed to improve his party's position in the House of Commons in every election but one, although the NDP share of the popular vote varied little. His successor, to be chosen at a convention in Winnipeg on 30 November to 3 December, will be the fourth leader in NDP history since the party was established in 1961.

13 March 1989
Byelection—
Federal; Reform
Party

The Reform Party of Canada wins its first seat in the House of Commons in a byelection in the Alberta riding of Beaver River. Deborah Grey replaces Conservative John Dahmer who died shortly after the November 1988 election. The Reform Party was founded by Preston Manning in 1988 on a platform of western disenchantment with the perceived centrist attitudes of the three traditional federal parties. The Reform Party is on record as opposing the Meech Lake Constitutional Accord and demanding Senate reform.

16 March 1989
Regional Develop-
ment—ERDA

Federal Public Works Minister Elmer MacKay confirms that the federal government has frozen talks with the provinces on regional development agreements. Confirmation of the freeze comes amid widespread talk about severe federal spending cuts anticipated in the upcoming federal budget next month. Sources in several provinces say they are deeply concerned that the federal government will slash its share of economic and regional development agreements (ERDAs), whose total value is roughly $6 billion. Currently, the federal government pays as much as two-thirds of the costs of ERDAs for poorer provinces, while richer provinces split the costs evenly with the federal government. On 31 March 1989 more than 40 such agreements worth about $1.5 billion will expire in eight provinces.

16 March 1989
Federal-Territorial
Relations

Pierre Cadieux, Federal Minister of Indian Affairs and Northern Development, announces that the federal government has ratified a November 1988 agreement-in-principle with 13 Indian bands to turn over more than 41,000 square kilometres of Yukon territory and $232 million in cash. The deal, which includes everything from mineral rights to royalties, has been negotiated over 15 years by Ottawa, the territorial government, and the Indian bands and allows for guaranteed representation on boards involving wildlife management and land-use planning.

20 March 1989
Elections—Alberta

The Alberta Progressive Conservative Party is swept back to power in its sixth straight majority government, but Premier Don Getty loses his own seat to a Liberal.

The Conservatives win 59 seats, the NDP are unchanged at 16 and the Liberals capture eight. The election of 24 NDP and Liberal members marks the first time since 1930 that Albertans have provided a significant opposition to the government in two consecutive elections. Alberta Premier Don Getty later wins a byelection 9 May in the rural riding of Stettler, enabling him to sit in the legislature almost two months later.

21 March 1989
Free Trade

The Ontario government announces that it will comply with GATT and FTA obligations requiring the province to phase out differences in retail prices between U.S. and EC wines and domestic products over a seven year period. For several months prior to the decision, Premier Peterson's Liberal government threatened confrontation or court action with the federal government over the threat to the province's grape and wine industries. Ontario backed down after Ottawa agreed to contribute an extra $5 million towards the marketing of Canadian wines as part of a $100 million federal-provincial, 12 year compensation package to help grape growers adjust to changing conditions.

21 March 1989
Regional Development— New Brunswick

New Brunswick Premier Frank McKenna tells the federal government that his province is willing to pay Ottawa's share of new federal-provincial regional development agreements on an interim basis if the federal government will sign the deals now. "We are interested in making as generous a gesture as we can to demonstrate how important it is to us to get these sub-agreements," says McKenna. The provincial proposal sees New Brunswick "front-ending" Ottawa's share of the agreements' costs until the federal government's financial problems have passed; then, Ottawa would compensate New Brunswick at a later date.

29 March 1989
Free Trade

The Advisory Council on Adjustment, chaired by industrialist Jean de Grandpré, releases its report. Appointed by the Prime Minister in December, 1988 to advise the government on labour adjustments under free trade, the Council rejects specific programs aimed only at workers or businesses hurt by the FTA, saying the concern is for *all* the unemployed. The report says that businesses which will not train or retrain their workers should pay a special free trade tax that could add up to $3 billion a year. Also, the Council recommends changes in unemployment insurance to encourage job retraining rather than treat UIC as an economic safety net.

31 March 1989
Supreme Court—
Appointments

Beverley McLachlin of the British Columbia Supreme Court is appointed to the Supreme Court of Canada by Prime Minister Mulroney. The appointment of the bilingual McLachlin, who succeeds retiring Justice William McIntyre of British Columbia, brings to three the number of women who now sit on the highest court in the country. The fact that MacLachlin is from British Columbia is significant in that it means Mulroney chose to ignore the tradition of rotating the two western positions on the Court among the four western provinces. Saskatchewan, which has not been represented on the Court since 1973, had been lobbying intensely for the seat.

1 April 1989
Fisheries

Newfoundland's Conservative Premier Thomas Rideout denounces the Canada-France agreement on cod, signed the previous day. Under the agreement, Canada will allow the French to almost double the amount of northern cod they can take from Canadian waters during the next three years while a special five-member independent tribunal settles who owns the waters around Newfoundland and the French islands of St-Pierre and Miquelon. Rideout says Ottawa should not have given the French access to the province's fishery, now suffering from reduced catch limits recently imposed by Ottawa to replenish cod stocks. "This is as totally unacceptable to me as it is to the people of Newfoundland and Labrador," says Rideout, who has been in office only ten days and is beginning a three-week election campaign.

3 April 1989
Council of
Maritime Premiers

The three Maritime premiers send a letter to Prime Minister Mulroney expressing concern over the expiry of a number of Economic Regional Development Agreements (ERDAs). The agreements, worth about $135 million annually to the three provinces, expire in four days. Nova Scotia Premier John Buchanan notes the dependence of the Maritime's economies on the ERDAs, particularly the resource development subsidiary agreements.

10 April 1989
Environment

A Federal Court judge quashes the federal licence for a $125 million dam project in southeastern Saskatchewan. In his ruling, Mr. Justice Bud Cullen finds that Federal Environment Minister Thomas McMillan "failed to comply with a statutory duty" and "exceeded his jurisdiction" when he failed to hold public hearings or appoint an independent panel to review the dam project. This opens the doors for full environmental hearings on federal projects ranging from oilsands megaprojects to nuclear submarines. The court challenge was seen as a test case because no one was certain whether the federal environmental guidelines were mandatory or voluntary.

11 April 1989
Unemployment
Insurance

Federal Employment Minister Barbara McDougall announces proposed changes to the unemployment insurance system. Highlights of the proposed reforms include:

• $1.3 billion will be cut from payments now made to unemployed workers under the $13-billion UI program and reallocated to other programs through changes to the qualification rules and benefit periods. Qualifying periods and benefit levels have been made more stringent, but on a sliding scale to reflect regional levels of unemployment.

• An additional $800-million will be spent on a variety of worker training schemes designed to train an additional 60,000 UI claimants a year, help laid-off older workers and provide financial assistance to those anxious to move to areas of lower unemployment.

• New rules will provide $500-million more in benefits for maternity and parental leave and sickness benefits, and extend payments to workers over the age of 65.

The changes will be put into legislation to be introduced in Parliament in June, aiming for implementation on 1 January 1990.

18 April 1989
Free Trade; GATT

International Trade Minister John Crosbie suggests that provincial governments will be kept informed, but not asked to participate, in coming negotiations with the United States over the definition of subsidies. "We believe quite clearly that international trade is under federal jurisdiction and falls under the Prime Minister and the Government of Canada, not the prime minster and the premiers," says Mr. Crosbie after a day-long meeting with provincial trade ministers and their officials.

The meeting also reviews the implementation of the Free Trade Agreement and the status of the GATT negotiations in Geneva, and discusses greater federal-provincial cooperation in trade promotion and international marketing in Europe and the Pacific Rim nations. Crosbie suggests that provincial involvement in the GATT negotiations will be in the same manner as with the FTA: during that two-year negotiating process, federal officials met with provincial trade officials to seek their opinions in advance and then reported to them after the meetings.

19 April 1989
Environment

Federal Environment Minister Lucien Bouchard announces that federal and provincial environment ministers have established a five-year, $250 million fund to clean up hazardous waste sites whose owners are unknown. The fund will give top priority to those sites which pose a serious threat to public health and the environment. The ministers also agree to work together to fight the breakdown of the ozone layer and to control the production, use and elimination of toxic substances. Calling Canada one of the most wasteful nations, the ministers set the year 2000 as a target date to reduce waste by 50 per cent through recycling projects.

20 April 1989
Regulation—Financial Institutions

Ten provincial ministers sign a memorandum of understanding in Vancouver providing for the sharing of information of financial institutions. The provincial effort to harmonize regulations is designed to avert the need for a federal securities and exchange commission. "We felt it was important that the provinces themselves show some leadership in terms of being willing to work together in the interests of the Canadian consumer," says Mel Couvelier, British Columbia's Minister of Finance and Corporate Relations and spokesperson for the other provincial ministers.

20 April 1989
Elections—Newfoundland; Meech Lake

Liberal leader Clyde Wells leads his party to electoral victory in Newfoundland, ending 17 years of Conservative government. Wells suffers personal defeat in his Humber East riding, but the Liberals take 30 of the 52 seats, leaving former premier Tom Rideout's Conservatives with 22 seats. The NDP, under the leadership of Cle Newhook, loses the only two seats it had held in the legislature before the election. The main issues in the campaign revolved around leadership and the record of the governing Tories. One month later, Premier Wells wins a byelection by acclamation in the riding of Bay of Islands, enabling him to sit in the legislature.

Within hours of his electoral victory, Wells says in an interview that he cannot support the Meech Lake Accord because it confers special status on Quebec, makes reform of the Senate next to impossible and weakens the position of the federal government; however, Wells says that he will not use his objection to the constitutional agreement to wring concessions from Prime Minister Brian Mulroney on issues important to Newfoundland.

26 April 1989
Budgets—Federal; Federal-Provincial Fiscal Relations

Federal Finance Minister Michael Wilson reads a lengthy statement featuring highlights of the federal budget at a news conference following a leak of budget details to Global Television News earlier in the day. The budget is aimed at reducing the growth of the federal deficit, which has increased unexpectedly in recent months due to higher interest rates. Highlights of the tax and expenditure policies include:

• the closing or reduction in size of 14 military bases;

- cuts in subsidies to VIA Rail by $500 million over four years as well as increasing fares and the closing, sale or transfer of substantial parts of the system;

- deferral of the Conservative government's election campaign pledge to launch a $6.4 billion day-care program;

- decrease in the transfers to the provinces for health and postsecondary education by one percentage point.

- increase from 3 to 5 per cent for the surtaxes on personal and corporate income tax and an additional 3 per cent surtax on high-income individuals;

- complete withdrawal of the federal government from financing the unemployment insurance program, adding at least $2 billion to the $10 billion now paid in Unemployment Insurance premiums by employers and employees.

2 May 1989
Meech Lake Accord
—Manitoba

The Manitoba government's public hearings on the Meech Lake Accord draw to a close in Winnipeg after a month-long tour of the province by an all-party committee to hear the opinion of Manitobans on the proposed constitutional amendment. The seven-member committee, chaired by University of Manitoba political scientist Waldron Fox-Decent, heard submissions from over 300 people, 25 per cent of whom said they would like the Accord passed without any changes.

2 May 1989
Elections—Prince
Edward Island

Prince Edward Island Premier Joe Ghiz announces a general election for 29 May, seeking a second term in office for the governing Liberal party. At dissolution, the Liberals hold 22 seats, the Conservatives, nine and there is one vacancy.

3 May 1989
Language Policy—
Quebec

Quebec cabinet minister Claude Ryan announces proposed regulations for Quebec's controversial language law (Bill 178), passed in December 1988, which declared that all outdoor signs in Quebec must be in French only. Under the regulations, Quebec stores with fewer than 50 employees will be permitted to post bilingual signs indoors, provided the French lettering is twice as large as the lettering in other languages. Ryan, the minister responsible for the province's language law, says that the public has 60 days to make its views known on the regulations before the cabinet makes a decision.

3 May 1989
Liberal Party—
Canada

Leader of the Opposition John Turner announces that he will be stepping down as Liberal leader as soon as a leadership convention to replace him can be held. Turner indicates that he will retain his Vancouver Quadra seat in the meantime.

5 May 1989
Environment

The Saskatchewan Government files an appeal in the Federal Court of Appeal from the 10 April court ruling that halted construction of the Rafferty Dam project (see entry for 10 April 1989). Eric Berntson, the Saskatchewan cabinet minister in charge of the project, says the province is losing $2 million a month by not proceeding with the dam, which was scheduled for completion by 1990.

15 May 1989
Regional Develop-
ment—ACOA

Federal cabinet minister Elmer MacKay tells the House of Commons committee on regional development that funding for the Atlantic Canada Opportunities Agency (ACOA) will be cut by as much as 28 per cent each year under deficit-reducing measures introduced in the federal budget last month. Mackay, the minister responsible for ACOA, says that the agency's original budget of $1.05 billion over five years will instead be spread over six to seven years, for an average annual payment of $150 million, down from $210 million under the old system.

18 May 1989
Throne Speech—
Manitoba

Manitoba Government opens a new session of its legislature with a throne speech pledging, among other things, to fight for better relations with Ottawa. This pledge includes the opening of a previously announced office in Ottawa to improve communications with federal officials.

23 May 1989
Federal-Provincial
Fiscal Relations

Auditor General Ken Dye, in testimony before the House of Commons public accounts committee, proposes that future spending agreements between Ottawa, the provinces and municipalities should contain provisions to ensure that taxpayers' funds are spent wisely. Dye says that existing agreements are not clear regarding who audits federal transfer payments, which in 1989-90 involve a total of $23.9 billion, most of which is received by provincial governments.

25 May 1989
Throne Speech—
Newfoundland;
Meech Lake Accord

A speech from the throne opens the first legislative session of the new government of Newfoundland Premier Clyde Wells pledging to make the province a full, participating member of Canada. Apart from emphasis on the troubled fishery and economic development, the speech stresses health and education, two areas Wells has targeted as major priorities for his month-old government.

The speech also contains a pledge to push for changes to the Meech Lake Accord and to ask the House of Assembly to rescind a resolution ratifying the agreement if such changes are not considered.

29 May 1989
Elections—Prince
Edward Island

Prince Edward Island's Liberal Party is returned to office in a landslide victory, capturing 30 of 32 seats in the province's general election. The majority is the largest in the province since 1935 when the Liberals took all the seats.

1 June 1989
Hydroelectricity;
Environment

Federal Environment Minister Lucien Bouchard tells a House of Commons environment committee that Ottawa has begun talks with the Quebec government and Hydro-Québec on how to ensure federal input into the evaluation of the James Bay II hydroelectric development. The talks are partly in response to a recent Hydro-Québec study which found that fish samples taken from reservoirs in the area contain mercury levels up to nine times higher than the maximum limit recommended by the federal government.

1 June 1989
Environment

Federal Transport Minister Benoit Bouchard and Environment Minister Lucien Bouchard indicate that the legal provisions for the transportation of hazardous goods have been made stronger. The new provisions were developed in cooperation with provincial officials and cover three areas: extension of existing rules governing the transportation of hazardous goods to cover materials destined for recycling; establishment of a uniform manifest document for shippers; and requirement of 30 day's notice for shipping PCBs between provinces.

3 June 1989
Meech Lake Accord

This marks the second anniversary of the approval in Ottawa by the Prime Minister and all the premiers on 3 June 1987 of the text of the *Constitution Amendment, 1987*. At this point two years later the Meech Lake Constitutional Accord has been ratified by eight provincial legislatures and the House of Commons. The Manitoba and New Brunswick legislatures have yet to ratify the agreement and the newly-elected premier of Newfoundland, Clyde Wells, is threatening to revoke his legislature's support for the Accord unless major changes are introduced. It is generally assumed that under the procedure for constitutional amendment adopted in 1982, the Constitution Amendment 1987 must be ratified by Ottawa and all ten provinces by 23 June 1990 in order to become law.

15 June 1989
Throne Speech—
Prince Edward
Island

Prince Edward Island's Liberal government unleashes a concentrated attack on the federal government in its first throne speech since re-election two weeks ago. One major focus of the province's discontent is the planned closure by Ottawa of Canadian Forces Base Summerside, announced in the 27 April federal budget, which could cost the province about 1300 jobs. Premier Ghiz says that while budget deficits are a concern to all provinces, deficit control can "not justify the government of Canada's attack on our region and our province."

20 June 1989
Regulation—Finan-
cial Services

The Conference Board of Canada releases a report citing a "pressing need" for intergovernmental cooperation in the financial services sector. Guy Glorieux, director of the Conference Board's financial services research program, notes that "while banks are under federal jurisdiction, their securities affiliates are governed by the provinces ... [and] without all of the players' involvement, the industry cannot achieve the necessary level of efficiency required to be competitive in the 1990s."

27 June 1989
Council of Mari-
time Premiers

The Council of Maritime Premiers meets in Mont Carmel, Prince Edward Island for its seventy-fourth session. Communiques are issued on such matters as interprovincial trade barriers, the closure of CFB Summerside and the question of jurisdiction over telephone utilities which is before the Supreme Court of Canada. In responding to questions from the media, the premiers express a general concern that Atlantic Canada is being asked to pay a disproportionate share of federal deficit reduction; as well, they are concerned about the delays in getting new ERDA agreements signed.

Chronology: Index

Meech Lake Accord: 26,28 January 1988; 17,30 March 1988; 21 April 1988; 13,25 May 1988; 2,22,29 June 1988; 8 July 1988; 19 December 1988; 27 February 1989; 3 March 1989; 20 April 1989; 2,25 May 1989; 3 June 1989
Megaprojects: 18 July 1988; 2,24 September 1988
Monetary Policy: 8 November 1988
National Parks: 12 July 1988
New Democratic Party: 8 March 1988; 4 March 1989
Parti Québécois: 26 November 1988
Procurement: 19 September 1988
Progressive Conservative Party: 21 January 1989
Provincial-International Relations: 7,19,26 April 1988; 4,16 January 1989
Reform Party: 13 March 1989
Regional Development: 18 January 1988; 4,15,29 February 1988; 26 May 1988; 9,23 June 1988; 18 August 1988; 28 September 1988; 16,21 March 1989; 15 May 1989
Regulation: 7 January 1988; 15 March 1988; 6 September 1988; 6 June 1988; 5 July 1988; 27 October 1988; 9 December 1988; 20 April 1989; 20 June 1989
Senate: 26 January 1988; 21 April 1988; 26 September 1988; 10 January 1989; 7 February 1989
Sports: 2 November 1988
Supreme Court: 28 January 1988; 25 February 1988; 24 May 1988; 2,9 June 1988; 15 December 1988; 23 January 1989; 31 March 1989
Tax Reform: 13 April 1988
Throne Speeches: 18,25 May 1989; 15 June 1989
Transportation: 20 June 1988
Unemployment Insurance: 11 April 1989
Western Premiers' Conference: 18-21 May 1988

List of Titles in Print

Institute of Intergovernmental Relations, *Annual Report to the Advisory Council, July, 1989*/Institut des relations intergouvernementales, *Rapport annuel au conseil consultatif, juillet 1989* (charge for postage only).

William M. Chandler and Christian W. Zöllner, *Challenges to Federalism: Policy-Making in Canada and the Federal Republic of Germany*, 1989. ($25)

Peter M. Leslie, *Rebuilding the Relationship: Quebec and its Confederation Partners/Une collaboration renouvelée: le Québec et ses partenaires dans la confédération*, 1987. ($8)

A. Paul Pross and Susan McCorquodale, *Economic Resurgence and the Constitutional Agenda: The Case of the East Coast Fisheries*, 1987. ($10)

Bruce G. Pollard, *Managing the Interface: Intergovernmental Affairs Agencies in Canada*, 1986. ($12)

Catherine A. Murray, *Managing Diversity: Federal-Provincial Collaboration and the Committee on Extension of Services to Northern and Remote Communities*, 1984. ($15)

Peter Russell et al, *The Court and the Constitution: Comments on the Supreme Court Reference on Constitutional Amendment*, 1982. (Paper $5, Cloth $10)

Allan Tupper, *Public Money in the Private Sector: Industrial Assistance Policy and Canadian Federalism*, 1982. ($12)

William P. Irvine, *Does Canada Need a New Electoral System?*, 1979. ($8)

Canada: The State of the Federation

Peter M. Leslie and Ronald M. Watts, editors, *Canada: The State of the Federation, 1987-88*. ($15)

Peter M. Leslie, editor, *Canada: The State of the Federation 1986*. ($15)

Peter M. Leslie, editor, *Canada: The State of the Federation 1985*. ($14)

Volumes I, II and III ($22)

Canada: L'état de la fédération 1985. ($14)

The Year in Review

Bruce G. Pollard, *The Year in Review 1983: Intergovernmental Relations in Canada*. ($16)

Revue de l'année 1983: les relations intergouvernementales au Canada. ($16)

S.M. Dunn, *The Year in Review 1982: Intergovernmental Relations in Canada.* ($12)

Revue de l'année 1982: les relations intergouvernementales au Canada. ($12)

S.M. Dunn, *The Year in Review 1981: Intergovernmental Relations in Canada.* ($10)

R.J. Zukowsky, *Intergovernmental Relations in Canada: The Year in Review 1980, Volume I: Policy and Politics.* ($8) (*Volume II not available*)

Research Papers/Notes de Recherche (formerly Discussion Papers)

25. Denis Robert, *L'ajustement structurel et le fédéralisme canadien: le cas de l'industrie du textile et du vêtement*, 1989. (forthcoming)
24. Peter M. Leslie, *Ethnonationalism in a Federal State: The Case of Canada*, 1988. ($4)
23. Peter M. Leslie, *National Citizenship and Provincial Communities: A Review of Canadian Fiscal Federalism*, 1988. ($4)
22. Robert L. Stanfield, *National Political Parties and Regional Diversity*, 1985. (Postage Only)
21. Donald Smiley, *An Elected Senate for Canada? Clues from the Australian Experience*, 1985. ($8)
20. Nicholas R. Sidor, *Consumer Policy in the Canadian Federal State*, 1984. ($8)
19. Thomas O. Hueglin, *Federalism and Fragmentation: A Comparative View of Political Accommodation in Canada*, 1984. ($8)
18. Allan Tupper, *Bill S-31 and the Federalism of State Capitalism*, 1983. ($7)
17. Reginald Whitaker, *Federalism and Democratic Theory*, 1983. ($7)
16. Roger Gibbins, *Senate Reform: Moving Towards the Slippery Slope*, 1983. ($7)
14. John Whyte, *The Constitution and Natural Resource Revenues*, 1982. ($7)

Reflections/Réflexions

3. Peter M. Leslie, *Federal Leadership in Economic and Social Policy*, 1988. ($3)
2. Clive Thomson, editor, *Navigating Meech Lake: The 1987 Constitutional Accord*, 1988. ($4)
1. Allan E. Blakeney, *Canada: Its Framework, Its Foibles, Its Future*, 1988. ($3)

Dean's Conference on Law and Policy

1. John D. Whyte and Ian Peach (eds.), *Re-forming Canada? The Meaning of the Meech Lake Accord and the Free Trade Agreement for the Canadian State*, 1989. ($6.00)

Bibliographies

Bibliography of Canadian and Comparative Federalism, 1986. ($20)

Bibliography of Canadian and Comparative Federalism, 1980-1985. ($39)

Aboriginal Self-Government in Canada: A Bibliography 1986. ($7)

A Supplementary Bibliography, 1979. ($5)

A Supplementary Bibliography, 1975. ($10)

Federalism and Intergovernmental Relations in Australia, Canada, the United States and Other Countries: A Bibliography, 1967. ($9)

Aboriginal Peoples and Constitutional Reform

Background Papers

16. Bradford W. Morse, *Providing Land and Resources for Aboriginal Peoples*, 1987. ($10)
15. Evelyn J. Peters, *Aboriginal Self-Government Arrangements in Canada*, 1987. ($7)
14. Delia Opekokew, *The Political and Legal Inequities Among Aboriginal Peoples in Canada*, 1987. ($7)
13. Ian B. Cowie, *Future Issues of Jurisdiction and Coordination Between Aboriginal and Non-Aboriginal Governments*, 1987. ($7)
12. C.E.S. Franks, *Public Administration Questions Relating to Aboriginal Self-Government*, 1987. ($10)
11. Richard H. Bartlett, *Subjugation, Self-Management and Self-Government of Aboriginal Lands and Resources in Canada*, 1986. ($10)
10. Jerry Paquette, *Aboriginal Self-Government and Education in Canada*, 1986. ($10)
9. Marc Malone, *Financing Aboriginal Self-Government in Canada*, 1986. ($7)
8. John Weinstein, *Aboriginal Self-Determination Off a Land Base*, 1986. ($7)
7. David C. Hawkes, *Negotiating Aboriginal Self-Government: Developments Surrounding the 1985 First Ministers' Conference*, 1985. ($5)
6. Bryan P. Schwartz, *First Principles: Constitutional Reform with Respect to the Aboriginal Peoples of Canada 1982-1984*, 1985. ($20)
5. Douglas E. Sanders, *Aboriginal Self-Government in the United States*, 1985. ($12)
4. Bradford Morse, *Aboriginal Self-Government in Australia and Canada*, 1985. ($12)
3. (not available).
2. David A. Boisvert, *Forms of Aboriginal Self-Government*, 1985. ($12)

1. Noel Lyon, *Aboriginal Self-Government: Rights of Citizenship and Access to Governmental Services,* 1984. ($12)

Discussion Papers

David C. Hawkes, *The Search for Accommodation,* 1987. ($7)

David C. Hawkes, *Aboriginal Self-Government: What Does It Mean?,* 1985. ($12)

Position Papers

Inuit Committee on National Issues, *Completing Canada: Inuit Approaches to Self-Government,* 1987. ($7)

Martin Dunn, *Access to Survival, A Perspective on Aboriginal Self-Government for the Constituency of the Native Council of Canada,* 1986. ($7)

Workshop Reports

David C. Hawkes and Evelyn J. Peters, *Issues in Entrenching Aboriginal Self-Government,* 1987. ($12)

David C. Hawkes and Evelyn J. Peters, *Implementing Aboriginal Self-Government: Problems and Prospects,* 1986. ($7)

Bibliography

Evelyn J. Peters, *Aboriginal Self-Government in Canada: A Bibliography 1986.* ($7)

Final Report

David C. Hawkes, *Aboriginal Peoples and Constitutional Reform: What Have We Learned?,* 1989. (forthcoming)

Publications may be ordered from:

Institute of Intergovernmental Relations
Queen's University
Kingston, Ontario, Canada
K7L 3N6